Enforced Marginality

Enforced Marginality

Jewish Narratives on Abandoned Wives

Bluma Goldstein

UNIVERSITY OF CALIFORNIA PRESS

Berkeley / Los Angeles / London

University of California Press, one of the most distinguished university presses in the United States, enriches lives around the world by advancing scholarship in the humanities, social sciences, and natural sciences. Its activities are supported by the UC Press Foundation and by philanthropic contributions from individuals and institutions. For more information, visit www.ucpress.edu.

University of California Press
Berkeley and Los Angeles, California

University of California Press, Ltd.
London, England

© 2007 by The Regents of the University of California

Library of Congress Cataloging-in-Publication Data

Goldstein, Bluma.
    Enforced marginality : Jewish narratives on abandoned wives / Bluma Goldstein.
        p.   cm.
    Includes bibliographical references and index.
    ISBN 978-0-520-24968-4 (cloth : alk. paper)
    1. Agunahs.   2. Jewish women—Legal status, laws, etc.   3. Jewish women in literature.   4. Jewish literature—History and criticism.   I. Title.

KBM550.5G65 2007
296.4'444—dc22   2006035371

Manufactured in the United States of America

16 15 14 13 12 11 10 09 08 07
10 9 8 7 6 5 4 3 2 1

Contents

Acknowledgments

This book took shape over more years than I care to remember. Indeed, I cannot actually recall when my interest in abandoned wives morphed into a serious study. At times it seems that I never actually chose to pursue the subject of abandonment, that instead it chose me and pursued me with a vengeance. My father deserted my mother and me when I was an infant, but for half of my life, abandonment was hardly a part of my vocabulary or concern. In fact, it was only when I began to teach courses with Jewish content—"Jewish Writers in the German-Speaking World" and "Yiddish Literature"—and encountered a number of texts about *agunes* that I began to take a scholarly interest in the subject. It was certainly disconcerting to discover how little had been written about *agunes,* how few representations of them existed, and how often critics, in writing about stories of desertion, overlooked the presence of the abandoned wives and their significance. It was then that I also began to explore the importance of Jewish family law and Jewish patriarchy for the plight of the *agune,* as well as the role of the National Desertion Bureau in tracking down many thousands of absconding Jewish husbands in the United States of the twentieth century. Moreover, when I observed how many of the deserted wives in the texts I examined were intimidated and silent, and also how many writers—literary critics, historians, sociologists, feminists, and so on—were silent about the predicament of these women, it seemed necessary for someone to speak when these others could not or did not.

I embarked on this study with two of the more literary chapters—the autobiographical writings of Glikl Hamel and Solomon Maimon, and

Eastern European Yiddish novels—primarily because those were texts I studied in my courses. For the chapter on autobiographical texts, I had some very useful assistance from a colleague and good friend, and one of the most eminent and erudite Jewish historians and thinkers, the late Amos Funkenstein. He read the chapter carefully, argued with me (very effectively) about Maimon's writings and intentions, enlightened me about some of Glikl's difficult *Jüdischdeutsch* (Old Yiddish) locutions, and made incisive comments and suggestions. Although Amos was himself a storehouse for an enormous amount of information about almost everything, and his time was fully occupied—with teaching and mentoring, researching in many fields, and writing—he seemed nonetheless always available for questions and discussion. His untimely death was shattering for many of us who knew him and often relied on him. He has a very significant place in my work and my heart.

I owe a special debt of gratitude to Chava Turniansky for her seminal work on Glikl and for her comments on my text. Jordan Finkin's extensive linguistic skills proved to be an unexpected blessing. He agreed to proofread the portion of my writing on Glikl, helped with linguistic anomalies of Glikl's text that were especially challenging, and improved upon my transliterations. Just when I thought that my manuscript was as it should be, Diane Wolf made a suggestion about reorganizing the chapter on Glikl, for which I am enormously grateful. Also her remarks regarding the structure of the family (Diane is a Professor of Sociology and Jewish Studies) proved very useful, particularly in the chapter on desertion in the United States.

Jennifer Sylvor's dissertation work on Sholem Aleykhem's *Menakhem-Mendl* and her exceptional insights into the ways in which variations in language create characters and contribute to the depiction of the social milieu informed my understanding of the novel's economic and social determinants more than I can say. Robert Peckerar's comments about the chapter on the Yiddish novels, which raised many interesting questions about the texts, were instrumental in my rethinking and reassessing the politics of the texts. Robert (Uri) Alter, a colleague and longtime friend, read and commented on this chapter, and I thank him generally for his many insights and particularly for drawing attention to some of my remarks about the history of the luftmentsh that needed further investigation and revision. It was in a summer seminar at Yale with Benjamin Harshav that I first articulated my thoughts about *agunes* in writing, and I owe a special debt to Professor Harshav for his focus on Jewish literary and linguistic concerns in the seminar, which contributed to the direction of my project. Naomi Seidman, who had once been my student in Berkeley and is now a professor and director of the Center of Jewish Studies at the Graduate Theological Union, was also a participant in the seminar, and I cannot express how much her interest in my work and her remarkably perceptive ideas meant to me. Since my background is completely secular (in my youth I thought that Esther, the one biblical book we read in the *arbeyter ring shuln* [Workmen's Circle Yiddish schools] because it contained no mention of God, was the only book of the Bible), and Naomi was reared in an intellectually vibrant religious family, she often provided me with valuable information about rituals, prayers, and, for me, arcane Judaica that was absolutely necessary for my work, particularly on *The Travels of Benjamin the Third* by Sholem Yakov Abramovitsh (Mendele Moykher Sforim). She has, in addition, been a warm, wonderful, and supportive friend for many a moon.

Eli Katz and I both came to the Department of German at Berkeley in the 1960s and remained very close friends and allies these many years. He was a linguist and a Yiddishist, and his lectures on the history of the Yiddish language and its literature provided me with an indispensable treasure trove of information and insights. He had an extraordinary familiarity with the nuances of the Yiddish language—what was high or low register; the dialect used and its particular contextual significance; the political and social implications of linguistic changes in a text—and a vast knowledge of Yiddish literature from the Middle Ages through the twentieth century. Eli was always ready to help with difficulties, to explain at length the intricacies of a dialogue or turn of phrase in a text, or to lend me a needed volume unavailable at the library (he possessed an extensive library of Yiddish language, literary, and reference texts). As a Germanist I had done virtually no work on Yiddish since my graduation from *mitlshule* (Yiddish "after-school" high school) at age thirteen, and I doubt whether I would have ventured into Yiddish literature had it not been for my wonderful and intellectually fruitful friendship with Eli. There is no day when I do not wish he were still here.

My indebtedness to my colleague and very good friend Chana Kronfeld eludes any language I can muster to express my gratitude for everything she has done to support me and my work. No matter how little time she had for herself or her own work, she always found time and made the effort to read and critique my work in exceptionally careful detail, an act that was, in fact, instrumental in shaping not only my ideas and arguments but also the structure and methodology of my writing. Although as a graduate student Chana asked me to be a member of her exam committees and asked to study Yiddish literature with me, it was clear to me that it was I who had much to gain from her knowledge and fine readings of Yiddish poetry and literary theory. I am convinced that our friendship, deep and long, has not only affected my life in ways I cannot convey but also inspired and rekindled my interest in and commitment to Yiddish literature and culture. (She is also responsible for awakening in her students an extraordinarily valuable concern for Yiddish cultural production.)

Many participants at a number of conferences (including the Association for Jewish Studies, Modern Language Association, and Annual Yiddish Conference in Berkeley) in which I presented papers related to the topic of this book contributed valuable comments, ideas, and insights into various aspects of this study, as did many of my students over the years. A number of libraries were extremely helpful in obtaining materials necessary for this book. The late Dina Abramowicz, a librarian at YIVO (*Yidische visnshaftlekhe organizatsyon*, the Jewish Research Institute), was especially helpful, finding original documents and reports of the National Desertion Bureau from the early decades of the twentieth century. More recently the YIVO library managed to unearth two of the Bureau's case studies, even though all the materials from the Bureau remain in storage at YIVO, not yet catalogued and therefore unavailable to the public. Also very helpful were the Judaica division of the New York Public Library and the library at the Leo Baeck Institute. The University of California has over the years supported this project with research funds and research assistants.

Tova Rosen, a Professor of Medieval Literature at Tel Aviv University, and I met for the first time just over a year ago when she was a visiting professor at the University of California, Berkeley. When we spent a day together visiting the wine country, she told me the story of the nineteen years she had spent as an *agune,* not the result of desertion but of a recalcitrant husband. Just listening to the restrictions and the pain she suffered as a result of being a "chained woman" made me all the more eager to finish this book. Public pressure finally convinced her husband to deliver a completed *get* (religious divorce) to the court, thereby "liberating" her. We questioned why, in an enlightened society in the twenty-first century, a woman is forced to wait for a man to "liberate" her—and to wait for two decades!

Allison Schachter, who is now a professor at Vanderbilt University, was very generous with her time and expertise when I needed research assistance. Kurt Beals made very good use of his remarkable eagle eye, knowledge of German, and perspicacity when he proofread the final version. I am especially grateful for the attentive work Eliyah Arnon did for me over a period of many years when he worked hard and long as my research assistant in Berkeley and, even at times, in New York. Apart from tracking down difficult-to-obtain books, documents, and early-twentieth-century Yiddish newspapers and helping fix my many computer glitches, he also corrected typographical and bibliographic errors, and he made useful suggestions. He surpassed the call of duty by leaps and bounds, and for that and everything else I cannot thank him enough. I also want to express my gratitude to the University of California Press's excellent editorial staff: to Chalon Emmons and Bonita Hurd for their many important efforts, and to Stan Holwitz for his interest in my project, his continuous support, and his very constructive, thoughtful suggestions and comments.

Prologue

Finally Out in the Open

My father deserted my mother when I was still in utero, returned when I was six months old, and left, never to be seen again, when I was about a year old. My mother raised me by herself, supporting us with strenuous work in garment factories as an "operator"—the term for a seamstress who operated machines. Gaining authority solely through absence, the invisible, missing husband and father became a potent center of our small family, but my mother and I developed very different sensibilities in response to this absent figure. She, devastated and humiliated by abandonment, saw herself as incompetent, incapable of "holding onto a husband," and felt both victimized and ashamed of her victimization. I, on the other hand, although always aware that I was a fatherless child, refused to see myself as a victim, and surely not the victim of an invisible phantom who had run out on me in some vague, unremembered past. But even as a phantom, he did nevertheless exist for us; and because he did, my mother—trying, I believe, to salvage some vestige of self-esteem in the eyes of others—swore me to secrecy and silence. I was to disclose to no one that my father had deserted us. He was to be considered dead, and although I was not an especially obedient child, I maintained the silence. But my unacknowledged rage at being left impoverished, vulnerable, and silenced was occasionally relieved by creating new, ever-more-dreadful causes of his death each time anyone asked about him. Only decades later, when I finally divested myself of the debilitating secrecy and silence imposed on me, could I begin to understand not only that the shame that was rightfully his had unjustifiably become the terrible burden of my mother but also how extensive the desertion by husbands was within the Jewish community and elsewhere.

Several decades ago, urged by my university department to teach two new courses, one on Jewish German writers, the other on Yiddish literature, I was confronted with a bevy of historical, cultural, legal, and literary texts that led me to surmise just how serious a problem desertion was within broad sectors of the Jewish community. Finding a reference to the National Desertion Bureau, a specifically Jewish organization, was my madeleine, kindling remembrances of the many childhood trips to that office with my mother. My recollection of the Bureau's large imposing offices and of the discussions with social workers about whether my father had been located yet, and about the disposition of the case, began to batter the ramparts that had secured my rejected memories of the upheaval that desertion had brought into my life.

Then, in the late 1970s and early 1980s, several series of lengthy articles about *agunes*[1]—"chained women," that is, women who under Jewish law could not obtain a divorce—appeared in the *Village Voice,* a popular weekly newspaper in New York City. That led me to search the New York Public Library and the library and archives at YIVO (*Yidische visnshaftlekhe organizatsyon,* or Jewish Research Institute) for records and files of the National Desertion Bureau, which had for almost half a century processed many thousands of cases a year, and for whatever else was available on the issue of desertion. I soon learned that for many decades *Der Forverts* (the *Jewish Daily Forward*)—the most widely read Yiddish newspaper in the United States—had run a feature called *A galeriye fun farshvundene mener* (A Gallery of Vanished Husbands) that appeared several times a week, each time highlighting many deserters (sometimes as many as thirty) by printing their portraits and abbreviated histories. This Gallery also appeared at least once a week in four other major Yiddish newspapers, in Chicago, Cleveland, Montreal, and Toronto, with a combined circulation of no fewer than 250,000. The Pandora's box was open and could no longer be closed.

While the subject of desertion also cropped up in many of the texts for my courses—in German, Yiddish, and English autobiographies, memoirs, and literary texts—critics, whether literary or cultural, rarely in these writings confronted with any gravity the socially prevalent problem of deserted wives and families, which may explain in part at least why the complex and painful issues of deserted families have for so long lingered silently in the shadows. Indeed, abandoned wives and children were as marginalized and invisible in written texts as in the social world. Even I, who in my own life had experienced the repercussions of desertion, at times overlooked or underestimated the significance of references to women as deserted wives, as *agunes*. Even I did not yet realize what a major social phenomenon desertion was and had been, especially in a community where Jewish law did not allow for divorce when the husband was not present to deliver the decree or refused to do so. Two main experiences strongly affected me. First, I was surprised that so many of my students, apparently accepting the commonplace view of the solidity of the Jewish family, were incredulous that the Jewish paterfamilias, known for his devotion to family, would abandon his wife and children. Yet for years even I thought of my family situation as an anomaly and had not realized that, for thousands of children like me, Jewish households were not generally the sites of happy families. Second, and perhaps more important, were the numbers of Jewish German and Yiddish texts that included instances of desertions, texts I revisited in light of insights I acquired from recent developments in feminist discourse, gender theory, and cultural studies, all of which insisted on the value of exploring textual and social problems from multiple interrelated perspectives.

It became clear to me—even or especially when issues of desertion and deserted wives might seem peripheral to the main focus of a text— that when gender was not a text's explicit subject, the reader would nonetheless be advised to make a conscious effort to read for it. "Gender," Myra Jehlen observes, "has emerged as a problem that is always implicit in any work. It is a quality of the literary voice hitherto masked by the static of common assumptions. And as a critical category gender is an additional lens, or a way of lifting the curtain to an unseen recess of the self and of society."[2] Of course, gender, understood as being culturally constructed (not as biologically or naturally determined), necessarily includes men as well as women along with the asymmetries and power differentials that develop within their social relationships. What is also important for an exploration of desertion, particularly within a Jewish context, is an analysis of the institutional relations and practices of power—be they social, political, or religious—that are deeply implicated, not only in autobiographical and fictional works about desertion that have absorbed significant aspects of the texts' cultural environment, but also in the culture within which those texts were produced. A large part of my effort in this work is devoted to an exploration—within historical and cultural contexts—of representations of the victims and the perpetrators of desertion over a period of four centuries by reinterpreting and reassessing selected well-known texts in the light of new avenues of approach to various forms of cultural production. These texts, whose depicted abandoned wives deserve recognition and a fair hearing, require close readings if one is to lay bare the extensive textual and social importance of desertion that has been concealed far too long. Beyond that, and perhaps more important, a contextual and interdiscursive reading provides access to significant historical moments—the effects of and changes in economic restrictions, religious practices, political regulation, or social institutions—that form the complex and intricate environment in which both the narrative and its value are embedded.

In this book, close readings of the autobiographical and literary texts take us on a historical and cultural journey through transformations in European society that resulted in significant structural changes for the Jewish community—the relaxation of residence restrictions, the development of accessible and effective means of transportation (railroads, steamships), and more diverse economic opportunities, to name a few. Witness, for example, the developments in the economic life of Jews over several centuries: In Glikl Hamel's seventeenth-century Germany, Jews were largely restricted to work as merchants and moneylenders, and yet less than a century later, during Solomon Maimon's years in Enlightenment Germany, Jews were doctors, philosophers, accountants, pharmacists, and so on, and Maimon was called to task for not undertaking a remunerative profession. In the later nineteenth century, however, Sholem Aleykhem's Menakhem-Mendl could wander around the financial and stock markets of Ukraine's metropolises trying to become a millionaire; and in twentieth-century America, while deserting husbands featured in the *Forverts'* "A Gallery of Vanished Husbands" seem generally impoverished, they also clearly work in a number of diverse, albeit often menial, jobs and are able to move about, freely changing workplace and occupation. Although these economic and monetary developments might appear to have little significance for issues of desertion, they are in fact aspects of the particular historical, social, and political contexts detailed in the texts that provide the cultural environment necessary for situating and understanding the narratives about the various *agunes.*

Thus this book covers a broad expanse of time and place, from the early modern period of Jewish (and European) history in seventeenth- and eighteenth-century Germany to late-nineteenth-century Eastern Europe and twentieth-century United States, a trajectory that traces the demographic movements of Jews in the West. Although this work generally advances chronologically and linearly, there is no continuous narrative exposition of abandoned *agunes* through the centuries. Instead, a transdisciplinary approach and the exploration of a range of texts at the intersection of disciplines—history, autobiography, literature, sociology, and gender and cultural studies—provide informative insights into the complex, serious consequences of spousal desertion over an extended period of time. Indeed, contending with the depiction and discussion of desertion in diverse texts from an interdisciplinary perspective more fully exposes the power differential and cultural asymmetries that inform the tensions in the public sphere concerning social life, cultural forms, and institutional regulation. But these differentiae also inform the conflicting interactions within and between families, communal life, and gender relationships "where power, dependence, and inequality are most at stake."[3] Thus, this study is committed to the consideration of powerless *agunes* marginalized within a male hegemonic situation, to the resuscitation of the suppressed, submerged, or obliterated voices of these women and the even more powerless children, whose voices were almost never heard.

In the first chapter, after a brief survey of the complicated corpus of Jewish family law related to issues of the *agune* and *aginut*[4] and of the fundamental legal basis and rabbinical arguments for the difficult, indeed impossible, circumstances confronting abandoned wives, I turn to two notable autobiographical works written in the seventeenth and eighteenth centuries in Germany. Glikl Hamel wrote her *Zikhroynes (Memoirs)* intermittently between 1690 and 1719 in Judeo-German, or *Jüdischdeutsch* (also known as Yiddish or, when distinguished from modern Yiddish, Old Yiddish), when she lived in Hamburg and Metz. Solomon Maimon, a learned religious Jew who had migrated from Poland to Berlin and whose native language was Yiddish, wrote his *Lebensgeschichte (Autobiography)* in German in 1792–93, during his stay in Brandenburg-Prussia. These autobiographical texts deliver a wealth of historical information about Jewish life in Germany and Eastern Europe during periods of important political changes for Western Europeans in general and Jews in particular, but they also contain surprisingly accomplished narratives that may best be understood as something more than historical documents. Because the embedded narratives about *agunes*—especially Glikl's story—have notably discrete literary structures, they require close interdiscursive readings that account for the intricate literary elements as well as historical and cultural environment.

Glikl was a mere three years old in 1648 at the end of the Thirty Years' War, a war that had raged through most of Europe, irrevocably rearranged its map, and brought rapid change to its Jewish population. The Thirty Years' War, usually characterized as a religious struggle between Catholics and Protestants, was also an imperialistic war for territorial gain, dynastic control, and commercial and economic advantage at a time when feudalism was in decline and mercantile capitalism was emerging. Two aspects of its peace settlement, the 1648 Treaty of Westphalia, proved particularly advantageous for Jews: although its doctrine of ecclesiastical tolerance applied only to three Christian communities (Catholic, Lutheran, and Calvinist), the implied separation of politics from religion had an important effect on a beleaguered Jewish population; and the establishment of member states of the Holy Roman Empire as sovereign entities instituted a direct relationship between individual subject and absolutist ruler, who now could, and at times did, protect Jews, usually because of their economic utility to the state. Thus, although in the years following the war Jews still had to contend with antisemitic onslaughts, residence restrictions, and interference with internal Jewish communal and religious practices, they gained access to formerly prohibited economic opportunities, formed new urban communities, found some entrée into non-Jewish culture, and were even permitted to attend a few universities in very limited programs. Of course, absolutist state policies, which sought to eliminate Jewish self-governance in their move toward direct relations between individual and state, also diminished the standing of Jewish communal organizations and weakened rabbinical authority, something which later became amply apparent in Solomon Maimon's Enlightenment Berlin.

Although some of these changes are already evident in Glikl's writings—she mentions her many commercial ventures and her factory, her stepsister's knowledge of French and music, and the nobles invited to her daughter's wedding—she and her community remained completely devoted to Jewish tradition and orthodoxy. Nevertheless, the story she relates about two *agunes* is a highly developed narrative that negotiates between her construction of an exemplary narrative about the power and empowerment of women and an accurate account of a notorious public event that occurred in her contemporary Hamburg. Glikl's account of a woman's activist intervention on behalf of a hapless *agune* and its power to encourage another *agune* to unearth the cause of her husband's disappearance may seem like a very modern feminist move.[5] The connection between historicity and exemplarity, however, actually corresponds to a traditional understanding of Jewish history not only as a historical report of what happened but also as an interpretation of it. What is radical about her account is that a woman, here Glikl, creatively intervenes in the history of a notorious event to produce an exemplary story about an indomitable woman, Rebekah, who herself intervened in that historical event by pursuing justice for an *agune* in defiance of the timid and resistant male members of the community. In doing so, Glikl asserts her affiliation and solidarity with the most marginalized of women and constructs an important example for actions other women might take.

Solomon Maimon, a brilliant young Polish Talmudist and rabbi, professed an indefatigable devotion to "truth" and maintained that his *Autobiography* presents an accurate and truthful account of his "spiritual [or intellectual] rebirth" as an enlightened individual.[6] Leaving his Eastern European shtetl (townlet), he abandoned his family, fatherland, and nation, he claims, because traditional religious, social, and family obligations challenged the Enlightenment ideal of the autonomy he desperately sought. What Maimon seemed not to realize is that—in a social arena rife with conflicting ideologies, a multiplicity of cultural norms, and struggles for power—complete autonomy is an unattainable ideal, and, furthermore, that autonomy necessitates supporting oneself, not always depending on charitable contributions.

By barely acknowledging, in his *Autobiography,* the wife and children he had deserted years earlier, Maimon virtually erases their existence from his writings and most likely from his consciousness. But when his wife finally does locate him and arrives in Germany pleading for a divorce, he is confronted with a dilemma that arises from the conflict between his "love of truth," his need to be an autonomous individual (a given of enlightened culture), and his inability to eradicate her existence from his life and his text. It may seem ironic that Maimon, who had abandoned his family and rejected Jewish Orthodox tradition, was unwilling or unable to part with his wife and the tradition she represented, but in fact his Eastern European heritage is precisely what he had to own as well as overcome in his quest for a "spiritual/intellectual rebirth." His effort to hold fast to the rejected traditions of his past might explain not only his resistance to granting the divorce but also the outrageous charade he orchestrates at the Jewish court where, after wily, albeit ultimately unsuccessful, machinations to avoid the rabbinic tribunal altogether, he wages against the rabbis a futile battle, the significance of which most Germans could hardly be expected to fathom. His description of his court appearances—which foregrounds the inadequate rationality of the rabbis and impugns Talmudic scholarship while never acknowledging the heavy burden borne by his wife as an *agune*—suggests that a prime function of his writing was probably not candor at all but an attempt to camouflage the truth and banish the past. His clever Talmudic argumentation may have stymied the rabbis, but it did not save him from having to confront his own vulnerability, even helplessness, when, after agreeing to a divorce, he remained as impoverished and alienated as before.

The ideology of the autonomous or sovereign individual, so important in eighteenth-century European thought and a driving force in Solomon Maimon's life, informs and favors the figure of the adventurer that, at the cusp between the nineteenth and twentieth centuries, appeared in many European and Eastern European literary works. In the third chapter I explore two highly regarded and widely read Eastern European Yiddish novels: one by S.Y. Abramovitsh (also known as Mendele Moykher Sforim, or Mendele the Bookpeddler) *Masoes benyomin hashlishi (The Travels of Benjamin the Third)*, published in 1895, and Sholem Aleykhem's *Menakhem-Mendl*, published in 1912. In each of these works, a protagonist's forays into self-serving adventurous exploits results in the permanent abandonment of his wife and family. The prototypical characteristic of the adventurer is a demand for sovereignty, for consummate freedom from all external control and dependencies, which then provides him (and the adventurer is most often a male) with the illusion of power, genius, heroism, and even cruelty. In the nineteenth century the ideology of the autonomous individual was displaced from social and political discourse into cultural discourse, where adventure may best be understood as an *imaginary* realm of freedom and pleasure, and the adventurer as a *fiction* whose fantasies of unconditional independence and fulfillment actually conceal the powerlessness, dependence, and alienation that are his true lot. Since, in a society rife with competing social and political interests, the modern adventurer's desire for total freedom and ubiquitous power can hardly be realized, his unfulfilled desire propels him into constant action, into obsession with conquest or acquisition and with the need to shed all binding commitments, including (or especially) those to women and family.

In the nineteenth century, when the elimination of residence restrictions on Jews and the greater availability of train and ship transportation made leaving the shtetl and ghetto more possible, the figure of the adventurer also wandered into Yiddish literature. In these two multi-faceted Yiddish novels, the inept and farcical protagonist-adventurers assume the roles of emancipated autonomous spirits, abandon wife and family, disregard the reality of their actual indigence and incompetence, and venture out of their impoverished *shtetlekh* into the "big world." Having cast off their burdensome familial responsibilities, Benjamin and Menakhem-Mendl feel free to pursue their fantastic, grandiose, and unrealizable goals; and although both fail miserably in their quest for a new identity of prominence, neither returns to his wife, leaving her to fend for herself as an *agune*. The victims of these adventurers are indeed the wives and children, who have been abandoned and discarded.

These parodic novels, which participate in modernist trends, negotiate a significant and complex social and cultural arena between Jewish literary genres and Western European ones, between Jewish traditional life in the Eastern European shtetl and escapades in the larger world, between the private and public spheres, and between women who remain embedded in domestic and communal life and men who seek new autonomous identities outside the shtetl. The texts are informed by a confluence of genres important within both European and Jewish literary traditions: in *Benjamin the Third,* chivalric romances (especially *Don Quixote*) and Jewish travel literature; and in *Menakhem-Mendl,* the epistolary novel, one of the earliest forms of the European novel, and the Jewish *brivnshteler,* a genre consisting of useful exemplars of letters. In these novels there is also a dual modeling in the figure of the adventurer-protagonist: he is, on the one hand, the luftmentsh of Jewish culture (a "person of air," a windbag, someone [almost always a male] with no stable occupation who seems to live only on air and who gives off a lot of "hot air") and, on the other, the modern adventurer on the lam in late-nineteenth- and early-twentieth-century European letters, most often an economic or erotic adventurer or a dandy.

Infused with far-fetched legends and completely ignorant of world geography, Benjamin and his companion, Senderl, leave their shtetl in Eastern Europe with the intention of reaching the Holy Land on foot. After trudging through a series of *shtetlekh* as ramshackle as their own, however, they are finally duped into joining the military. In the later novel, Menakhem-Mendl also leaves his home, but he travels to large cities that were being transformed by advancing capitalist enterprise and financial speculation. Although both protagonists are generally ignorant of the world outside the shtetl, untutored in any profession, and impecunious, each is driven by a desire to attain an identity of great renown and be worshipped by others. Benjamin hopes that, upon finding the legendary Red Jews (the Ten Lost Tribes) he had read about in old books, and bringing great prosperity to his impoverished and miserable coreligionists, he will be hailed as another Alexander the Great. And Menakhem-Mendl, given less to fantasy than Benjamin but no more practical, plunges—with almost no money and absolutely no knowledge about financial markets—into stock trading in his newly discovered capitalist paradises of Odessa and Yehupets (Kiev), confident he will soon earn the millions needed to become another Rothschild. Although both fail miserably in their pursuits, neither returns home, abandoning wives and children who are ensconced in the shtetl. The same contrast that exists between Benjamin's pomposity and garrulousness about his fantasized Herculean abilities and his wife Zelda's virtually silent presence as a hardworking, devoted wife (she is only spoken about; her words are never heard) is repeated and intensified in *Menakhem-Mendl*. Here letters alternate between the spouses during the first four of the six books in the volume, but the wife, Sheyne-Sheyndl, finally realizing after many attempts to entice her husband home that he has no intention of returning, removes herself from their epistolary exchange—"I am writing you, that I have nothing to write you"—and her letters are completely absent from the final two books. Menakhem-Mendl's practice of writing letters almost exclusively about himself to his wife then evolves into writing very long letters about himself to himself. What is silenced with the disappearance of Sheyne-Sheyndl's voice is not only the plight of the *agune* and her world of the shtetl, with its Yiddish idiom (*mame-loshn*, or "language of the mothers"), but also any interactive dialogue between the woman and man, between shtetl and metropolis, between domestic private domain and public arena, and between traditional communality and modern individualism. The seeds sown by Solomon Maimon a hundred years earlier reach full flower in Menakhem-Mendl. This impoverished blowhard of a luftmentsh—having failed in every enterprise he has undertaken (and there were many) and now ready to set sail for America, the "genuine" capitalist paradise, where, "gold, they say, is rolling in the streets"[7]—detaches himself completely from all his responsibilities, finally attaining the only kind of autonomy (the autonomy of powerlessness) and freedom (freedom in a vacuum) that modernity and capitalism can furnish him. When his wife, Sheyne-Sheyndl, is victimized, discarded, silenced, and forever marginalized as an "eternal *agune*," the novel is transformed from a dialogue, albeit an inadequate one, into a long, overbearing, narcissistic male monologue.[8]

Chapter 4 moves, like Menakhem-Mendl, to the New World, the United States, where, in response to a burgeoning number of abandoned women and the burden on public charities, the National Desertion Bureau was founded in 1911 with its main mission to find and bring to justice deserting Jewish husbands. Although up to this point I have focused on representations of a few isolated deserters, and perhaps given the impression that desertion was not a widespread problem, the Bureau's records indicate that it was in fact a problem of major proportions. For many years the Bureau processed more than five thousand cases annually, which were probably the tip of the iceberg, only the cases reported to its office. It also supplied the deserters' portraits, names, and other information to the *Forverts* and four other Yiddish newspapers for their ongoing feature, A Gallery of Vanished Husbands. But while the Gallery and the Bureau brought the issue of desertion into the broad public arena, they did not address with equal forthrightness and candor the predicament of the victims, the abandoned wives and children. The brief histories accompanying the deserters' pictures described these renegades as energetic men who had crossed a big ocean and settled in the United States, men who had worked, married, fathered children, deserted their families, sometimes married again, produced more children, and left those families too. The wives are inserted into these short biographies as faceless ciphers: they have no defining characteristics other than their first names and great need, evidenced by their seeking help from the charities. Once again the notoriously irresponsible deserters are portrayed as akin to adventurers, as having accomplished something, as having histories, while the women, with no portraits or histories, remain powerless and static, caring for their children, waiting for their husbands to return, waiting for assistance. There is no "Gallery of Abandoned Wives," no "Gallery of Abandoned Children." Indeed, the documents of the National Desertion Bureau—with their apologetics for the men who deserted their families and their sympathy for the weakness or depravity that caused men to yield to their "wandering proclivity"[9]—tend to sustain the impression that the Bureau's social (and at times self-serving) agenda was more concerned with the reputation of its directors and with relieving the monetary burden of the charities than with the plight of the women and children. Its rather patriarchal mission was to apprehend and "tame" the deserter, restore the family by the husband's return, and, accomplishing this, avoid any antisemitism that could arise from the encumbrance on the charities, an encumbrance that might reflect negatively on the Bureau's socially prominent founders. Since virtually all the deserters were poor, recent Yiddish-speaking immigrants living in New York's Lower East Side, and those pursuing them were already-acculturated professional German Jews (called "uptown Jews") in positions of power and concerned with their own public stature, one begins to understand that what happened here may have been not so much a struggle for the restoration of the family as a complex ethnic, class, and gender struggle. The family may best be regarded here as the occasion for one class of wealthy, eminent men bringing into line a class of impoverished men who were perceived as uncultured. Thus the victimized women and children comprise the arena for the struggle between these two groups of men, the privileged and the indigent.

In this chapter, I chart the social and cultural terrain of desertion by reviewing the Bureau's own literature and reports and assessing the impact of media representations of deserters and desertion. I also retrieve some of the submerged experiences and suppressed voices of the victimized and marginalized women and children from the newspapers' personal ads and letters to the editor, where the voices of those who had been overlooked could be found. But even in the letters of women and children, the fear of revealing anger and offending the deserter resulted in self-censorship and appeasement, which stood in sharp contrast to the open aggression articulated in a very long letter to the editor written by thirty-seven scofflaw husbands jailed for nonsupport of their families. The prisoners heap abuse on their wives, reject all responsibility for their own behavior and for the welfare of their families, and threaten their wives with enchainment as "eternal *agunes*." It becomes clear in this letter and in the Bureau's documents that the politics of gender among traditional Jews, as in many cultures, is closely allied with the politics of patriarchal power and property rights, for no matter how powerless or subjugated the Jewish male is in the social world, he always knows he has complete power over his wife, whose marital destiny he legally owns and controls.

Finally, chapter 5 focuses on the relationship between my mother, who was deserted by my father when I was an infant, and me. My original intention was to write an account only of my victimized mother as an abandoned woman, but during the writing I realized that, although I could recount many of my mother's experiences in detail, I often did not actually know what she thought or felt; and my presence intruded everywhere into what was intended to be her story. Realizing that I was a poor ventriloquist, and that her story was clearly not mine to tell, I changed course and wrote *our* story, an intertwining narrative of mother and daughter filtered through the experience of a daughter who, refusing to be a victim, nevertheless had to come to grips with a woman shrouded in her sense of unrelenting victimization. Like many, if not most, deserted or abused women, my mother felt she had to conceal the shame of having been deserted and of being so impoverished. I too, of course, was constrained to keep her secret, and even now I can hardly believe that I was obedient and silent, hiding the truth until I was an adult professional woman teaching at a university. Had I thought my journey into the past was uncommon or atypical, I would have yielded to my original misgivings about including a personal biographical essay in a generally scholarly text about representations of desertion. But writing this book—about the social marginality imposed on so many abandoned wives, who were positioned at the periphery of communal life and even of the texts about them—helped me to recognize that for years I had actually experienced myself as having been different, discarded, even an outcast. In fact, the sense of being marginal had consumed a large part of my life as well as my mother's. It became clear to me that an appropriate place for this narrative was precisely where one would not expect to find it: in a scholarly text in which deserted wives and children are the central focus.

To conclude, these multiple approaches—historical, cultural, literary, and autobiographical—present new and decidedly different views of Jewish men, Jewish women, and most certainly their families. Far from creating families that were havens in a heartless world, deserting fathers contributed to a long history of female-headed households. Indeed, too often these one-parent households experienced the feminization of poverty decades before the concept was created. However, although women and children were the victims of a patriarchal religious system and society, they were not solely victims. Thus, Glikl's story focuses on the solidarity among women that resulted in their empowerment, and my own narrative attends to the family dynamics in a female-headed household and injects a sense of agency from the child's perspective. While the scarce literature on the history and sociology of the Jewish family concentrates largely on the normative two-parent, intact nuclear family, this book opens a window into the lives of some of the thousands of Jewish families who over many centuries were forced to live otherwise.

CHAPTER I

Abandoned Wives in Jewish Family Law

An Introduction to the Agune

For two millennia, from Talmudic times well into the twentieth century, the *agune,* a woman "chained" or "anchored" to her husband because she is unable to divorce or remarry, has been regarded as a figure of considerable interest and importance for Jewish religious and legal authorities. Although *agunes* have suffered mightily because of their marginal position in the largely family-oriented Jewish community, it is perhaps the embarrassment of that community in the face of patent injustice against these women that accounts for the scant attention their plight has received from cultural, social, and literary historians and critics. Despite the fact that the *agune* is accorded considerable importance in many Jewish writings—rabbinical *responsa,* treatises on family law, and institutional social documents—she rarely emerges as a figure of central importance in historical or literary texts. Instead, she is often found hovering, silent or silenced, at the margins of those works. Even though, for example, the title of Khayim Grade's novel *Die agune (The Agune)* heralds the importance of the protagonist, her relevance is substantially diminished by her function as the occasion for an extended narrative about the disastrous confrontation between two generations of rabbinic authorities with opposing views, and for a comprehensive depiction of Vilna's social, religious, and moral tensions.[1] The *agune* in Grade's novel may be divested of her titular prominence, but her textual marginality nonetheless reflects the reality of her position within the social milieu and religious practices of the traditionally patriarchal Jewish society. The story of a bereft woman who has lost her primary social identity and status—as a wife—is thus transmuted into a narrative about powerful men of the community, rabbis, seeking to control the woman's fate. Paradoxically, however, although the *agune* is relegated to the margins of traditional society, her situation has for centuries actually garnered significant attention from Jewish legal authorities: the *Encyclopedia Judaica* notes that "the problem of the *agunah* is one of the most complex in halakhic [Jewish legal] discussions and is treated in great detail in halakhic literature."[2] Moreover, the extensive concern with the ostensibly halakhically insoluble problem of the abandoned *agune* does indeed disclose, even acknowledge, the serious consequences of the unalterable gender and power differential operative at the very foundation of the Jewish legal system.

In Jewish law, only the husband has the prerogative of executing and delivering a divorce, or *get,* and there are essentially four reasons why a woman may be unable to obtain a Jewish divorce: the husband is mentally ill, thus legally incompetent to grant a divorce; the husband has died but there is no legally valid evidence of his death; a recalcitrant husband refuses to divorce his wife; or the husband abandons her and disappears. Of these reasons, the one that has virtually no halakhic solution is that of the abandoned wife, a situation whose considerable repercussions are explored here in this discussion of the relevant aspects of Jewish law. Whereas the extensive halakhic consideration of the problem of the *agune* in the Talmud, and in the rabbinical *responsa* literature from the Middle Ages to the present, focuses largely on recalcitrant and deserting husbands, my study concentrates primarily on representations of the abandoned *agune* in selected texts from early modern Jewish history in the seventeenth century well into the twentieth.[3]

The broad range of writings that I consider in this book includes the diverse social and individual situations of a number of *agunes;* different genres—autobiographical texts, novels, institutional social documents, and a personal narrative; and texts in German, Yiddish, and English written in Germany, Eastern Europe, and the United States. While the book's structure embraces a range of perspectives on the *agune* figure and on the religious, social, and political dynamics of *aginut,* all the *agunes* in this study—the considerable disparity among the individual texts notwithstanding—share a common experience of marginality. Marginality is evident not only in the subaltern legal status of women within traditional Judaism but also in their marginal positions as *agunes* in the particular social environments and narratives they inhabit. But in order to engage in a meaningful discourse about the *agune* and *aginut,* some relevant knowledge of Jewish family law is necessary, for only then can one comprehend the fundamental issues confronting deserted wives and the consequences of the many futile challenges to any halakhically acceptable resolution.

In Jewish law, marriage creates a contract in which the wife (and all her property) is possessed by the husband, and only he has the prerogative to dispose of his possessions (including his wife), only he—not the courts or the wife—may nullify that contract by divorce. The biblical source for Jewish divorce (*get*) is Deuteronomy 24:1–2: "A man takes a wife and possesses her. She fails to please him because he finds something obnoxious about her, and he writes her a bill of divorcement, hands it to her, and sends her away from his house; she leaves his household and becomes the wife of another man."[4] Under Jewish law a marriage may be terminated by either the death of a spouse or divorce. Annulment is another possibility, but because sufficient grounds for this decree are difficult to sustain, only in very rare cases did the Orthodox rabbinate recognize legally inappropriate marriages that could be annulled. Thus, a woman had to rely on her husband for a divorce.[5] Yet, in the eleventh century, in a decidedly radical move, Rabbenu Gershom of Mainz, intending to support the rights of women as much as possible within the limitations of halakha, issued a *takana* (rabbinic directive with the force of law) that required the consent of the woman for a divorce to be legal.[6] This meant that, while the man retained the prerogative to grant a divorce, the woman could now consent to the divorce or refuse it. This liberalizing act was, however, overturned in the twelfth century by an influential French authority, Rabbenu Jacob Tam.

The difficulty in releasing an *agune* from her marriage derives essentially from the fundamentally unalterable corpus of Jewish law, at whose core is an unequal gender and power differential. Moshe Meiselman explains the reasons for the inflexibility of this law as follows: "The legislative prerogative granted to rabbinic authorities came to an end with the termination of the talmudic period. Among the many reasons the legislative prerogative came to a close is the fact that subsequent to the talmudic period no beth-din [rabbinic court] was universally accepted by all Jews, and universal acceptance is a sine qua non for legislation. Hence, no legislative prerogative to change the basic marriage and divorce laws was granted to any rabbi or group of rabbis subsequent to the talmudic period."[7] Rabbi and religious scholar Boaz Cohen affirmed the inalterability of Jewish divorce law in a 1953 Joint Conference of the Rabbinical Assembly (the international association of Conservative rabbis): "We cannot graft upon the tree of Jewish law a foreign branch, such as the principle of granting to women equal rights with the husband to *issue* a divorce."[8] In the many hundreds of years since Talmudic times, the inflexibility of the law has not, however, ended serious attempts to "alleviate" the plight of the *agune*. But Reuven Yaron indicates that, in the sphere of the abandoned *agune,* "there has been less change, less innovation, than in any other," and that "one encounters again and again the same tendency to strictness, the same horror at going beyond the principles laid down in the Talmud itself." In examining the numerous rabbinical decisions, he takes note of "the anguish and regret of the authors, the conflict between their humane desire to help and the overriding obedience to what they consider their duty," but he also recognizes that "this is poor consolation indeed for the woman whom the decision may condemn to a lifetime of celibacy,"[9] not to mention the shame, social ostracism, and loss of self-esteem and status she would suffer.

An oft-repeated explanation of why the rabbis were so reluctant to declare a deserted husband dead even after years of absence and to grant the *agune* permission to marry was the fear that, should the wife remarry and the former husband reappear, she would be an adulteress and any offspring of her new marriage would be *mamzerim.* A *mamzer,* a child of a forbidden union (here marriage with an adulterous woman), is not considered a normative Jew and is permitted to marry only another *mamzer* or a convert to Judaism. Moreover, the stigma of the *mamzer* remains with the family for ten generations.[10] In such cases, upon the first husband's return, the new husband must divorce the adulterous woman, who is then not permitted to remarry her first husband. Given the grave consequences of adulterous marriage, the rabbis were loath to verify a death without great certainty, even though, from the Talmudic period onward, rabbis counseled leniency in efforts to release an *agune.*

One important way in which the early rabbis sought to relieve the plight of an *agune* whose husband had disappeared was to relax the halakhic rules concerning acceptable witnesses (two Jewish males who were neither slaves nor relatives) for verifying a person's death. In litigation cases involving *agunes,* one witness (instead of two), slaves, relatives of the married couple, women, non-Jews, and apostates were permitted to testify. Even the *agune* could bear witness, provided she could prove that she had been on good terms with her husband and that he had not disappeared during wartime. Although Maimonides had ruled that "one does not examine the witnesses thoroughly in agunah cases because the Sages said to be lenient in order to release *agunot*,"[11] Rachel Biale notes that, "while the requirements concerning witnesses are lax because of the danger of *aginut* (Yevamot 93b), the standards demanding direct evidence of death remain firm, and these were sometimes impossible to meet."[12] The absentee husband's death or his funeral had to have been witnessed or his corpse indisputably identified; and while hearsay testimony was permitted, it had to be substantiated by direct evidence. Yael Levy of the Georgetown University Law Center notes, however, that, "in most situations where the husband is 'missing,' there is not a single witness to his death (or whereabouts), even among women and apostates. Consequently the relaxed evidentiary standards do not alleviate the predicament of most agunot."[13]

Many recommended modern solutions to the *agune* problem concerned recalcitrant husbands who refused to grant divorces to their wives, but several significant proposals involving abandoned wives are worth noting. In the nineteenth century the Reform Judaism movement declared that, if the laws of a country presumed a person dead after a specific number of years of unexplained absence, its *beyt din* could decide to release the *agune* from her marriage and permit her to marry again. This was, however, rejected by both the Conservative and Orthodox rabbinates. Taking up a similar argument about the husband's presumed death, Levy in 1993 submitted to Israel's religious courts a *takana* that she knew would not resolve problems concerning recalcitrant or mentally incompetent husbands, but which she thought "would at least provide a comprehensive solution to the problem of aginut resulting from a husband's disappearance." Her *takana* was based on the presumption of death after the passage of a length of time stipulated by the laws of different states in the United States. It required

(1) that any man who disappears from home for a stipulated period of time be declared dead; (2) that if facts and circumstances indicate the probability that he died prior to the expiration of the stipulated period he be declared dead at the earlier time which the facts and circumstances point to as the time of death; and (3) that if the woman has remarried under the assumption that her husband is dead, her second marriage shall be presumed valid and her first marriage dissolved, not to be reinstated even if her first husband reappears.[14]

There is no evidence that this *takana* was even considered by the Israeli courts. Concluding remarks in her article indicate that Levy's interest in resolving the problem of the deserted Jewish wife is grounded in an issue with significant ramifications for Jews and Judaism. "The problem of the agunah whose husband has disappeared," she writes, "is a compelling one requiring immediate solution. The longer Jewish lawmakers wait to implement a workable solution, the more cases of aginut arise and the more shameful Judaism appears to the rest of the world because of the shoddy way it treats its women. . . . For halakhah to retain its credibility it needs to be amended by takkanah, to redress this problem completely, not just artfully manipulated to cure bits and pieces of it."[15]

Other important resolutions for the problem of missing husbands were largely prophylactic—that is, intended to prevent a woman from becoming an *agune* rather than to release an existing *agune* from her plight. Two such recommended solutions were conditional marriage and conditional divorce, both of which the rabbinate ultimately deemed halakhically unsound. In 1884 the French rabbinate approved a declaration stating that a civil divorce would automatically be acceptable as a *get* under Jewish law because a rabbi had the power to annul a marriage terminated in civil court. Furthermore, the French Rabbi Michael Weil also suggested that all marriages be made conditional by the groom's promise to his bride during the wedding ceremony that "if the judges of the *state* shall divorce us and I not give you a *Jewish* divorce, this marriage will be retroactively invalid."[16] A similar solution had been tendered fifteen years earlier, in 1869, by the Reform movement at a rabbinical conference in Philadelphia, in which Jewish divorce was relegated to the civil courts, making the *get* altogether obsolete.[17] The Reform movement's proposal was rejected by both the Orthodox and Conservative movements, and at the beginning of the twentieth century the entire European rabbinate opposed the French proposal, therewith dismissing the whole matter. The main objection was that such conditionality undermined the unconditional commitment required for a Jewish marriage.

Proposals for conditional divorce fared no better than those for conditional marriage. Basically, two kinds of conditional divorces were proposed—one written at the time of the marriage would have permitted an agent, selected by the husband, to deliver the divorce to the wife if the husband did not return from a war or long journey; the other was a divorce issued when the husband was about to go to war or to embark on a journey. Both forms of divorce were rejected by the rabbinical authorities. In the former instance, it was argued that a *get* could not be used to protect against possible impending adversity, and that, once written, a *get* delivered to a woman would actually end the marriage immediately. In the latter case, the parties were expected to agree to remarry if the husband returned home, but a *kohen* (priest), for example, could not marry a divorcée even if she had once been his wife. Moreover, there was always the danger that one of the parties might decide not to honor the agreement to remarry.[18] Conditional marriage and conditional divorce were both attempts to prevent the woman from becoming an *agune,* but for a woman who was already an *agune,* particularly one who was abandoned, there was virtually no available halakhic solution. "Once a woman has become an agunah," Biale writes, "there are certain circumstances where there is absolutely no valid halakhic way of releasing her and permitting her to remarry. The only possible remedy for such circumstances would be a revolutionary change in the Halakhah, giving women or the Jewish courts the power to divorce a man without his consent."[19]

Of course, the legal right of a woman to divorce her husband would require the recognition of equality between men and women, which those who upheld the intransigent hierarchical and patriarchal characteristics of Jewish family law were no doubt loath to accept.[20] There had actually been a period of about five hundred years (from about the seventh to the eleventh century), however, during the ascendancy of the Geonim—they headed Babylonian academies and were authoritative interpreters of Talmudic law—when "spectacular achievements in this area of the law consisted in the fact that for the first and unfortunately last time in Jewish jurisprudence, almost complete equality was effected between men and women as regards the rules to *get*."[21] Although the husband's right to divorce his wife remained intact, and only he could prepare and deliver the *get* at will, she was granted the right to demand a *get* and, should her husband refuse, petition the court to compel him. She was also guaranteed the entire sum of the alimony provided for in their marriage contract.[22] The tide turned away from Geonic liberalism when Rabbenu Jacob Tam, the influential twelfth-century French authority, ruled against any coercion of recalcitrant husbands and against the right of women to initiate divorce proceedings. Shlomo Riskin indicates that Rabbenu Tam's legal position was readily accepted at the time, and for many generations, because of the social and political situation of the Jews in the Diaspora, where "small, cohesive Jewish communities, generally bound together by familial ties, isolated from the surrounding Gentile society by external anti-Semitism and internal religious strength, existed primarily against a backdrop of a culture that insisted upon the permanence of the marriage bond and family life."[23] The Geonim's liberalism about Jewish divorce was probably a reaction to the same social circumstances: they too were concerned with communal maintenance but feared that Jewish women who could not receive *gets* might make social connections outside Judaism that were more amenable to them.

The marked power differential between men and women under Jewish law is at the core of the *agune* problem, which has for centuries generated attempts by rabbis, feminists, lawyers, and organized groups[24] to find acceptable halakhic solutions for *agunes*. There has, however, been very little success in adopting legislation in which men and women would be entitled to the same justice; and the inequities are considerable. Consider, for example, the male version of the *agune,* a man whose wife is unwilling or unable to accept a divorce. Unlike the *agune,* he could, with the consent of a hundred rabbis (as difficult as this may be to acquire), be granted permission to marry again. But even without a dispensation to marry, any children he has with another (unmarried) Jewish woman would not be *mamzerim* excluded from normative Jewish practices. (A *mamzer* is the offspring of a man and a "forbidden" woman—namely, an adulterous woman; but, according to the Bible, there are no "forbidden" men.)[25] Blu Greenberg recognizes that the rabbis who "did not go the final step in equalizing divorce law" were guided not by a concern for gender equality but by "principles of paternalism and hierarchy," and yet, according to her apologetics, they "cannot be faulted, given the almost universal nature of sexual hierarchy."[26] Sexual hierarchy is, of course, not a natural phenomenon but a socially and politically constructed one and, as such, can be constructed differently. In fact, it was possible for five hundred years during the Geonic period to make significant gains in parity and protection for women, so it seems logical that now—in an atmosphere of continuing progress toward gender equality in Western societies—the adoption of similarly reasoned solutions might be possible. There could be emendations to the *ketuba* (marriage contract), forms of conditional marriage or divorce, or the presumption of the legal death of a person missing for a specific period of time. The explanation that the actions of the rabbis solely concern the well-being, protection, and status of the *agune* seems hollow, even disingenuous, especially when the rulings most often support a status quo that affirms the exclusive rights, advantages, and power of men. Greenberg claims that the traditional *ketuba*—with its provision that, upon divorce, the man return his wife's dowry and other properties and provide alimony until she remarries—"discouraged divorce by levying economic sanctions."[27] These sanctions may at times have discouraged divorce, but they may also encourage recalcitrance and desertion. Indeed, in the twentieth-century United States, which saw a very large number of desertions, desertion was often referred to as the "poor man's divorce" because it was considered an alternative to divorce for impoverished Eastern European immigrants who could not afford to honor the monetary commitments of the *ketuba* (see chapter 4).

CHAPTER 2

Doubly Exiled in Germany

Abandoned Wives in Glikl Hamel's Memoirs
and Solomon Maimon's Autobiography

Within the century spanning the final years of the seventeenth century and those of the eighteenth, two autobiographical works written by Jews living in Germany contained significant accounts of women whose husbands had deserted them or otherwise disappeared. Under traditional Jewish law, these *agunes* were unable to obtain a divorce and, therefore, to marry again. Although these particular incidents involving *agunes* comprise only a small part of the texts in which they appear, they nevertheless proffer important insights into the complex discourse of gender relations among Jews and into the interactions between German Jews and German Christians in a world in which the social, political, and cultural sands were beginning to shift toward modernity. The earlier of these texts, written intermittently between 1690 and 1719 in Judeo-German by Glikl Hamel,[1] a relatively well-to-do Jew from Hamburg, came to be known as her memoirs.[2] In 1792–93 Solomon Maimon, a brilliant former Talmudist and rabbi originally from Poland, published an autobiography *(Lebensgeschichte)* in German.

Each of these works is in part concerned with separate yet interactive contexts of Jewish community and tradition, on the one hand, and the dominant German society and culture, on the other. The texts and what they communicate are also markedly distinct from one another, partly because of differences in genre and style and in the gender, status, and interests of the writers. But these texts were also affected by the enormous political and economic upheavals resulting from the Thirty Years' War that ravaged the European continent during Glikl's lifetime and, later, by the Enlightenment and the French Revolution, which generated significant cultural and ideological developments in eighteenth-century Europe during Maimon's lifetime. Glikl—a widowed mother of twelve living children and an able businesswoman—wrote the "seven small books" of her *Zikhroynes (Memoirs)* between 1690 and 1719. It was a project that she hoped would not only dissipate the melancholia she suffered following her husband's untimely death but also inform her children of their family history and the moral behavior she regarded as necessary for an ethical Jewish life. Glikl wrote in Yiddish, her native tongue and the language common to the Jews of Germany at the time, and intended to have her writings circulate only within her own large family. In his midtwenties, Maimon—a product of an Orthodox Jewish Eastern European environment and a devotee of Moses Maimonides, in whose honor he adopted the name "Maimon"—moved to Germany, where he was an ardent supporter of the European Enlightenment; his ideas were highly regarded by contemporary philosophers such as Kant and Fichte. Although his native language was Yiddish and he was fluent in Hebrew, he wrote his major philosophical treatises and autobiography in German and, of course, intended to publish them.

Prominent among the differences in the autobiographical writings of Glikl and Maimon is their treatment of the tragic situation of the deserted *agune,* a marginalized woman in a family-oriented and male-dominated society. By moving the *agune*'s desperate predicament into the foreground of one of her narratives, Glikl transmutes, without undermining its historicity, the factual record of an infamous event of 1687 about two murdered Jews into an account of a traditional Jewish housewife's extraordinary prowess in search of justice. In *Salomon Maimons Lebensgeschichte, Von ihm selbst geschrieben (Solomon Maimon's Autobiography, Written by Himself),* on the other hand, the deserted wife—left behind in Poland when her husband makes the great "leap into the alien history" *(dieser Sprung in fremde Geschichte)* of eighteenth-century enlightened Germany[3]—disappears from its pages when he leaves for Germany. She does, however, reappear at the end of the *Autobiography,* when she confronts him on German soil. But even in the textual recognition of her presence, the narrator's suppressions, evasions, and satirical antics obscure both the *agune*'s plight and his own complicity in it from German readers who were, in large part, uninformed about Jewish law and religious practices. Indeed, Maimon's silence about the predicament of the wife and family he abandoned, as well as critics' inattention to the significance of the *agunes* in both his and Glikl's writings, make undoing this erasure all the more necessary, if only in critical recognition of the profound effects of such erasures.

Glikl's *Agunes*

One narrative in Glikl's *Memoirs* focuses on the *agune* and concerns actual events that took place several years earlier in Hamburg and attracted considerable interest because they involved the disappearance and murder of two local Jews, three years apart. Although Glikl purports merely to record the details of what she calls a "great" (or "very important") "story" (or "event") (*a grous mayse; mayse* may designate a "story" or "event"),[4] the narrative's structure and its deviations from a contemporaneous Hebrew account by Samuel ben Meir Hekscher— written at the time of the event in 1687 and therefore considered by some to be the more reliable of the two[5]—suggest that Glikl's text is something more than a factual account.[6] Her narrative may also be read as an exemplary tale, or perhaps as both an event and a story—a *mayse* in both of its senses. This connection between historicity and exemplarity of Glikl's *agune* story actually corresponds to a traditional understanding of Jewish history as both a record and an interpretation of what has happened, and it informs the overall structure of the *Memoirs,* two of whose significant levels of representation—factual, experiential report, on the one hand, and moralizing commentary and exemplary stories, on the other—have generally been noted by critics.[7] Indeed, the story about the *agunes* may be read as an interesting paradigm for the textual cooperation of historicity and exemplarity.

The design of the opening chapters of the *Memoirs* identifies Glikl's concern with both of these aspects. Thus, the text does not commence with moral admonitions but rather with a disclaimer: "I do not intend to make and write you a book of morals." *(ikh bin akh nit oyzn aykh ayn seyfer muser tsu makhn un tsu shraybn.)*[8] Nonetheless Glikl clearly expects that "writing about all the troubles and sorrows that a sinful person must suffer" *(vos zol ikh ale tsores un inuim shraybn di der zindige mentsh muz oys shteyn)*[9] will set her children on the proper ethical path through life. Indeed, the content and organization of the opening book—the space devoted to the narration of four exemplary tales (one third of book 1), the copious discussions about learning from moral texts, and the absence of experiential or historical material—indicate that one of her primary interests in the *Memoirs* is the fundamental importance of exemplary writings in learning to live a pious life. The stories, ethical commentary, and moral counsel in book I constitute a homiletic overture and major structural pillar for the presentation of the family history that follows. Not until the second book does Glikl begin to chronicle her family's life in the social and political milieu of seventeenth-century Germany. From that point on, she interweaves historical and experiential accounts with exemplary tales and moral commentary, as she does in the narrative about the *agunes* and the disappearance of their husbands.

Glikl's *agune* narrative may best be understood as the historical account of two notorious murders and as an exemplary story both about the unacknowledged empowering resources of women in a traditional Jewish society that regards them as subordinate and about the tragedy of exile. Read in this way, the personal fate of the *agunes* in Glikl's tale resembles the fate of the Jews in the Diaspora. This connection recalls the traditional topos that describes the relationship of God with the Jewish people as a marriage and the exiled people as an abandoned wife, an *agune*. The complex political, cultural, and aesthetic dynamics of a narrative that lays claim to historicity even as poetic license is taken to create a story of special, more encompassing significance warrant particularly close scrutiny, as do the differences between the accounts of Glikl and Hekscher, which invite speculation about important gender and status issues within the Jewish community.

Glikl's account of the historical event is clearly presented as a "story"—it begins: "About this time there took place in Hamburg a great story [or event]." *(in der tsayt leerekh izt behamburg akh a grous mayse gesheyen.)*[10] It may, therefore, be best, especially after the introductory episode, in which Glikl details her knowledge of the Metz family, to regard the narrator as an integral part of the story, and not as the memoirist Glikl but as a figure whom Glikl has also created to tell the story. Because the narrative is both subtle and complex and requires a detailed exploration,[11] I include here a translation of the entire text:

About this time [1687] there took place in Hamburg a great story [or event]. There lived in Altona a man, Abraham Metz by name, may God avenge his blood! He was married to my kinswoman Sarah, daughter of Elijah Cohen. Before he moved to Hamburg, he had lived in Herford and was married to the daughter of Leyb Herford. She died two years after the marriage, and he then moved to Hamburg and married Sarah. He brought with him a fortune of three thousand reichstaler. But he was a stranger here and knew nothing of the manners and the business ways of the Hamburgers, and within a few years had lost his entire fortune. He was a money changer and lived at that time in Altona.

One morning his wife came into town and asked all her friends whether her husband had stayed the night at any of their houses, but after innumerable enquiries, found no one with whom he had stayed. She was greatly alarmed. Many said she had quarreled with him and he had run away from her. It was three years to the time of the incident of which I am now writing, and nothing more was heard of this Abraham Metz. Everyone had his own opinion and said just what he liked. Many spoke evil of him, which I do not care to repeat or mention in connection with such a martyr. But because of our sins, our human weakness is such that we often speak with our mouth of what our eyes have not seen. Thus poor Sarah was for more than three years a "living widow" with her sad orphans and had to let the people speak as they liked and pass judgment on her husband, may God avenge his blood!

There was in the Hamburg community a head of household, an honest man who, although he was not rich, supported his wife and four children quite comfortably. He was a money changer. Every money changer rushes around all day for his living, and toward evening, at the time of afternoon prayers, goes home and thence to synagogue. Each one belongs to a *chevra*[12] and studies with the other members, and after studying returns home. It was very late on this particular night when the wife waited for her husband's return from the *chevra* so that they could have their supper together. Her waiting was in vain. She ran to all their friends' houses, but could not find him. He was, through our sins, sad to tell, lost.

The next day there were rumors flying about the town. One said he had seen him here, the other that he had seen him somewhere else. At midday they spoke of it at the bourse. Zanvil, the son of Reb Meir Hekscher, related, "Yesterday a woman came up to me and asked whether I had six hundred or seven hundred reichstaler with me; if I had, I should go with her—a distinguished stranger was in her house and had much gold and precious stones to sell. But I had no cash and so did not go with her." As he finished saying this a man named Lipman who stood nearby asked him what sort of a person she was and what she wore. Zanvil answered, "She wore this and that." Upon which Lipman said, "I know the woman! and also know whom she serves. I do not trust her master. Good cannot come of it." And with such talk they left the bourse, everyone going to his own house.

When Lipman reached home, he said to his wife, "Do you know what I am going to tell you? The woman who is a servant of the son of the owner of the Mariners' Tavern went to Zanvil Hekscher and would have taken him with her if he had had six or seven hundred reichstaler on him. I am really afraid that the man who is missing went with her and has been murdered." Upon hearing this, his wife beat her hands on her head and cried, "Through our sins! I've just remembered: the same person was also here and wanted you or me to go with her. You know very well what an evil man her master is; he is a murderer; it is certain that the upright, pious man was killed in her house." The woman, who was a very capable woman [or housewife], continued, "I will not rest or be still until I bring the whole thing to light."

"My crazy woman!" cried her husband. "If it is true, what are we to do? This is Hamburg, and one cannot even utter a word [because Jews had no residency rights, but lived in Hamburg on sufferance]." So, things remained as they were for some days. However, with a beat of the drum the town council proclaimed that anyone who knew anything of the missing Jew, dead or alive, should come forward and say what he knew: he would receive one hundred ducats reward, and his name would be kept secret. But no one came forward. Thus it was simply forgotten, that's the way of the world. No matter how intense and important something is, if there is no effect, it falls into oblivion. But the living widow and her orphans remained sitting in distress.

It happened that one early Sabbath morning in the summer, Lipman's wife could not sleep, just as once happened to the King of Spain. He once asked a Jewish scholar, "What is the meaning of the verse, *hineh lo yonum v'lo yishon shomer yisroel*?" The scholar translated: "He neither sleeps nor slumbers, the guardian of Israel." The King answered: "That is not what it means. The real meaning is that God the guardian lets one neither sleep nor slumber. Had I slept as usual this night, you would all have been lost as a result of a blood-libel. But God, your guardian, made me unable to sleep, and I saw how a child was thrown into a Jewish house. Had I not been witness to this, all Jews would have been put to death."

In the same way, Lipman's wife was unable to sleep. Early in the morning she stood at her window. She lived in the Ellern Steinway [Old Stoneway], a passageway through which everyone going in or out of Altona had to pass.

It was on Friday night that she could not sleep and drove everyone mad. Her husband reproached her, asking what sort of a game this was; she would really become crazy. But she answered that nothing would help her as long as the murder was not avenged, for she knew quite well, her heart told her, that *that* man was the murderer.

Day dawned, and she still stood at the window looking out onto the street. And there she saw the man whom she took to be the murderer, his wife, and a servant go by, carrying a large box. When she saw this, she cried out, "Oh God, stand by me now! This is the beginning of my satisfaction!" She rushed and straightway snatched up her apron and rain cloak and ran out of the room. Her husband sprang from his bed to restrain her, but could do nothing. She ran after those people, followed them to Altona, to the river Elbe, and saw them place the box upon the bank. Rebekah—that's what the woman was called— persuaded herself that nothing other was in the box than the murdered man.

She ran to the people of Altona and begged them, for God's sake, to help her; she knew for certain who was the murderer. But they were unwilling and said, "It is easy to begin anything, but one cannot foretell the end." But she insisted that they should go to the president with her, and at length two house-holders went with her. They appeared before the president and told him every-thing. He said to them, "If you cannot prove your accusation, I will confiscate your goods and chattels." Rebekah would not allow herself to be turned aside by this, but answered that she not only risked her property but her blood as well. "I beg you, for God's sake, Herr President, send for the murderer and take him with all that he has with him."

Upon this, watchmen and soldiers were sent to the Elbe. But they arrived just in time to see them go on board a ship for Harburg, an hour's journey from Altona. If they reached Harburg they would be free, for Harburg was under another jurisdiction. But the soldiers arrived in time and took the murderer, together with his wife and box, and brought them before the president, who ordered the box to be opened. Naught but the clothes of the murderer and his wife were found!

The fear and anxiety that fell on the poor Jews can be imagined! The man was closely examined and questioned but would confess nothing. On the contrary, he used threats, and terror fell on every Jew, for he came of a large, well-known family in Hamburg. All fled in fear, but Rebekah kept saying, "I beg you, dear folk, do not despair; you will see how God will help us." In her great anxiety she ran from Altona to town. As she came into the field between Altona and Hamburg, she came face to face with the woman who was in the murderer's service. Rebekah recognized her; she was the one who had gone to the sons of Israel asking which one had about seven hundred reichstaler and had taken him to her master's house. Rebekah went up to her and said, "It is lucky for you and your master and his wife that you have met me. They are both imprisoned in Altona for the murder they have committed. They have confessed everything, only your confession is missing. When you have confessed there is a ship waiting for you and your master and mistress to sail away in. For we Jews desire only to know that Abraham is dead, so that his wife may take another man. Other than that, we desire nothing from you."

She spoke more to the woman, for Rebekah was very clever and persuasive. Because of her words, the woman too began to talk and told her everything: how she had met Abraham at the bourse after she had called on Rebekah's husband Reb Lipman and other Jews. But no one else was so unlucky as Reb Abraham when, to his undoing, he had a full purse on him. She had shown him a small gold chain and told him that an officer in her master's house had much gold and diamonds to sell. "So Abraham came with me and when he entered the house, his slaughter bench was ready. My master led him down to his room, and together we took his life. We buried him under the threshold." Then the woman added, "Rebekah, I am telling you all this in confidence. Do not betray me." Rebekah answered her, "Are you a fool? Don't you know my honest heart? Everything I do is for your master and mistress, so that they may soon be released and out of Altona. As soon as you tell all this before our people, everything will be all right."

So the servant went to the house of the president with Rebekah. He heard out the former, and though now she stammered, repenting what she had said, still, everything was out. Most important of all, she had already revealed the burial place of the murdered man. In the end, she confessed everything to the president as she had to Rebekah. After this he again examined the master and mistress separately, but they denied everything and said, "All that the maid has told, the hussy has herself invented." Fear again fell on us. The president said to us, "I can help you no further. Shall I torture these two on the bare word of their servant? And if he does not confess on the rack, what then? You must see to your rights in Hamburg, and as soon as possible you must get permission from the council there to search the house for the corpse. If you find it, as the maid says, you can leave the rest to me."

The *parnassim* [elected leaders of the Jewish community] immediately got busy and tried to get hold of twenty soldiers to dig the place that the maid had mentioned. They obtained permission to bury the corpse, if it was found, in the Jewish cemetery in Altona. At the same time they were told: "Think about this very carefully, for if you do not find the murdered man, you are all lost. You know very well about the mob here in Hamburg. It would be impossible for us to restrain it."

Now we were all in great distress, but Rebekah was on all paths, in front and in back, and said we should not despair. She knew for certain that the murdered man would be found, for the maid had sworn on her own life and had given her full particulars. Ten trusted men and several sailors who were known for their trustworthiness went, in God's name, into the murderer's house that was not far from Alten Schragen—the old shambles.

Meanwhile there was an uproar in the entire place. There came from everywhere workers, canaille, and countless others in front of the murderer's door, and all agreed together: if the Jews find the murdered man, then it will all go well for them, but if not, there will remain of all the children of Israel not one hoof, God forbid. But God, blessed be He, did not leave us in our misery for long. As soon as our people came into the house, they opened the designated place and found what they wanted. But the eye cries, and the heart is happy. They cried that they had found the pious young man of twenty-four years in such a wretched condition, and nevertheless they rejoiced that the community was out of danger and they would soon witness revenge. The whole town council was summoned, and the corpse shown them and also the place where it had been found, all according to the maid's statement. The council registered and attested to this. The corpse was then placed on a wagon and brought to Altona. A multitude of sailors and apprentices was present. The sight was indescribable; perhaps there were a hundred thousand people present, but not one bad word was uttered. Though they are a rough people and in quiet times we suffer much harm and distress through them, still this time everything passed off quietly and each person went his way peacefully.

The next day the *parnassim* brought the attestation to the president of Altona, who had the murderer within his jurisdiction. The Jews preferred that judgment should be given in Altona. Again he had the murderer brought before him and informed him of what had occurred. On this he made a full confession. The widow received a part of her murdered husband's money, which was still there. The murderer, poor thing, was in prison till the time of his trial.

Meanwhile Sarah was still a "living widow." No news of her husband was to be had, and, as already related, there were many rumors. After this new murder, when everyone knew the murderer so well, it was remembered that, before he moved into the house near the Alten Schragen, he lived with his father, who owned the Mariners' Tavern, the best known inn in the whole of Hamburg. It is quite near the bourse, and Jewish as well as gentile merchants who had business, or a reckoning with one another, went there, and they used to drink there of silver dishes. The son was therefore well known to Jews. When it became known that this very son was a murderer, and remembered that Sarah's husband was a money changer, it was also remembered that the changers used to meet in that inn and do their business there, counting out money, for the place was well known for its security. Sarah knew also that her husband had been quite friendly with this son. She therefore went to her friends and said, "You know that my husband was lost a few years ago. Now it has come to light. My husband went often in and out of that house. I believe that the same man killed my husband. Help me, perhaps we may find that my husband lost his life by the same hand."

What need have I to dwell long on this? They went to the president and put this before him. He spoke to the murderers with good and bad words, threatened them with torture, to confess that he had killed Abraham Metz. For long he would not confess and only agreed that he had known him well. But the president spoke to him so long until he confessed that he had killed Abraham Metz in the Mariners' Tavern. He had buried him in a deep hole in the room kept only for cheeses and filled it up with lime before closing it up.

As soon as this was known, the *parnassim* went to the Hamburg Council and, as before, asked for permission to make a search. Again Jews were in dire peril, worse than before, that such a well-esteemed and distinguished house should be turned into a den of murderers. It was dangerous in case the corpse should not be found. Luckily for us, it was found; he still wore his red underwaistcoat with silver buttons and *arbakanfos* [a four-cornered garment that every Jewish man, according to biblical command, must wear]. He also was given a Jewish burial.

There was great mourning in our community, as though they had been killed that day. The friends of my kinswoman Sarah, before they allowed the burial, examined the corpse well, for Sarah told of certain marks on his body that it might be known for certain that he was indeed her dead husband and that she was really widowed. These were found, and she had permission to marry again. After this the result of the trial was made known: the murderer was to be broken on the wheel and his body, bound round with iron bands, placed on a stake, that he should be an example for a long time. His wife and servant were freed, but had to leave the country. On the day the murderer was executed, there was an uproar in all Hamburg such as had not occurred at an execution for a hundred years. But all the Jews were in deadly danger, because the entire populace had then stirred up great malice toward the Jews. In short, at the execution of the murderer we were in great danger. But

God, praised be He, the Shepherd, and from His great mercy that He has for us sinful people, and day after day proved true to us; as it is said "when they were in the land of their enemies, I did not despise nor forsake them"—that is what we experienced on that day. Praised be God, who always grants us his mercy.

If we sinful people could only recognize the great miracles and miraculous deeds, which God, praised be He, shows us poor people every day. That is the way it also happened for the good and without harm for us Jews.

The story revolves around two disappearances in Hamburg and the adjacent city of Altona in the late seventeenth century, when, three years apart, two Jewish men from neighboring communities failed to return home in the evening, leaving their wives as *agunes*. The text begins chronologically with the first disappearance, that of Abraham Metz, whose wife, Sarah, was related to Glikl. Nothing had been heard of him when the second man disappeared, three years later, in the summer of 1687. Although the first victimized husband and wife are specifically identified by name, only the bare facts of the event are reported; but the narrator's concern is clearly for the abandoned wife, a concern that is critical to an understanding of the entire narrative. Indeed, almost half the account of the initial incident, which in its entirety covers but a single page, is devoted to the *agune* Sarah, the "living widow" *(almone khaye)* whose quarrelsome nature was rumored to have been responsible for her husband's departure, and to her subsequent humiliation, pain, and difficult life.[13] The conclusion to this brief account articulates the narrator's concern for the personal and social anguish Sarah was made to suffer: "But because of our sins, our human weakness is such that we often speak with our mouth of what our eyes have not seen. Thus poor Sarah was for more than three years a 'living widow' with her sad orphans and had to let the people speak as they liked and pass judgment on her husband, may God avenge his blood!" *(ober unzer mentshlikhe shvakhheyt be avonoseynu horabim izt alzo dos mir oft mit unzere maul reydn dos unzer agn nit hobn gezeyen alzo izt di sore nebekh yoser als gimel shonim almone khaye gevezn mit ire betribte yesomim un di layt nokh ir gefalnis nokh min balo hashem yikom damo reydn un yuditsiren lozn.)*[14] With these words the story of Abraham and Sarah disappears from the body of the narrative. In fact, this first event forms part of a meager frame around the clearly more compelling account of the second incident: of the eleven pages devoted to the entire story, the case of Abraham and Sarah Metz is given only one page at the beginning and two pages at the conclusion. The greater portion of the narrative—the eight intervening pages—is devoted to the second disappearance, which is told continuously from start to finish, and its structure reveals a complex interaction between historical report and exemplary tale.

What is immediately striking when comparing the narratives of the two incidents is the marked difference between two interrelated areas: the function of names and naming, and the construction of the protagonist, Rebekah, as independent actor. In contrast to the first incident, the second victimized husband and wife are not named, although other, less central figures are specifically identified. At the time, the Hamburg Jewish community was relatively small—in 1670 it consisted of twenty-three households[15]—and it is clear from Glikl's *Memoirs* that she was acquainted with virtually everyone within the community. It is also obvious from those named, and from the reported details of the event, that Glikl remembered the particulars of the circumstances very well. This event was, moreover, a very prominent public affair that brought crowds (the text claims perhaps a hundred thousand) to the scene of the crime, and the narrator notes that, "on the day the murderer was executed, there was an uproar in all Hamburg such as had not occurred at an execution for a hundred years." *(beose yom als der retseyekh izt niden gevorn izt zo ayn mehume tokh hamburg gevezn als in meye shonim iber kaynem den man hot dan gevezn nit gevezn izt.)*[16] If needed or desired, the names could no doubt easily have been retrieved from community or family members. But the omission of the names of major figures and the references to the victim merely as "head of household" *(balebos)* or "pious young man" *(frume menkhi),* and to the wife as "his wife" *(zayn frou)* or "living widow" *(almone khaye),* are certainly significant, especially within the context of a specific cast of named characters. The omission serves an important aesthetic and political purpose in the narrative—namely, to create out of specifically historical reportage an exemplary tale that generally heralds the cause of the *agune* and the possibility of empowering the disenfranchised.

An examination of the assignment of names in the *agune* story reveals their social and aesthetic significance. Hekscher's report identifies the second man, who disappeared in July 1687, as Aaron ben Moshe, a money changer. Although his identity is not revealed in Glikl's account, there is the curious incident in which Rebekah, the woman seeking to extract information about his disappearance from the suspected murderer's maid, refers to the victim as "Abraham," which was of course the name of the first casualty, Abraham Metz, to which the maid responds, using the same name. Two translators of the *Memoirs* regard this as an oversight or failure of Glikl's memory. But as mentioned earlier, it is highly unlikely that she, who knew everyone in her small Jewish community, would have forgotten, or not retrieved, the name of the most recent victim. A German translator, Alfred Feilchenfeld, concludes that Glikl made an error, that she confused the two victims.[17] While he may be correct, his reasoning and conclusion remain problematic, since nowhere else in the text is the victim referred to either by name or by the name Abraham. A translation into English by Marvin Lowenthal goes one step further and conceals the "error" from the reader by identifying the man as Aaron ben Moses in the first line of the account and referring to him throughout as Reb Aaron, clearly undermining the complexity of the narrative structure.[18] If, however, one understands Glikl's account exemplarily, then the name Abraham, which refers to the first patriarch, may function archetypically—particularly in a conversation between Jew and gentile—to refer generically to any Jewish "man of the house," especially perhaps to one living in a condition of exile. It is, then, a felicitous coincidence that Abraham and Sarah Metz of the first episode bear the names of the first biblical patriarch and matriarch.

Another shift in character naming and function, which distinguishes Glikl's text from Hekscher's, highlights her overt focus on the plight of the *agune* and the value of solidarity among women. In both accounts, the wife of one Lipman deduces from her husband's account of the disappearance the identity of the murderer and, later, witnesses the suspected murderer's attempt to leave town. While in Hekscher's account, Aaron's wife—that is, the *agune* herself—pursues the investigation and is responsible for uncovering the evidence, in Glikl's narrative it is not the *agune* but Lipman's wife who, moved by compassion for the abandoned woman and her children, garners the evidence and pursues a resolution against all odds. Moreover, in Glikl's account, the given name of this woman, Rebekah—identified only as Lipman's wife in Hekscher's rendition—is revealed at a significant moment in the narrative. Initially, in Glikl's story, the protagonist Rebekah is referred to only as Lipman's wife. She first appears in the text when Lipman returns home from the bourse, or stock exchange, and describes the circumstances of the disappearance. Concluding from this that the murderer was a gentile innkeeper's son, she announces that she will not rest until the murder is resolved, to which her husband responds by calling her "my crazy woman" *(meshugeste)* and warning that, even if she were correct about the murderer's identity, nothing could be done: "This is Hamburg, and one cannot even utter a word." *(es izt hamburg, kayn os derfte man tsu zogn.)*"[19] Since almost all Jews resided in Hamburg on sufferance, had earlier been driven out more than once, and lived in constant fear of expulsion, Lipman, like the rest of the Jewish community, would prefer to remain inactive and silent, to provoke nothing and no one there.[20] But soon thereafter Lipman's wife is stirred to action when she sees through the window the suspected murderer and his spouse about to leave town with a huge crate. Although her husband tries to restrain her from confronting them, she breaks away from him and leaves. The next sentence reads: "Rebekah—that's what the woman was called—persuaded herself that nothing other was in the box than the murdered man." *(di rivke zo hayst di frou hot zikh nit andersht ayn gebild dos der mentsh den horeg dar in der kist hot.)*[21] Thus, precisely at the moment when Lipman's wife frees herself from her husband's attempt to detain her at home, the narrator announces her given name, thereby detaching her from a relational identity as Lipman's wife and establishing her independent status. This move by a woman, which is important for Rebekah's solitary, adamant pursuit of justice, surely presents a remarkable challenge to a manifestly patriarchal society.

It may be fortuitous, and certainly propitious, that Rebekah resembles her namesake in the Bible in her ability to maneuver cleverly— here to elicit from the purported murderer's maid the condemning information. The biblical Rebekah, as Robert Alter notes, is but one in "a remarkable gallery of women—Rebekah, Tamar, Deborah, Ruth— who are not content with a vegetative existence in a corner of the house but, when thwarted by the male world or when they find it lacking in moral insight or practical initiative, do not hesitate to take their destiny, or their nation's, into their own hands."[22] The act of naming and its timing in Glikl's narrative underline Rebekah's declaration of independence and resoluteness, as well as her adherence to Jewish tradition, albeit to a radical one of activist women. Yet the differences between the Glikl and Hekscher accounts suggest that perhaps equally important in the *Memoirs* are the narrator's creative interventions into an infamous historical event to produce atypical, even radical, levels of meaning and significance.

The connection in Glikl's text between the status of the protagonist, Rebekah, and the significance of the *agune* becomes clear from the narrator's story and Rebekah's role in it. After Rebekah seems to obey her husband's caution about the necessity of silence, the narrator first expresses the fear that the memory of the event would also disappear, because no one had responded to the government's offer of a reward for information about the man who disappeared: "Thus it was simply forgotten, that's the way of the world. No matter how intense and important something is, if there is no effect, it falls into oblivion." *(alzo izt es fast fargesen voren vi der seyder olem izt, ven ayn zakh nokh zo ayvrik un vikhtik izt ven kayn afekten filgen [sic], shtelt man es in fargesung.)* But then, the narrative notes the continued plight of the unfortunate *agune* and her family, accentuating Rebekah's earlier response of concern: "But the living widow and her orphans remained sitting in distress." *(ober di almone khaye un ire yesomim zenen betrifter heyt gezesn.)*[23] The realization that the pain experienced by the *agune* and her children persists like a thorn embedded in the minds of some—notably, the narrator and the protagonist—marks the beginning of two prominent interventions: the narrator's into the history of the events, and Rebekah's into the second unsolved disappearance.

The double intervention of narrator and protagonist commences with the narrator's observation that Lipman's wife cannot sleep—a disclosure that confirms the wife's previous assertion that she will not rest until the case is resolved—and the startling allusion to a situation in a folktale, in which Rebekah's sleeplessness is compared to that of the king of Spain.[24] The narrator explains that this king inquired of a learned Jew about the meaning of the Hebrew expression *hineh lo yonum v'lo yishon shomer yisroel*,[25] which the Jew translated accurately as "He neither sleeps nor slumbers, the guardian of Israel." *(er shloft un shlumt nit der hiter fon yisroel.)* The king, however, insisted that it meant "God the guardian lets one neither sleep nor slumber" *(got der hiter er lozt nit shlofn nokh shlumen)* and discloses that insomnia had allowed him to witness a child being thrown into a Jewish house and, therefore, to save the Jews from a false blood-libel accusation that would have resulted in the destruction of their community. It was, he tells the learned Jew, because "God, *your* guardian" *(got ayer hiter)* had kept him awake so that he could save the Jewish people.[26] The narrator's analogy between Lipman's wife and the king of Spain suggests two contrary, yet not necessarily contradictory, tendencies in the presentation of Rebekah as protagonist. On the one hand, it invites three rather daring and unconventional comparisons: the woman—described earlier merely as "a very capable woman [or housewife]" *(ayn grouse berye)*[27]—with a Spanish king; a competent Jewish woman with European royalty; and a woman who has no official power in her traditional Jewish community with a man who is a regent with full power. On the other hand, the analogy suggests that, like the king whom God had assisted, Rebekah too will save the Jewish people, not as an act of individual ingenuity but as the activity of a devout Jew relying on God's help. Whether or not her actions may be attributed to God's will, the analogy to a king in the dominant society highlights her power and independence. Moreover, she shares with the king a kind of noble selflessness: referring to the God who kept him awake as "God, *your* guardian" suggests he sought justice not for his own people but for others; and Rebekah acts only to alleviate the burden of the *agune* and to obtain communal justice.

Rebekah, in her efforts, certainly exceeds the social commitment expected of women and even that expected of men in a hostile Hamburg. After all, she must not only unearth the explanation for the disappearance but also contend with a recalcitrant Jewish community that, not without justification, fears both the German people and their authorities. Antisemitism and physical threats to Jews in Germany do appear elsewhere in the *Memoirs,* but markedly so in this narrative. Here the president of Altona,[28] to whom representatives of the Jewish community bring their complaint, warns them that if their accusations are not verified the Jews will surely be divested of everything they own. The suspected murderer also threatens them, and when members of the Jewish community, coerced by Rebekah, ask to have the alleged burial site of the victim exhumed, the government authorities warn them of a possible pogrom should the body not be found: "Think about this very carefully, for if you do not find the murdered man, you are all lost. You know very well about the mob here in Hamburg. It would be impossible for us to restrain it." *(zekht aykh vol fir zolte ir den horeg nit finden es ver um aykh ale getan den ir vist vol fon den pebel vos hir in hamburg izt es ver unz un meglikh tsu veren.)* Rebekah, however, does not relent; she is certain about what must be done: "Now we were all in great distress," the narration continues, "but Rebekah was on all paths, in front and in back, and said we should not despair. She knew for certain that the murdered man would be found." *(nun mir zenen ale betsore gedole gevezn ober di rivke izt aler vegn hinten un foren gevezn, un gezogt man zole nit far tsogen zi viste gevis dos man den horeg dar finden vert.)*[29] The sense of danger, expressed once again when the body of Abraham Metz is to be exhumed, is evident even at the execution of the confessed murderer of the two men: "On the day the murderer was executed, there was an uproar in Hamburg such as had not occurred at an execution for a hundred years. But all the Jews were in deadly danger, because the entire populace had then stirred up great malice toward the Jews. In short, at the execution of the murderer we were in great danger." *(beose yom als der retseyekh izt niden gevorn izt zo ayn mehume tokh hamburg gevezn als in meye shonim iber kaynem den man hot dan gevezn nit gevezn izt ober beney yisroel bikhlal zenen tokh sakones nefoshes gevezn den hot zikh grous rishes misorer gevezn lekitser beyom haniden haretseyekh zenen mir tokh godl sakone gevezn.)*[30] While the repeated threats and the ongoing fear correspond to the situation of the Jews in seventeenth-century Hamburg, where they had been harassed and driven out and now lived under frequent threats of violence and expulsion, they also function in this story to draw attention to the enormous courage and determination of Rebekah, who refuses, in the face of injustice and in sympathy for the plight of the *agune,* to capitulate to those threats.

Two major differences between Hekscher's and Glikl's accounts of this incident illuminate not only the kind of probity apparent in Rebekah's behavior but also Glikl's conception of history and the significance of writing it.[31] The first glaring difference is the role played by Lipman's wife. In Hekscher's report, she appears briefly when Hekscher meets her outside her house and gives her the details about Aaron's disappearance, from which she immediately concludes, like Rebekah in Glikl's text, that the innkeeper's son is the murderer. Her principal action, however, is to call together the Jews when she sees the suspected murderer and his wife about to leave the city; and it is not she, but the group of Jewish men, who prevents the couple from leaving. In Glikl's text, however, members of the Jewish community only very reluctantly, and after considerable pressure from Rebekah, agree to approach the authorities. The second significant difference occurs at the end of Hekscher's account. There, as noted earlier, the *agune* (the wife of the disappeared Aaron ben Moshe), not Lipman's wife (the given names of these women do not appear in Hekscher's text), is responsible for extracting information from the maid of the innkeeper's son about the murder and the location of the corpse. While other variations in the texts, such as the prominence accorded Hekscher and other men of the community in his version, might be open to question because they tend to serve the interests of the reporter, there seem to be no grounds to doubt his veracity about the role of the *agune,* who, after all, stood to benefit the most from determining precisely what had happened to her husband. It is noteworthy, however, that in her conversation with the maid about her husband's disappearance she never alludes to her own status as *agune,* while in Glikl's story Rebekah almost immediately apprises the maid of the *agune*'s plight: "For we Jews desire only to know that Abraham is dead, so that his wife may take another man. Other than that, we desire nothing from you." *(den mir yehudim begeren nur tsu visen das der avrom tot izt das di frou derf vider ayn man nemen zonsten begeren mir niks andersht fon aykh.)*[32]

What becomes clear from these differences between the Hekscher and Glikl texts, as well as from the narrative structure in the *Memoirs,* is the significance of creative intervention and interpretation in Glikl's rendition. Narrated history there comprises both a factual report of events that had occurred several years earlier and an interpretative formulation of those events that functions exemplarily, corresponding, as already noted, to the traditional understanding of Jewish history as a record of what happened and an interpretation of that. In Glikl's text the coexistence of historicity and exemplarity may be understood as two alternative modes of consciousness and representation that elicit different, yet not necessarily contradictory, responses. Relying on logical reasoning to identify the murderer and on ingenious casuistry to extract the needed information from the suspected murderer's servant, the Rebekah of the *Memoirs* is, in part at least, an interesting composite of the wives of Lipman and Aaron described in Hekscher's report. In fact, the deviations from the Hekscher account reinforce the perception—already apparent in the structure of Glikl's story—that her narrative presents a confluence of a historical account and a story about ethically ideal behavior. Thus, while the story documents events important for Hamburg Jewry, Rebekah, presented as the historical figure she is—that is, as Lipman's spouse—is nonetheless reconstructed as a paragon of intrepid social and ethical behavior. Within the contexts of patriarchal Jewish tradition and a hostile German environment, she is a social anomaly, an indomitable female protagonist who, by her radical yet tradition-bound activism, constantly reminds members of her community of their moral obligation to pursue justice, whether on behalf of an *agune* or the community. Despite her subaltern status within Jewish patriarchy, Rebekah assumes authority that surpasses the traditional communal social codes, not for self-serving purposes, but in an act of affiliation and solidarity with others. Seeking to alleviate not her own situation but another woman's burden, she ultimately attains justice for the entire community.

Until now I have focused primarily on Glikl's attention to the plight of the *agune* and the unacknowledged resources of a woman (here Rebekah) in a patriarchal society. But equally compelling is the tragedy of exile that *agunes* share with the many Jews in the Diaspora. Although subtly articulated, the connection between the fates of the *agune* and of

Jews in the Diaspora is a central part of Glikl's narrative. Consider, for example, the social, moral, and political complexity of the scene when, largely through the insistence of Rebekah, the body of the second victim is exhumed despite the threat to the Jewish community:

Meanwhile there was an uproar in the entire place. There came from everywhere workers, canaille, and countless others in front of the murderer's door, and all agreed together: if the Jews find the murdered man, then it will all go well for them, but if not, there will remain of all the children of Israel not one hoof, God forbid. But God, blessed be He, did not leave us in our misery for long. As soon as our people came into the house, they opened the designated place and found what they wanted. But the eye cries, and the heart is happy. They cried that they had found the pious young man of twenty-four years in such a wretched condition, and nevertheless they rejoiced that the community was out of danger and they would soon witness revenge.

beyn kakh izt di getseke im gantsen mokem gekumen zenen aler hant verkis layt ale kanalim shishim ribo zikh far zamelt un far dem retseyekh zayn tir gekumen vehiskimu kulom be'ekhod veren di beney yisroel den horeg dar finden mutov ve'im lav lo nishar parso akhas mibney yisroel khas ve kholile ober hamokem borekh hashem der unz nit lang in unzere tsores gelozn zo bald unzere layt in dos bayis gekumen zayn hobn zi dos beshtimte ort geefnet un gefunden vos zi far langt hobn ober ayin bokho vehalev someyakh zi hobn geveynt das zi den frumen yungen man min kaf daled shonim le'eyrekh zo elendiklekh gefunden un vider mesameyakh gevezn dos di kehile oys der sakone gevezn un dos man vert bald nekome zehen.[33]

The circumstances, in which a dreadful situation elicits joy merely because a greater tragedy—here the decimation of the entire community—has been averted, represent one of the bitter consequences of a disenfranchised minority living, unwanted and constantly harassed, within a hostile dominant society. This reaction also replicates that of the *agune* to the discovery of her husband's body: she too grieves because of her great loss but is relieved that she no longer lives in limbo, that she can remarry, should she so desire, or remain a respected widow. Thus the *agune*—subordinate and powerless within traditional Judaism, a "living widow" unable to reconstitute a conventional Jewish family life—experiences the degradation and helplessness not only as a Jew living in a perilous Diaspora but also as a woman living a marginal life within her community. She is doubly exiled: as a woman within the traditional Jewish community, and as a Jew in Germany.

Embedded in Glikl's account of historical events in Hamburg is a story of a female protagonist whose deliberative and principled behavior attests to the obligation to respond morally to the predicament of the disenfranchised. Thus, within the social context of this narrative, Rebekah, depicted as unique within her Jewish community, performs a special function: she forges her own identity by taking ethical action despite the opposition of her husband and the overt threats to herself and her community. Provoked by concern for the hapless *agune* and the injustice suffered by the Jews of Hamburg, Rebekah's actions create the possibility for justice for both of these "exiles."

While the story about the disappearances presents a particular instance of the intersection of historical and exemplary narratives, it may also register how readers could respond to that textual cooperation. In fact, within the text itself, attention to a possible reader response suggests that there may indeed be two different, yet interrelated, reactions to the narrative: one to an exemplary story involving the protagonist Rebekah, the other to the historical account of the event.

The concluding pages of the narrative suggest how an exemplary story might function for a reading public. After withstanding all pressures from the government authorities and the Jewish community, which feared antisemitic retaliation because the suspected murderer was a gentile, Rebekah uncovers the body of the murdered man, thereby averting a pogrom and enabling the *agune,* who now becomes a widow, to remarry. Furthermore, apparently as a result of witnessing the success of Rebekah's endeavors, Sarah Metz, the first *agune,* who had languished for years tolerating abusive rumors, becomes energized, uncovers her husband's murderer, and locates her husband's corpse. Seemingly following Rebekah's example, Sarah models an effective response to an exemplary story about the necessity of determined action to bring about justice. Like Rebekah, she first uses reason to determine who murdered her husband and then seeks the assistance of friends to bring the case before the government authorities. Because Abraham's body was said to have been buried in the tavern of the murderer's father, a "well-esteemed and distinguished house" *(ayn khoshev for nem bayis),* there was an even greater threat of violence to the Jews. But the body is recovered, and Sarah, no longer an *agune,* becomes a widow with "permission to marry again" *(zi hasore bekomen ayn man tsu nemen)*.[34] Thus, in the final pages of the text, the incident with which the narrative began is brought to a conclusion. Apparently as a result of her "reading" of Rebekah's exemplary behavior, the previously inert and silent Sarah learned how to pursue justice in spite of all obstacles, thereby presenting the reader of Glikl's text with an effective, pragmatic response to an exemplary story.

The closing moments of the narrative, which provide a resolution to both the historical account and the exemplary story, include a perfunctory report about criminal penalties meted out (execution for the murderer, banishment for his wife and servant); a brief description of the mode of execution; a report about the great menace Jews experienced on the day of execution; and, finally, homage to the God who alone creates "great miracles and miraculous deeds" *(di grouse nisim venifloes)*[35] and has once again shielded Jews from harm in the land of the enemy.[36] This invocation, in which God is presented as the One who directs our lives and creates all miracles, would seem to undercut the value of heroic actions by the protagonists (who bear the matriarchal names of Rebekah and Sarah). Yet it actually functions as a largely superfluous and perfunctory coda because of its formulaic praise and position at the very end of the narrative. What reverberates vividly at the conclusion of this text is not only the historical record of the tragic circumstances of Jews in the Diaspora and of *agunes* as exiles within the community but also the overwhelming presence of Rebekah, whose action on behalf of one *agune* is powerful enough to motivate another to seek justice and to succeed. The resolution to the two disappearances presents a paradigm for that kind of exemplary ethical intervention in a continuing situation of powerlessness that can dissolve, perhaps only temporarily, or at least alleviate the paralysis of marginalized, disenfranchised, and subjugated people—be they *agunes,* women in a traditional Jewish community, or all Jews living in exile.[37]

Solomon Maimon

Among the differences between Glikl Hamel's *Memoirs* and Solomon Maimon's *Autobiography* in how they present the problem of the *agune,* two stand out above all others. Glikl's narrative and its protagonist remain firmly within the orbit of Jewish tradition, even though Rebekah defies the Jewish community's quiescent response to the *agunes.* In contrast, Maimon moves to the margins of Jewish tradition when he attacks the logic and religious foundations of rabbinic studies and voices his disdain for Jewish marriage and divorce conventions, but avoids their effect on the predicament of *agunes.* Second, by constructing an exemplary narrative within a historical account, Glikl creates a large, compassionate voice for the victimized and silent *agunes,* whereas Maimon's references to his deserted wife account for but a few sentences in the text, virtually silencing her, thereby repressing or camouflaging her difficult and disabling situation as an *agune*. However, his inclusion of historical, religious, and cultural perspectives does call greater attention to matrimonial matters than their meager share of the text would seem to warrant. The complex positions regarding marriage and divorce articulated in the *Autobiography* may best be elucidated by focusing on two prominent interrelated issues: first, the connection of Maimon's critique of marriage customs and his own marital status to his attack on Talmudic studies; and second, the evasions in the text that minimize the significance of his wife and conceal (especially from non-Jewish readers) what she as an *agune* suffers, even while Maimon enhances his own image as a clever and committed adherent of the Enlightenment.

Before I turn to the specifics of the text, a few observations on some of the difficulties of Maimon as autobiographer are in order. Although he viewed his *Autobiography* as an accurate record of his "spiritual [or intellectual] rebirth" (*geistige Wiedergeburt;* the term *geistige* may signify either "spiritual" or "intellectual"),[38] there is evidence throughout this work of the continuing and seemingly unresolvable tension he experienced between the Eastern European Orthodox heritage he wanted to discard and the enlightened German culture he sought to embrace. The preface *(Vorrede)* to the second part of the *Autobiography* indicates that the primary motivating force of this work and indeed of Maimon's life was an avid search for truth. He writes that his love of truth was so great that, for its sake, he would "even defy the devil and his grandmother" (*frage ich selbst nach dem Teufel und seiner Grossmutter nicht*),[39] and that his text delivers "an accurate description" (*eine treue Beschreibung)* of his activities and indeed of life itself.[40] As both an admission and justification of previous offensive behavior, Maimon claims that his life story (or history of a life; *Lebensgeschichte* may mean either) presents a constructive "inventory" *(Inventarium)* of what he has already achieved in the course of fulfilling his destiny and of what he still needs to accomplish.[41] Maimon's practice of taking an inventory of his progress toward "spiritual rebirth" resembles the concept of autobiography as a process of reflection directed at self-confirmation, which was a relatively new phenomenon in eighteenth-century European letters.[42] Yet it is also reminiscent of a ritual of Yom Kippur, one of the most important Jewish holy days, which commemorates the beginning of the new year, when Jews take stock of their past behavior, pray to have transgressions forgiven, and plan to reform their future lives.[43] It is thus difficult to know whether Maimon's enterprise to justify or merely account for his behavior and work was inspired by his contemporary German cultural milieu, or by the Eastern European tradition he was trying to overcome, or more likely, by both. Here, as elsewhere in this text, Maimon's behavior seems to negotiate an arena of tension between Jewish and non-Jewish traditions, between religious and secular ways of life, and more generally, between Eastern and Western European cultures.

Maimon's insistence on the accuracy of the autobiographical content in his work raises an important issue. If autobiography is a form of invention that constructs a different, an alternative life—that is, if, as one critic has noted, it is "one way of making life matter" when life seems insufficiently rewarding[44]—then claims of factuality and reliability would no doubt prove problematic. Critics and Maimon's contemporaries in Germany have noted errors, lapses, and exaggerations, especially concerning his activities in Germany, and insufficient information makes it difficult to verify his statements about his earlier life in Poland. If, however, autobiography is understood, as it already was in the eighteenth century, as a literary text, a narrative that presents the writer's own reconstruction and interpretation of a remembered past, then even significant discrepancies between factual data and written text would not necessarily undermine its validity. The inaccuracies and inventions notwithstanding, the text may be valuable in itself, interesting for the complex life and story it constructs. Thus, any misrepresentations of the details of an event or argument, for example, need not negate the possibility of an accurate, though not completely factual, portrayal of the social and intellectual milieu or undermine the writer's perception of the meaning of his life and work. Of course, ostensible falsifications may, at times, be the result of differences in perception between Maimon as a Polish Jew who had not fully divested himself of his Orthodox shtetl upbringing and the views of his cosmopolitan German Jewish contemporaries about Ostjuden (Eastern European Jews), in general, and Maimon, in particular. Moreover, whether conscious or unconscious, invention and distortion often reveal as much as they conceal and therefore require especially cautious scrutiny and interpretation.

Although the primary focus of this study is Maimon's discourse in the *Autobiography*, I call attention here to the pertinent inconsistencies between fact and his "fictions." Of special importance here is the significance of Maimon's behavior and values, which can be educed from the representation of his marital relations and response to his wife's quest for a divorce and, more generally, from both the narrative structure and the social and psychological dynamics of this portrayed life. No less vital, however, is the historical context that resonates in Maimon's conscious reflections on his experiences—that is, the discourse within the narrative about the complex reality of Jewish life in the Diaspora during the Enlightenment period in Europe, a time of major political and social transformations.

AN UNYIELDING PAST: MARRIAGE CONTRACTS, DIVORCE LAWS, AND TALMUD STUDIES

Solomon Maimon explains the motivation for his difficult decision to leave "the darkness of superstition and ignorance" *(Finsternis des Aberglaubens und der Unwissenheit)*[45] of Lithuanian Jewish orthodoxy in order to devote himself to secular studies in Germany: "Since to search for the truth now, I have abandoned my nation, my fatherland, and my family, then one can't expect me for trivial motives to compromise the truth." *(Da ich nun die Wahrheit aufzusuchen, meine Nation, mein Vaterland und meine Familie verlassen habe, so kann man mir nicht zumuten, daß ich geringfügiger Motive halber der Wahrheit etwas vergeben sollte.)*[46] In 1777, when he was twenty-four years old, he left his family, which included a wife of thirteen years, a ten-year-old son named David, and several other children. He does not disclose how many, but mentions that his wedded life was "rather fruitful" *(ziemlich fruchtbar)*[47] and later speaks of David as the eldest son.[48] Although there is no record of what he told his family when he departed for Königsberg, his words about his departure convey little more than consuming self-interest, certainly no concern for the needs of his wife and children: "Since my external circumstances continually grew worse because I no longer wanted to put up with my ordinary occupations and therefore found myself everywhere outside of my circle; also, on the other hand, I could not sufficiently satisfy my favorite inclination for scientific studies where I lived, I decided to go to Germany and there study medicine and, given this opportunity, also other sciences." *(Da meine äußern Umstände immer schlechter wurden, weil ich mir nicht mehr zu meinen gewöhnlichen Geschäften schicken wollte und mich daher überall aus meiner Sphäre befand; ich auch von der andern Seite meine Lieblingsneigung zum Studium der Wissenschaften in meinem Wohnorte nicht genug befriedigen konnte, so beschloß ich, mich nach Deutschland zu begeben und da Medizin und bei dieser Gelegenheit auch andere Wissenschaften zu studieren.)*[49] There are, in addition, several instances in the text that suggest he neither discussed his departure with his wife nor ever contacted her thereafter. In one instance, when still in Poland and clearly preoccupied only with his own needs and passions, Maimon admits that, upon learning that a rabbi who lived at some distance was in possession of German books, he left home "without saying a word about it to my family" *(ohne meiner Familie ein Wort zu sagen)*;[50] and later a Polish Jew commissioned by Maimon's wife to request that her husband return to the family or deliver a letter of divorcement, and who did not know Maimon's whereabouts in Germany, had first to search for his place of residence. In a third instance, the chief judge of the Jewish court in Breslau accused him of desertion and of never having contacted or supported his wife and family, charges Maimon did not deny.[51]

Although in Germany Maimon dedicated himself to secular studies and the ideas of the Enlightenment, his behavior betrays a continued adherence to aspects of the Eastern European Jewish culture in which he had been reared. For example, he abided by an ongoing Jewish tradition that Daniel Boyarin calls that of the "married monk": "the practice of husbands leaving their wives for very extended periods to study Torah."[52] The wives of "married monks," however, willingly took upon themselves the financial burden of the family in return for the prestige of being related to and supporting a distinguished scholar. But when Maimon abandoned his Talmudic studies, his wife was excluded from such recognition, and he was not prepared to return to fulfill his social and conjugal duties. Although Maimon had overtly disavowed his Orthodox beliefs for secular culture, the confluence of his earlier rigorous traditional practices and his current impoverished situation may have caused him to overlook the needs of his wife and children. But it is clear in the context of secular and bourgeois Berlin that his acquaintances expected him to seek out a profession or job that could support him and his family. Yet there are, in the *Autobiography,* no detectable signs of concern or guilt about the family he had abandoned or, for that matter, any indications that he would agree to do anything other than devote himself to his secular studies.

Maimon's continued struggle to detach himself completely from his Orthodox past, and his inability to do so, is reflected in much of his behavior in the *Autobiography,* but his particular conception of

Eastern European tradition articulated in this text helps to explain his problematic response to issues of marriage and divorce. In the introductory chapter of the *Autobiography,* Maimon enumerates three classes of Jews in Poland: uneducated workers; the educated who use their learning to support themselves as rabbis, teachers, judges, and so forth; and those who dedicate themselves completely to study and are supported by the working class. He elaborates on this latter group:

The third class consists of those scholars who, because of their outstanding talents and scholarship, draw the attention of the uneducated to themselves, are taken by these into their homes, married to their daughters, and with wife and children are completely supported for some years. Afterward, however, the wife must take upon herself the support of her holy idler and their children (which are usually very numerous in this class), for which, as is reasonable, she will feel great pride.

Die dritte Klasse besteht aus denjenigen Gelehrten, die wegen ihrer vorzüglichen Talente und Gelehrsamkeit die Aufmerksamkeit der Ungelehrten auf sich ziehen, von diesem in ihre Häuser genommen, mit ihren Töchtern verheiratet und einige Jahre auf eigene Unkosten mit Frau und Kindern unterhalten werden. Nachher, aber muß diese Frau die Ernährung ihres heiligen Müßiggängers und ihre Kinder (die gemeiniglich bei dieser Klasse sehr zahlreich sind) auf sich nehmen, worauf sie sich, wie billig, sehr viel einbildet.[53]

And some six chapters later, just prior to a discussion of his own marriage, which according to custom was negotiated by his father, Maimon returns to the subject of Talmudists who were celebrated for their great learning, once again in relation to marriage and financial support. He writes of their desirability as sons-in-law, the large dowry each can expect, and finally the role of the wife who "undertakes the arrangement of the household and management of business and is satisfied if, for all her labors, she will partake just to some extent in the fame and future blessedness of her husband" *(übernimmt die Frau die Einrichtung des Hauswesens und Führung der Geschäfte und ist zufrieden, wenn sie für alle Mühseligkeiten nur einigermaßen des Ruhmes und der zukünftigen Seligkeit ihres Mannes teilhaftig wird).*[54] Juxtaposed, however, with this discussion of the conventions of marital arrangements is a threefold attack that Maimon launches on Talmud studies: Talmudists, he notes, expend great intellectual effort on trivial subjects, contribute nothing to systematic studies of history and nature, and practice a kind of Talmudic skepticism that is "for the most part contrary to the expedient systematic study" *(dem zweckmäßigen systematische Studium am meisten zuwider).*[55]

What is curious about this coupling of a Talmudist's lucrative marriage contract and the assault on the institution and utility of Talmud studies is Maimon's ambivalent involvement with each aspect. On the one hand, he is not averse to a marital situation that would provide him with the means to study without having to work; on the other, such an endowment could be achieved only by pursuing something he considers to be without value, that is, rabbinical studies. Should a Talmudist enter a marriage negotiated on the grounds of his scholarly acclaim—as Maimon, a rabbi at age eleven and regarded as brilliant, actually did—and instead pursue secular studies, then his wife, who in that community would be compensated for her toil only by his prestige as a Talmudist, is condemned to a life of privation, drudgery, and social degradation with no recognized social reward. Although Maimon does not openly admit it, his preoccupation with both Eastern European marriage arrangements and the negative aspects of Talmud studies reveals a person fully cognizant of the contradictions in his struggle against traditional orthodoxy and of the humiliation his wife must suffer as a result of his rebellion.

As mentioned earlier, one cannot be certain whether the behavior Maimon describes was provoked by the cultural environment in Germany or kindled by his Eastern European Orthodox heritage. The almost complete exclusion of Maimon's wife from the pages of his biography as well as his evasive deportment when confronted in Germany first by his wife's envoy and later by his wife and oldest son betray both a persistent effort to forget his miserable life in Poland and a frustrating failure to accomplish that. Indeed, in this text his shtetl mentality repeatedly undermines his efforts to assimilate into the German Jewish intelligentsia, nowhere more apparent perhaps than when his wife appears in Breslau to request that he return home or divorce her. Challenged by her needs and his dereliction of family responsibility, and by the contradictions he experienced as a Polish shtetl Jew living in cosmopolitan Germany, Maimon admits that he knows no satisfactory resolution for his dilemma. He confesses that he does not want "to lose a woman whom I had once loved" *(eine Frau, der ich einstens gut gewesen war, zu verlieren)*,[56] but indicates that she does not understand the impossibility inherent in the idea

that a man of my kind, who had already lived for some years in Germany, happily freed himself from the chains of superstition and religious prejudices, laid aside his crude customs and manners, and widely expanded his knowledge of many things, should voluntarily return again to the former barbaric and miserable situation, deprive himself of all the advantages he had acquired, and expose himself to rabbinical rage at the smallest deviation from ceremonial law and the articulation of a free idea.

daß ein Mann von meiner Art, der sich schon seit einigen Jahren in Deutschland aufgehalten, sich von den Fesseln des Aberglaubens und der Religionsvorurteile glücklich losgemacht, seine rohe Sitten und Lebensart abgelegt und seine Kenntnisse um vieles erweitert hatte, freiwillig wieder in den vorigen barbarischen und elenden Zustand sich zurückbegeben, aller erworbnen Vorteile sich berauben und der rabbinischen Wut sich bei der kleinsten Abweichung vom Zeremonialgesetz und bei Äußerung eines freien Gedankens aussetzen sollte.[57]

Although he finally concludes that "among the two evils here the lesser one was to be chosen, and I agreed to a divorce" *(Hier war also unter zwei Übeln das kleinere zu wählen, und ich willigte in die Scheidung),*[58] he does not readily relinquish his bond with his past. Instead, he continues to erect many obstacles to divorce, including an unnecessary court proceeding at the *beyt din* (the religious court), which merely provides him with an opportunity to wrestle once again with the rabbis, to humiliate and defeat them.

It is clear from the text that the confrontation with his wife in Germany activated an already existent dilemma—that is, his desire for a Talmudist's lucrative marriage contract and his enormous disdain for Talmud studies. Because his ambition was to pursue secular studies and enjoy autonomy without, however, assuming the responsibility for supporting himself or his family, he wished to be a fully supported "married monk," but one who would not need to expend his intellectual energies on the Talmud. The absence of any apparent concern for the plight of his abandoned wife and family suggests that they had little importance for him.

But not only is the *Autobiography* silent about the dire situation of his abandoned family, it also obscures the significance of relevant aspects of Jewish tradition and practice, such as divorce laws, the status of the *agune,* and the function of the religious court *(beyt din).* Such omissions in a work that otherwise explains to a non-Jewish audience many difficult and arcane areas of Judaism and Jewish life—among them, the education system, marriage contracts, Kabbalah, forms of Chasidism, and Maimonides's philosophy—conceal from the reader, and perhaps even from the writer himself, the degradation to which he subjects his wife by his desertion and unwillingness to grant a divorce. Readers not versed in Jewish law may not know, for example, that no one but the husband—not even the *beyt din*—can execute a divorce *(get),* or that without a *get* an *agune* is not permitted to remarry; and they may be bewildered by Maimon's obscure disputations with the *beyt din* judges, who are rabbis. The culmination of two encounters with the rabbis, in which he apparently prevails in debate against them, illuminates his problematic relationship with rabbinic Judaism and his own unhappy predicament of hovering uneasily between two worlds, at home in neither. But ridiculing the practices of Judaism and demonstrating the impotence of the rabbis who have no authority to coerce him to divorce did not change the reality of either Maimon's own powerlessness and poverty or his wife's refusal to remain an *agune.*

MAIMON CONFRONTS THE RABBIS: AN EXERCISE IN FUTILITY

The two incidents, in which Maimon is requested—first by his wife's envoy, and subsequently by his wife and son—to return to his wife or divorce her, disclose a pattern of behavior already apparent in his earlier preoccupation with the traditions of Talmud studies and marriage. These episodes not only emphasize his attachment to past traditions, which persists despite great changes in his cultural environment and activity in Germany, but also illuminate the historical and social context of a person struggling with two seemingly mutually exclusive worlds—the narrow and enclosed world of Eastern European religious orthodoxy and the enlightened culture of Germany. Moreover, the repetition of structural elements in the narration of the two incidents accentuates Maimon's tenuous and troubling reactions when confronted simultaneously with both worlds, and it suggests that his particular behavior may represent a larger cultural and historic condition of Jews in eighteenth-century Europe.

Because a reader unfamiliar with Jewish law and tradition may not recognize the significance of seemingly minor or harmless events, whose importance Maimon may have wanted to conceal, they merit exploration in detail. In each instance, Maimon is overtly confronted with the same major decision about his life—to return to Poland or divorce his wife. In each he interprets his dilemma as having to opt for one of two mutually exclusive forms of life. Each instance culminates in an encounter with a rabbi whom Maimon challenges by employing the Talmudist's skill of disputation, apparently assuming that brilliant debate alone would invalidate or obliterate established rabbinic law and authority; and in each instance Maimon's masterful, perhaps decimating performance leaves him feeling no more content or powerful, possibly even less so.

The first incident, which begins with the arrival of the Polish Jew sent by Maimon's wife, is reported in a chapter in which Maimon grapples with the unhappiness and sense of inadequacy he has experienced in Germany. The chapter commences with the painful admission that, after years spent in Germany, he feels alienated from the German cultural world as well as from the Jewish traditional one:

> Happily I returned to Hamburg, but here I fell into the most distressing conditions. I lived in a miserable inn, had nothing to eat, and did not know what I should begin to do. I was too enlightened to return to Poland, to spend my life in misery, without any rational occupations and robbed of any society, and to sink back into the darkness of superstition and ignorance, from which, with so much effort, I had barely freed myself. In Germany I also could not count on making progress because of my lack of knowledge of the language, customs, and lifestyle, to which I did not even until now actually want to acquiesce. I had not learned a specific profession, had distinguished myself in no particular science, indeed I did not even know any language in which I could make myself completely understood.

> *Glücklich kam ich wieder nach Hamburg, geriet hier aber in die allerbedrängtesten Umstände. Ich logierte in einem Wirtshause, hatte nichts zu zehren und wußte nicht, was ich anfangen sollte. Ich war zu aufgeklärt, um zurück nach Polen zu gehen, in Elend, Mangel an allen vernünftigen Beschäftigungen und jedes Umgangs beraubt mein Leben zuzubringen und in die Finsternis des Aberglaubens und der Unwissenheit, woraus ich mich mit so vieler Mühe kaum losgemacht hatte, zurückzusinken. In Deutschland fortzukommen durfte ich mir auch aus Mangel an Kenntnis der Sprache, Sitten und Lebensart, worin ich mich noch bis jetzt nicht recht fügen wollte, keine Rechnung machen. Eine bestimmte Profession hatte ich nicht gelernt, in keiner besondern Wissenschaft mich hervorgetan, ja ich verstand nicht einmal irgendeine Sprache, worin ich mich ganz verständlich machen konnte.*[59]

After this introductory lament, Maimon explains that for practical reasons he decided it would be useful to convert to Christianity, but a pastor, offended by Maimon's opportunism, refused to baptize him. Subsequently, an acquaintance arranged to have Maimon reside and study languages and other subjects at a gymnasium, where, he says, he "lived peacefully and contented for a few years" *(lebte ich ein paar Jahre ruhig und zufrieden).*[60]

It was at this time that the Polish envoy arrived with the request from Maimon's wife that he "either return home immediately or send through him a letter of divorcement" *(entweder ohne Verzug nach Hause zu kommen oder ihr durch ihn einen Scheidebrief zu schicken).* Not able to take either course, however, Maimon remained suspended between his attachment to an immobilized and immobilizing Polish shtetl and his uncertain opportunities in an enlightened Germany: "But at that time I could as little do the one as the other. I was not inclined to let myself be divorced from my wife without cause, and it was impossible for me right on the spot to return to Poland, where I had not the least prospect of continuing my progress and leading a rational life." *(Ich konnte damals aber so wenig das eine als das andere tun. Mich von meiner Frau ohne Ursache Scheide zu lassen, war ich nicht geneigt, und gleich auf der Stelle nach Polen zurückzukehren, wo ich noch nicht die mindeste Aussicht hatte, mir mein Fortkommen zu verschaffen und ein vernünftiges Leben zu führen, war mir unmöglich.)*[61] Because Maimon's assertion that he must first consult with friends in Berlin is interpreted as an attempt to avoid making a decision, the envoy has him summoned before the court of the chief rabbi. Claiming that his gymnasium is exempt from the intrusion of Jewish law, Maimon refuses to appear at court but does accept the chief rabbi's invitation for an informal discussion, during which he learns that the rabbi knew his father and even remembered the young Maimon as a very promising scholar. During the lengthy dispute about Maimon's religiosity, which the rabbi questions because of Maimon's clean-shaven face (all Orthodox men traditionally wear beards) and his absence from the synagogue, Maimon argues that his actions were "as little opposed to (properly understood) religion as they were to reason" *(so wenig der [wohl verstandenen] Religion als der Vernunft zuwider).* In addition, given his circumstances, the Talmud permits such conduct. But Maimon's unrelenting insistence on the correctness of his position finally causes the chief rabbi to cry out, "Shofar! Shofar!" *(Schoffer! Schoffer!)* Maimon explains, "That is namely what the horn is called which is blown in the synagogue as an exhortation to repent and of which Satan is supposed to be terribly afraid." *(So heißt nämlich das Horn, worin die Ermahnung zur Buße in der Synagoge geblasen wird und vor dem sich der Satan ganz abscheulich fürchten soll.)* When, Maimon claims, he was asked to identify the shofar and referred to it as a "ram's horn" *(Horn von einem Bock)* and not a "shofar" (the sacred term for this kind of horn), the chief rabbi "fell back into his chair and began to lament my lost soul" *(fiel der Oberrabbiner auf seinen Stuhl zurück und fing an, meine verlorene Seele zu beklagen).* At this point, Maimon says that he "let him lament for as long as he desired, and took my leave" *(ließ ihn klagen, solange er Lust hatte, und empfahl mich).*[62] No further word about this episode appears in the text, whose narration returns immediately to a discussion of his life in the gymnasium.

If the reader is to make sense of this episode and its significance, two central issues here and elsewhere in the *Autobiography* need to be elucidated: marriage conventions and Talmudic studies. Since the wife, by virtue of the Jewish marriage contract, is a legal possession of her husband and only he can release her, the abandoned wife can under no circumstances receive a divorce. If the absent husband is found, however, and if certain circumstances pertain, the wife may register a complaint with the *beyt din* against her husband, but the court can only coerce the man to grant a divorce "of his own free will." Maimon's intransigence, his refusal to grant a divorce—seemingly the result of abundant self-interest—leaves his wife in a state of limbo, powerless to change her situation.

One aspect of this episode that remains obscure for an audience untutored in Jewish traditions is the unresolved tension between the two rabbis—the chief rabbi and Maimon, the Polish rabbi who had drifted away from orthodoxy: one bearded and carrying the weight of orthodoxy, the other clean-shaven and engrossed in Enlightenment philosophy and culture. Despite these differences, however, both rely upon Jewish religious texts and codes in their disputation. This would of course be expected of the chief rabbi, but Maimon might have taken quite a different course, arguing perhaps from enlightened philosophical conceptions of religion and ethics. That he does not is noteworthy, for, by drawing justification from the Talmud and the methods of Talmudic disputation, Maimon can, if his position prevails, be victorious on the chief rabbi's territory—that is, within the compass of Orthodox Judaism. He would then remain true to the primacy of reason associated with the Enlightenment, but within the context of accepted Jewish tradition. It is not clear, however, when the chief rabbi concludes the debate by calling out "Shofar! Shofar!" just who has been successful and who defeated. Significantly, Maimon's explanation of the shofar refers to its function during the Jewish High Holy Days but neglects its important use in the rite of excommunication, which seems to be precisely what the chief rabbi is implying by drawing attention to it.[63] The idea of excommunication may have threatened Maimon, who, while critical of the practices of the Judaism, had not actually abandoned the religion and, for that matter, some of its practices—Talmudic disputation, for instance.[64] In addition, Maimon's identification of the shofar as an instrument of which "Satan is supposed to be terribly afraid" refers to an idea in Orthodox Judaism that he condemns repeatedly in the *Autobiography*—that is, the idea of prevailing religious superstition.

Other unanswered, perhaps unanswerable, questions about this episode still linger. In a text that adequately explains to a non-Jewish audience many difficult and recondite areas of Judaism and Jewish life, why do aspects of the tradition—such as divorce law, the *agune,* the *beyt din,* the shofar—remain obscure? How do the kinds of things concealed and revealed function within the framework of the narrative? And what do patterns of masking or limited exposition disclose about the narrator and the representation of his interaction with the two markedly different environments he has experienced in the Diaspora—Poland and Germany? Similar questions also emerge from the second episode, Maimon's encounter with his wife and son in Germany and his appearance before the *beyt din.* The answers to these questions can perhaps be found by scrutinizing the event.

At a later date, when Maimon was living in Breslau and his financial condition had once again just begun to deteriorate, his wife, accompanied by their oldest son, arrived and demanded that her husband return immediately to Poland or divorce her. It is interesting and disturbing that Ralph-Rainer Wuthenow, the same critic who incorrectly referred to Maimon's wife as "homely," also notes that the wife "tried . . . to induce him to return to Poland,"[65] when, in fact, she presented an alternative—divorce. The text states that she "disclosed her decision to obtain a divorce, if I would not go with her immediately" *(eröffnete mir ihren Entschluß, sich von mir, wenn ich mit ihr nicht gleich reisen wollte, scheiden zu lassen).*[66] But even before Maimon reveals his wife's request, his assessment of his wife and himself offers clues to the reasons why reaching a decision was so difficult. Maimon describes her as "a woman of crude education and manners, but of great common sense and Amazonian courage" *(ein Frauenzimmer von rauher Erziehung und Lebensart, aber von sehr vielem bon sens und Amazonenmut),* and himself as a man "who had already lived for some years in Germany, happily freed himself from the chains of superstition and religious prejudices, laid aside his crude customs and manners, and widely expanded his knowledge of many things" *(der sich schon seit einigen Jahren in Deutschland aufgehalten, sich von den Fesseln des Aberglaubens und der Religionsvorurteile glücklich losgemacht, seine rohen Sitten und Lebensart abgelegt und seine Kenntnisse um vieles erweitert hatte).*[67] Here the dilemma that beleaguers Maimon surfaces once again: he maintains a strong appreciation for his wife's vitality and general intelligence but has outgrown her Eastern European environment. He admits that he does not want "to lose a woman whom I had once loved" *(eine Frau, der ich einstens gut gewesen war, zu verlieren)*,[68] but he knows that he could not "voluntarily return again to the former barbaric and miserable situation, deprive himself of all the advantages he had acquired, and expose himself to rabbinical rage at the smallest deviation from ceremonial law and the articulation of a free idea" *(freiwillig wieder in den vorigen barbarischen und elenden Zustand sich zurückbegeben, aller erworbnen Vorteile sich berauben und der rabbinischen Wut sich bei der kleinsten Abweichung vom Zeremonialgesetz und bei Äußerung eines freien Gedanken aussetzen sollte)*.[69] Although it is obvious in this text that Maimon cannot and will not return to Poland, in a number of ways he endeavors to inhibit any motion toward divorce—he asks for time to travel to Berlin to raise money for her, tries in vain to convince the son to remain in Germany, and finally, when his wife refuses to wait any longer, accedes to a divorce. But then he erects yet another obstacle and decides he "would only agree to a divorce if it is imposed on him by the court" *(daß ich nur dann in eine Ehescheidung willigen würde, wenn sie mir von den Gerichten auferlegt würde)*,[70] even though he is fully cognizant of the fact that issuing a divorce is outside the purview of the court.

Maimon's agenda seems to be twofold: not to lose his wife, but if he must divorce her, at least to impugn the court and ridicule the rabbis. The text is completely silent about the hardship and dismay that court action might cause his family. It is before the tribunal of the *beyt din* that the two major issues—marriage and divorce law, and Talmudic tradition—coalesce and that Maimon's social attitudes and conduct are clearly exposed. These proceedings may also strike a general audience as obscure, farcical, and harmless, but a reading informed by Jewish tradition unfolds a narrative in which Maimon's behavior camouflages not only the wife's deplorable situation as an *agune* but his own powerlessness as well.

Since within Jewish law only the husband may execute a divorce and the court can only advise and attempt to coerce, the judge—after hearing the wife's complaint at the tribunal—does indeed advise *(raten)* that there be a divorce. But when Maimon counters that "we did not come here to *ask for advice,* but to obtain a *judicial sentence*" (*wir kamen hier nicht her, um* Rat zu fragen *sondern um eine* richterliche Sentenz *zu erhalten* [emphases in the text]), the chief judge stands up and points to a passage in the legal codes which states: "A vagabond, who leaves his wife for many years, does not write to her, and sends her no money should, if he be found, be legally coerced to grant a divorce." *(Ein Vagabund, der seine Frau auf viele Jahre verläßt, ihr nicht schreibt und kein Geld schickt, soll, wenn er aufgefunden wird, zur Ehescheidung gerichtlich gezwungen werden.)* Maimon claims that the judge stood because the judge knew that his remarks could have no judicial authority. Indeed Maimon's request that the judge sit down and deliver the "judicial sentence" *(richterliche Sentenz),* which he knows the judge cannot do in a marital contractual case, elicits a furious response from the judge, who calls Maimon "a damned *heretic*" (*verdammter* Ketzer) and curses him "in the name of the Lord" *(im Namen des Herren).*[71] Although Maimon soon thereafter leaves the court, noting that nothing had changed, he does subsequently agree to the divorce, provided that they appear before a different judge. (In Jewish tradition, the divorce document is given, in the presence of witnesses, to the wife who then hands it over to the *beyt din* for the ritual closure.)[72] Despite the rather laconic and seemingly opaque report with which the episode concludes, the text betrays the narrator's isolation and vulnerability: "After the divorce my wife traveled with my son back to Poland. I remained for some time in Breslau; but since my situation continued to worsen, I decided to return once again to Berlin." *(Nach der Ehescheidung reiste meine Frau mit meinem Sohn nach Polen zurück. Ich blieb noch einige Zeit in Breslau; da sich aber mein Zustand immer mehr verschlimmerte, so beschloß ich, wieder nach Berlin zurückzukehren.)*[73]

The encounter at the *beyt din* with this chief judge is both similar to and an intensification of Maimon's earlier discussion with the chief rabbi in Hamburg. While previously Maimon had avoided a court appearance and met informally with the rabbi, he initiated the court proceeding by stipulating that he would grant a divorce only if it were imposed by the court. Because he knows full well that, in issues involving contractual rights, the court may order but not actually enforce the decision,[74] his behavior in court seems designed to provoke the tribunal and to demonstrate both the powerlessness of the rabbis and the irrationality of the legal system. Thus, when Maimon tells the chief judge to "sit down again at your place and deliver your *judicial sentence* about this matter" (*Setzen Sie sich also wieder an ihren Platz und sprechen hierüber Ihre* richterliche Sentenz),[75] he indicates that he knows the prescript that in court the judges sit, while those appearing before the court stand. But there is also a linguistic ploy involved here, for Maimon wants the court to observe literally a convention that is expressed figuratively: "to sit in judgment"; and it is probably no coincidence that, when summoned before the *beyt din* in the previous episode, Maimon does not use the term *Gericht* (court) to refer to the tribunal but the metaphorical *Richterstuhl* (literally, "judge's seat").[76] Maimon's interaction with the chief judge seems to be designed to ridicule the conventions of the court and the validity of its judgments, as well as to display his own astuteness and linguistic dexterity.

The culmination of these encounters with the rabbis underscores Maimon's own unhappy predicament and his problematic relationship with them. Just as the chief rabbi had concluded the discussion by tacitly threatening Maimon with excommunication, so too does the chief judge here retreat from the proceedings, once again implying heresy. And Maimon's final comment on what he calls "this strange trial" *(dieser seltsame Prozeß)*—"Everything remained as before" *(Es blieb alles beim alten)*[77]—may, in fact, refer both to the outcome of the proceedings and the motive for his conduct. After all, at the conclusion of both episodes, after ridiculing the practices of Judaism and demonstrating the impotence of the rabbis, he is still married to his wife, which is precisely what he says he wants, and still impoverished and alone. But nowhere does Maimon acknowledge his wife's burden of supporting a family, or the recriminations *she* may harbor against a society and religion that allow only the husband to release her from her status as *agune*. Moreover, from her actions—sending an envoy in search of her husband, traveling to a foreign country, appearing before the *beyt din,* and finally begging Maimon to release her—one can educe the despair that she, as an *agune,* suffers, even though the narrator in his silence does not acknowledge her predicament. His is the kind of silence or evasion which Glikl's Rebekah would not tolerate and which needs to be challenged, if only in critical recognition of the erasure.

EVASIONS, REPRESSION, SILENCE

Tracing the presence and absence of Maimon's wife in the pages of this *Autobiography* is instructive. Her lengthiest appearance occurs in one small paragraph in which Maimon explains how he tried to gain dominance over his bride by stepping on her foot during the marriage service. But because she stepped on his foot first, he saw himself destined to be his wife's slave for a lifetime. His final comment—"From my cowardice and the heroic fortitude of my wife, the reader can readily grasp why this prophesy would actually be fulfilled" *(Aus meiner*

Feigheit und dem Heldenmut meiner Frau kann der Leser leicht begreifen, warum diese Prophezeiung wirklich eintreffen mußte)[78]—seems deeply ironic, given his abandonment of wife and children. Prior to her arrival in Germany she materializes once again in the course of Maimon's lengthy narrative about the escapades of the marauding, drunken local Polish ruler, Prince Radzivill. When for a moment his wife becomes the object of a suggestive gesture from the prince, Maimon comments briefly on her great natural beauty. But references to her activities, her thoughts, or their family life are not to be found in this text. She has almost no life in this narrative, and she is virtually nameless: her name, Sarah, is mentioned once, when she is first introduced as the daughter of Madame Rissa, who seeks Maimon as a son-in-law; thereafter, she is repeatedly referred to merely as his wife. Maimon also erases their children. While the text states that his son David was born when Maimon was fourteen years old[79] (this is the only instance in which his name is mentioned), that David was his oldest son,[80] and that Maimon's marriage was fruitful, no further information about the children is given. Only when the wife and eldest son appear in Breslau do these family members seem to possess any subjectivity whatsoever; and even then they appear as little more than one-dimensional figures who merely exacerbate Maimon's difficulties.

Some of the readers of Maimon's *Autobiography* seem to replicate his neglect of his family. Only one critic even mentions the wife, and then only to note that "he easily allowed himself to be dominated by his homely wife,"[81] a blatant misrepresentation of the text; for while Maimon does refer to both his wife and mother-in-law as amazons when he notes their daring and courage, he describes his wife specifically as "a beauty of the first order" *(eine Schönheit vom ersten Range)*.[82] But even though only a small portion of the *Autobiography* is devoted to the wife and their relationship, those segments gain greater significance because the textual repression of the wife and her emergence in Germany mirror Maimon's continuous struggle to eradicate the memory of his miserable youth in Eastern Europe and his frustrating inability to expunge it. Indeed, this *Autobiography,* written in German for a learned German audience, may be viewed as a futile and anguished attempt to bury that past—a past poignantly represented by his wife and the rabbis—in a contemporary form of secular European writing. Again and again in his behavior and his efforts to assimilate into German intellectual circles, the shtetl mentality he tries to crush returns to haunt his life amid the culturally enlightened elite. Thus, when his wife finally appears in Breslau, Maimon is confronted not only by his wife and his dereliction of familial responsibility but also with everything he had tried to eradicate—all the contradictions he experienced both as a Jew in the Diaspora and as a Polish Jew in exile among the cosmopolitan Jews and gentiles in Germany.

The question arises about how to reconcile, in the *Autobiography,* the silences, evasions, and camouflage concerning family matters with the overall candid renderings of even embarrassing and unflattering situations. Moreover, textual silences seem to contradict Maimon's repeated assertion in the preface to part 2 of the text that the motivating force behind this work and indeed his life is his search for truth. But scrutiny of the two general conceptions of truth articulated in the preface suggests that there may, in fact, be no inconsistency between his expressed allegiance to truth and the evasions and erasures. On the one hand, truth is understood as an abstract concept connected with Western philosophy and with Maimonides's acknowledged "*love of truth,* which surpasses all else" (*die* Liebe zur Wahrheit, *die über alles geht* [emphases in the text]).[83] On the other hand, truth refers to the accurate description of Maimon's own experiences, which comprise not his social interactions and responsibilities but primarily what he calls his "spiritual [or intellectual] rebirth." Indeed, one of his statements identifies a truth that excludes personal and social responsibilities: "Since to search for the truth now, I have abandoned my nation, my fatherland, and my family, then one cannot expect of me that I should for trivial motives compromise the truth." *(Da ich nun die Wahrheit aufzusuchen, meine Nation, mein Vaterland und meine Familie verlassen habe, so kann man mir nicht zumuten, daß ich geringfügiger Motive halber der Wahrheit etwas vergeben sollte.)*[84]

It is not surprising in the context of Maimon's Eastern European world, in which women gain recognition largely by their service to men (especially learned ones), that the affliction of an *agune* would have—as his wife's virtual absence from the text testifies—no significant value as truth. But it seems remarkable that Maimon's residency in Germany for more than a dozen years should have so little influenced his behavior and values concerning issues of gender, given his dedication to the Enlightenment and his association with the Berlin elite, who often mingled with such prominent women as Henrietta Herz (the wife of the physician Marcus Herz, who was a student of Kant and who held many serious discussions with Maimon),[85] Dorothea Schlegel (Moses Mendelssohn's daughter), and Rahel Varhagen at Berlin cultural salons. While his suppressions and evasions about his wife as *agune* underscore the prerogatives of male authority in Orthodox Judaism, they also relate to the enhanced importance, in eighteenth-century Germany, of the idea of a discrete individual released from former religious, social, and political definition. Wuthenow notes that, during this period, the process of self-reflection, which was critical for the development of autobiography, "should be viewed in connection with the liberation—from tutelage of religion and social class—of the individual for whom, with the loss of ties as well as the means of production, nothing remains other than the certainty of his own self."[86] Written in an age in which the concept of an individual emancipated from communal definition was becoming prominent, at a time when the French Revolution was brewing and capitalism expanding, Maimon's *Autobiography* is haunted by the narrator's drive to develop and secure his own subjectivity through self-reflection, specifically, written self-reflection. Although Maimon conceives of himself as an autonomous individual, which to him was a given of enlightened culture, his *Autobiography* reveals that this narrator as independent entity is actually a construction that heavily depends on the repression and evasion of the aspects of his life that would challenge his sovereignty, namely, traditional religious, social, and family obligations. Maimon's dilemma arises from the conflict between his "love of truth," his need to be an autonomous individual, and his inability to erase completely his wife's presence from his life and his text. To the extent that what is repressed continues to erupt into his life and inform both his self-image and behavior, past traditions constantly threaten to destabilize his life and identity.

Maimon maintains, of course, that candor is the motivating force behind the *Autobiography,* but there is convincing textual evidence that a prime function of its writing may have been to camouflage or banish past experience. He actually acknowledges the potential power of a discarded or repressed past—his constricting and miserable life in Eastern Europe—to shatter his current life as a German writer; and although he twice employs the commonplace literary convention of the reluctant writing hand, his deep anxiety about the return of the repressed, which causes his hand to falter, is apparent. In one instance, for example, Maimon registers the nightmare of his youth in Poland, "whose description causes the pen to fall from my hands and whose painful memory I seek to stifle in me" *(bei deren Beschreibung mir die Feder aus den Händen fallt und deren schmerzhafte Zurückerinnerung ich in mir zu ersticken suche).*[87] The pen and the autobiography are thus designed not only to silence an Eastern European past that includes his wife, family, and the rabbis but also to construct the narrator as a discrete German-writing subject as well.

If the *agunes* in Glikl's *Memoirs* may be understood as doubly exiled—exiled as Jews in the Diaspora, and as *agunes* within the Jewish community—then Maimon's wife suffers a threefold exile: in the Diaspora, within the Jewish community, and finally from her husband's *Lebensgeschichte* (life story or history). But her misfortune also signifies his tragedy, for if her fate is determined by being "chained" to her husband, Maimon's fate is determined by his inability to unchain himself from the Eastern European heritage they both shared, by the impossibility of writing his past out of the script of his life. Moreover, in order to fulfill his conception of himself as author of his life, he would have to eradicate all that his wife and the rabbis represent, but he cannot, for their presence is the obstacle he needs to surmount. Indeed, without negating or overcoming their presence, he could not lay claim to a "spiritual rebirth" as an autonomous individual. And since he cannot eliminate, but can only evade, mask, and silence his family's existence, the *agune* still stands, albeit in the shadows, as a stubborn reminder of his shattered self-image as independent and enlightened German thinker.

CHAPTER 3

The Victims of Adventure

Abandoned Wives in Abramovitsh's Benjamin the
Third *and Sholem Aleykhem's* Menakhem-Mendl

In two major Yiddish novels, both of them parodic and written around
the turn of the twentieth century, protagonists who leave wife and
home behind them are presented as adventurers: Benjamin of Tuneyadevke in S. Y. Abramovitsh's *The Travels of Benjamin the Third* (*Masoes
benyomin hashlishi,* published in 1895) and Menakhem-Mendl in Sholem
Aleykhem's *Menakhem-Mendl* (published in 1912; the titles of the two
English translations are *The Adventures of Menahem-Mendl* [1969] and
The Letters of Menakhem-Mendl and Sheyne-Sheyndl [2002]). Each protagonist ventures out of his shtetl in the Pale of Settlement—an area
within czarist Russia where Jews were legally permitted to live—in part
to improve the circumstances of his life. Benjamin makes grandiose
plans to find the Red Jews (the Ten Lost Tribes) and enlist their military forces in liberating the people of Israel, thereby hoping to alleviate the oppression of his fellow Jews living in exile under czarist rule.
Menakhem-Mendl, with no such grandiose national agenda, leaves his
shtetl, Kasrilevke, merely to collect a debt owed him. He finds himself
in the capitalist marketplaces of modernizing urban centers, where he
thinks he can earn a living or, more accurately, make or acquire money,
which he sorely lacks. In addition, the texts make it clear that a major motivation—and perhaps even the only one—for their adventurous undertakings in the seemingly vast, unpredictable world outside
their narrow *shtetlekh* is the acquisition of an identity of eminence and
stature. In *Menakhem-Mendl,* moreover, the conventional roles of husband, father, and coreligionist, considered adequate in an impoverished

and systemically unproductive shtetl, no longer sufficed in the larger world being transformed by advancing capitalist production. Indeed, not unlike the requirements for autonomy during the Enlightenment, those traditional roles were actually experienced as obstacles to a sense of individual prominence or self-importance in burgeoning metropolitan arenas.

Since robust youth and social savoir faire are salient characteristics of adventurers, these two figures from backwoods *shtetlekh* may at first, because of their age, marital state, and the limitations of their extraordinarily provincial lives, appear to be unlikely candidates.[1] On closer scrutiny, however, their status as travelers and adventurers participates in the modern discourses of both Jewish tradition and European culture. Indeed, the texts in which they appear reveal a partial, simultaneous patterning of affiliations to multiple cultures, literary genres, and trends. In each text there is a confluence of genres important within both the European and Jewish literary traditions of the late nineteenth and early twentieth centuries: in *Benjamin the Third*, chivalric romances and Jewish travel literature (also thematized in the novel); and in *Menakhem-Mendl*, the epistolary novel and the Jewish *brivnshteler*, a genre that offers useful exemplars of letters.[2] There is, however, also a fundamental dual modeling in the presentation of the figure of the adventurer, as the luftmentsh ("a person of air," or a windbag, almost always male) of Jewish tradition and as the modern adventurer (most often an erotic or economic adventurer or a dandy) in European letters of that period. Furthermore, just as the European genres of the chivalric and picaresque romances and the epistolary novel take on cultural specificity when modeled with Jewish traditional genres important within the specific sociocultural framework of Eastern European Jewry, so too does the figure of the modern European adventurer reveal a similar cultural specificity when it emerges within the modern Jewish figuration of the luftmentsh. Let me focus briefly on the European adventurer.

A prototypical characteristic of the adventurer in European culture is his sense of freedom from external control that provides him with an aura of power, genius, heroism, and even cruelty.[3] To attain such sovereignty, however, the individual must distance himself from his dependencies and petty quotidian concerns, something especially difficult for the Eastern European Jewish adventurer, given the confinement and abject poverty of the shtetl. The ideology of the autonomous individual, so prominent in eighteenth-century European Enlightenment thought, informs and favors the figure of the adventurer, which in the nineteenth century is displaced from social and political discourse into cultural discourse. Adventure may be understood as an imaginary realm of freedom and pleasure, and the adventurer as a fiction whose fantasies of consummate independence and fulfillment actually conceal the powerlessness, dependence, and isolation that are his true lot.

With the exception of the satiric *Don Quixote,* which Abramovitsh parodies, the modern adventurer—unlike the knight-errant in medieval romances, who was motivated by socially prescribed duty and etiquette, and who participated in adventurous activity in order to protect society and its institutions—is neither impelled by duty nor particularly concerned about his society, which he more often than not impugns or opposes. He is instead driven by desire, by a sense of incompletion or emptiness within himself (or within society) that sends him out to conquer or appropriate whatever he experiences as "other"—be that rivals, women, or money—in order to construct or affirm a sense of his own importance and power, which is, however, almost always predicated on loss. Because he must still forge an identity within the social arena, such self-affirmation often entails violating the social codes and institutions that inhibit his success, notably codes that regulate family life and social services. The medieval knight who, for example, was rewarded for protecting women's virtue has been replaced in more recent times by an erotic adventurer who gains stature by making sexual conquests, especially of young virgins and respectable married women, and by outdoing (or doing in) protective fathers and husbands. Since within a society rife with competing social needs and interests the modern adventurer's expectations—total freedom, complete sovereignty, and ubiquitous power—are hardly achievable, perpetually recurring desire propels him into action, into obsession with conquest or acquisition, and creates his need to shed all binding commitments, including (or especially) those to women and family.

Both Benjamin and Menakhem-Mendl are generally regarded as typical luftmentshn, a term within modern Jewish culture commonly used to refer to those who, removed as they are from the material realities necessary for survival, have no stable profession and seem to live merely on air.[4] In the past, the Hebrew term *batlan* (idler) often also referred to someone who did not pursue a remunerative trade or profession but—unlike the luftmentsh—occupied himself with religious study. If he was truly a serious Talmud or Torah student and practiced "spiritual idleness" (*batala ruchanit,* in modern Hebrew), he would be so highly valued by family and community that they would be willing to support him. With the European Enlightenment in the eighteenth century, the Jewish Enlightenment (the *haskole*) in the nineteenth century, the rise of secular modernity in general, and the decline of the former reverence for exclusive religious study, the *batlan* became an unacceptable social encumbrance, a luftmentsh characterized by practical ineptitude and the inability to fulfill the productive expectations of modernity. In nineteenth-century Jewish cultural discourse, the luftmentsh was perceived as a blusterer whose articulated intentions were rarely realized but continually circulated within the realm of language.

Within Jewish communities, the expansion of capitalism, secularization, and urban life occasioned a shift in the understanding and value of "masculinity," from the adulation of the religious scholar to that of the economically competent and successful man—a Rothschild or an Israel Brodsky, a magnate of the sugar industry. Both the esoteric religious scholar of pre-Enlightenment tradition and the modern capitalist or erotic adventurer, however, shared at least one salient characteristic: their sense that they owned the male privilege of freedom to carry on their activities without interference. Indeed, this idealized autonomous or sovereign identity, whose masculine entitlement excluded all those feminized spaces usually inhabited by women and children, provided a critical nexus between the cultural discourse of the luftmentsh of Jewish tradition and that of the modern European adventurer. What is so important in *Benjamin the Third* and *Menakhem-Mendl* is precisely this confluence of adventurer and luftmentsh in one figure, his preoccupation with his own identity and status, and his problematic relationship to his wife and the institution of the family.

The Travels of Benjamin the Third

In the story that Mendele the Bookpeddler (Mendele Moykher Sforim),[5] the fictional narrator of *Benjamin the Third,* relates in ordinary Yiddish—quoting at times from the protagonist Benjamin the Third's own memoirs—it is Benjamin himself who at the outset articulates in inflated language the special significance that wife and marriage have for him. But the irony and hypocrisy of exalted pronouncements in praise of his spouse in the first chapter, titled "Who This Benjamin Is, Where He Came From, and How His Travels Suddenly Took Hold of Him" *(ver der binyomin iz, fun vanen er iz un vi di nesiye hot plutslim tsu im zikh genumen),*[6] soon become glaringly manifest when he abandons her in order to venture out in search of the Red Jews *(royte yidelekh)*. Using traditional formal Hebrew locutions and ostentatiously extolling his wife as the chaste Mrs. Zelda, Benjamin first announces that he lives in Tuneyadevke: "There I was born, there I was brought up, and there I fortunately married my wife [Hebrew], my missus [mixed Aramaic-Yiddish], the chaste Mrs. [Hebrew] Zelda, long may she live [Hebrew]." *(dort bin ikh geboyrn gevorn, dort bin ikh dertsoygn gevorn, un dort hob ikh lemazl khasene gehat im ishti mit mayn ployneste hatsnue mores Zelda tkhie.)*[7] Although Benjamin's words suggest spousal devotion, Mendele's depiction of life in Tuneyadevke makes it clear that abandoning one's family is actually part of the routine of daily life. After all, the narrator Mendele notes, the unemployed men of the impoverished town congregate in the study house or public bath, where they "sit constantly all day long until late at night, abandoning wife as well as children" *(vos zitsn shtendik a gantsn tog biz shpet in der nakht, zaynen mafker vayb i kinder)*[8] and discuss international politics and finance. Not only is the abandonment of the family during the course of daily life represented as completely acceptable behavior, the community actually provides public spaces—the synagogue or study house and the bathhouse—for male retreats.

Indeed, Tuneyadevke's ubiquitous poverty does not preclude a sociopolitical hierarchical structure that places women outside the "polis," outside those places where the men generate what they deem important political decisions. Although discussion generally begins in the homes, where women may be present, it eventually moves to the synagogue and its stove, where the men deliberate the serious contemporary issues: "domestic secrets, as well as the politics of Istanbul, about Turkey and about Austria, as well as about financial matters, about Rothschild's fortune in comparison with the great lords and the other great rich men, as well as rumors about the evil decrees and about the little Red Jews and so on" *(heyn soydes fun shtubzakhn, heyn politike mikoyekh stambul, mikoyekh dem toyger, vemikoyekh kiren, heyn gelt-gesheftn, mikoyekh rotshilds farmegn in farglaykh mit di groyse pritsim un di andere groyse negidim, veheyn potshtn mikoyekh di gzeyres vemikoyekh di royte yidelekh vekedoyme)*. Then the special committee of "respectable venerable Jews" *(sheyne batogte yidn)*, who have abandoned their wives and children in order to pursue these issues into the night, bring their ruminations for final resolution to "a full assembly of city burghers" *(a fuler asife fun shtot-balebatim)* seated on the most desirable top benches of the bathhouse.[9] In this caricature of a parliamentary system in one of the most impoverished and debased communities of Jews, the shtetl men play out the farce of settling the major political and financial problems of the capitalist-imperialistic world, while the women remain invisible, ensconced as they are in the domestic sphere. Here, within the traditional Jewish community, the special prerogatives of men are obvious, as are the unequal privileges and status of men and women.

There are also in this text other aspects of Jewish tradition that support the social acceptance, even glorification, of such spousal desertion. Two such aspects are prominent: the first refers to a long tradition of religious scholars who leave wives and families in order to pursue their studies elsewhere, often in distant locations.[10] In such cases, wives willingly accepted the burden of sustaining the family, financially and otherwise, in return for the prestige of being related to and supporting a distinguished scholar. While the wives in this tradition and in the daily routine of Tuneyadevke have not been technically or legally deserted, this conventional male behavior suggests a model for the relationship between spouses in which men alone have the prerogative of leaving their wives to go off on their own to study or while away the days and nights in the bath and study houses, where the fate of the Crimean War or of the Rothschilds is decided.[11] Indeed, the narrator Mendele explicitly identifies this male behavior as family abandonment. On another level, of course, this practice may be related to a larger phenomenon within Jewish tradition—namely, the cross purposes that arise when a national or religious mission conflicts with family responsibility. Such tensions appear, for example, in the Bible in the *lekh lekho* ("Go forth from your land and your birthplace and your father's house" [Genesis 12:1]) episode, when God tells Abraham to leave home and country, and in traditional commentaries on the *akeda* (the binding of Isaac), where Sarah, who seems not to have been told what was to happen to her son Isaac, is said to have died of a broken heart after learning of his binding.[12]

The second relevant aspect of Jewish tradition that may dignify abandonment involves the *shekhine* of the religious mystical tradition. In the teachings of the Kabbalah, the *shekhine* is often understood as the feminine divine principle, which is closest to the created world (the divine manifestation as opposed to divine transcendence) and is identified, in her exile from God, with the nation Israel.[13] Relating to a traditional topos, noted in chapter 2, that describes the relationship between God and the Jewish people as a marriage, and this people, when exiled, as an abandoned woman, the *shekhine* is, at times, figured in literary texts as an *agune* exiled from the center of meaning. A small but salient instance early in *Benjamin the Third* reveals the importance of this connection in the text. There, in order to convince his friend to join him in his projected travels, Benjamin visits Senderl and finds him sitting dejected "like a young woman whose husband discarded her and went off to countries beyond the sea" *(vi a yugnt, vos der man irer hot zi avekgevorfn un iz avekgegangen lemedines hayam).*[14] This passage about a deserting husband who sailed away alludes to a Talmudic midrash in which the grieving abandoned woman is likened to the exiled nation Israel and the *shekhine.* The midrash tells of a wailing woman, who calls herself Mother Zion, whose husband had gone "away to a far city by the sea," and whose seven sons were subsequently killed in a house that collapsed. (Some fifty years after *Benjamin the Third* appeared, Dvora Baron, in a Hebrew story titled *Aguna* [in English translation, "Deserted Wife"], alludes to the same midrash and to an *agune*'s husband who "left her and sailed off to a land across the seas.")[15] Thus, Senderl is identified with an abhorrent personal, national, and spiritual state of abandonment. Of course, identifying the passive and abused Senderl with the exalted *shekhine* is grotesquely humorous and ironic, but a feminized and submissive shtetl resident living under oppressive czarist rule may, nonetheless, be an entirely appropriate figure to represent Israel in its miserable exilic condition. Indeed, the midrashic allusion is both preceded and followed by an alternate description of a feminized Senderl. In the first instance, he is referred to as a *yidene,* a linguistically correct term for a "Jewish woman," but one most often used derogatorily to signify a person who is uneducated and insignificant in the communal polity. In the second, he is described as looking "like a woman [or wife] whose husband has slapped her" *(vi an ishe, vos der man hot ir derlangt a patsh),*[16] a simile which, by foregrounding his demeaning feminization, undermines any exalted implication in the comparison of Senderl to the *shekhine.*[17] The marked differences between the two descriptions notwithstanding, both the midrashic allusion and the analogy with domestic abuse alert the reader once again to the fact that, within the Eastern European Jewish community, the plight of the *agune* and gender inequality are rooted in generally acceptable, even exalted, Jewish practices and traditions.

The intimate connection between luftmentsh/adventurer and abandoned woman is evident in the second chapter, "How Benjamin Becomes a Martyr and Zelda an *Agune*" *(vi binyomen vert a koydesh un zelda an agune),*[18] though the pronouncement in the title is both misleading and markedly ironic. After all, the incredibly fearful Benjamin's very first attempt to leave the shtetl by himself for only a brief time ends in a debacle worthy of a village comic opera or farce: a terrified Benjamin gets lost, passes out in a paroxysm of fear when he sees a peasant's wagon approaching, and is hauled back to town atop a sack of potatoes on the wagon. Because Benjamin, widely known to be a coward, had been absent from his daily routine at the study house and bath and could not be found, "he was already considered a martyr and his wife a desolate *agune*" *(men hot im shoyn gehaltn far a koydesh un zayn vayb far a viste agune).*[19] Indeed, from that day forth he and Zelda were known as *koydesh* and *agune,* titles that *his* actions alone had earned for both of them. But the fact that *he* was awarded a title of honor, whether deserved or not, while *she* was given merely an appellation of loss and degradation, highlights not only her subaltern status and powerlessness as a woman and potential *agune* within that community but also the glorification of the deserter.

Although, in the novel, Zelda remains a character only spoken about and whose own words are never heard, there is an important interaction between Benjamin's garrulous heroic pretensions and her virtually silent presence as a hardworking, devoted wife. He concedes that she may, in fact, be a "woman of valor" *(eyshes khayil),* a biblical term for a husband's praise of his wife. The praise, actually marked in song at the beginning of every Sabbath, is offered largely in recognition of the woman's ability to maintain a fine household for husband and family; but in Benjamin's eyes, even such a woman of valor "is nonetheless nothing more than a *yidene*" *(iz zi dokh fort nisht mer vi a yidene).*[20] He then adds, "What the lowliest man has in his nail, the finest and smartest *yidene* cannot have at all even in her head." *(vos der mindester mansbil hot in nogl, hot es nisht, un ken es gor nisht hobn, di faynste un di kligste yidene afile in ir kop.)*[21]

The nearer Benjamin's impending departure for the East, however, the more overtly does he begin to construct an image of himself as the quintessential adventurer, "as a hero, as a speculative thinker" *(far a giber, far a khakren),* a Columbus or a king, but most often as Alexander the Great—namely, as a hero who one day will return "with honor and with a good name in the world" *(mit koved un mit a gutn nomen in der velt).*[22] Simultaneously, in a bid for autonomy, he also begins to erase the presence of his wife, first by maligning her in unconscionable terms, then, from a position of patriarchal male superiority, by denigrating her as a woman, and eventually by deserting her completely. Indeed, when he and Senderl finally decide to leave together, Zelda is, in a few brief phrases, virtually eliminated from the text and seemingly from

Benjamin's life. Thereafter, he refers to her neither as wife nor as Zelda, but only as something that he owns: "I will say it now as you did," he tells Senderl. "As to her? Mine, I mean. What kind of concern do I have? There is, however, another question: how can we cover expenses?" *(ikh zog itst oykh azoy vi du: ay zi? mayne meyn ikh. vos far a dayge ikh hob? s'iz ober do nokh a kashe: vu nemt men af hetsoes?)*[23] Thus, in his desire to undertake adventures and to acquire status and power associated with sovereignty, Benjamin presents himself quite literally as a kind of luft-mentsh, or creature of the air, as "a free bird, like the little field birds here" (*a frayer foygl, glaykh vi di feldfeygelekh do;*[24] in Yiddish, "free bird" *[frayer foygl]* is used idiomatically to designate a person without attach-ments or responsibilities). Calling attention to the inanity of Benjamin's anticipated great triumphs, the narrator Mendele asks birds to join him in a paean to Benjamin and his imminent venture, thereby both parody-ing adventure romances, particularly the already parodic *Don Quixote*, and bitterly satirizing the protagonist's heroic pretensions:

—Come, let us sing as well as exult and bring joy to the fine person near the windmill. He is Benjamin himself. That is Benjamin of Tuneyadevke, the Alex-ander of Macedon of his time, who is leaving his fatherland, discarding wife and children, and is going on a mission, wherever the eyes carry him! There stands the great Benjamin, who like the sun came out of his tent and like a hero pre-pares to run down the road with his bundle in hand! He is strong as a leopard and light as an eagle to do the will of our Father in heaven! Sing, play: trililili, trril, tril, sing and bring joy to his heart!

—*kumt, lomir zingen i shaln un derfreyen dem faynem parshoyn nebn der vintmil. dos iz binyomen aleyn. dos iz benyomin der tuneyadevker, der aleksander mukden fun zayn tsayt, vos er farlozt zayn foterland, varft avek vayb un kinder un geyt in shlikhes, vohin di oygn trogn! ot shteyt der groyser binyomen, vos er iz vi di zun aroys fun zayn getselt un greyt zikh vi a giber tsu loyfn in veg mit zayn pekl in der hant! er iz shtark vi a lempert un gring vi an odler tsu tun dem rotsn fun undzer foter in himl! zingt, shpilt: trililili, trril, tril, zingt un derfreyt zayn harts!*[25]

The narrator Mendele is clearly cognizant that Benjamin, as modern adventurer, is mightily concerned not only with his identity as hero and with his grandiose mission as redeemer of his people but also with the necessity of eradicating—by abandoning wife and family—all traces of his inadequacy and dependency and of transforming his fictional free-dom into reality.

But victory and fame were not to be. After wandering through sev-eral impoverished *shtetlekh,* each one as decrepit or even more so than their own, the gullible pair are finally duped by two Jews and forced into the army. Only in the final chapters, after Benjamin and Senderl are in military service, does Benjamin's quest for accomplishing a holy mission seem to have disappeared from his consciousness. The narrator characterizes the disposition of these two travelers, and Benjamin's conception of freedom, by alluding once again to the natures of different kinds of birds. Senderl, true to his adaptive disposition and not unlike many kinds of creatures, conforms all too readily to any environment, even captivity: "Need one be freer than a bird," the narrator notes; "however, when one catches it and places it in a little cage, it adapts bit by bit, begins to nibble kernels with relish, jumps and sings happy songs, just as if the whole world with its fields and forests is present for it in the narrow little cage." *(bedarf men mer fray vi a foygl iz, fun destvegn, az men fangt im un men zetst im arayn in a shtaygele, gevoynt er zikh tsubislekh, heybt on tsu pikn kerner mit apetit, shpringt un zingt freylekhe lider, glaykh vi di gantse velt mit ire felder un velder iz far im do in dem engn shtaygele.)*[26] Unlike Senderl, however, who had begun to conform to military life like a bird that cannot fly, "a puffed up turkey" *(a ongeblozener indik),*[27] Benjamin's nature is likened to that of

one of those birds, which are called migratory birds, that is, whose nature it is every year at the end of summer to fly away and spend the winter there in far-away, warm places. The habit of wandering afflicts such a bird so strongly that, if one holds it captive in a cage, its life is so disagreeable, it doesn't eat, doesn't drink, it clambers up the bare walls and seeks somewhere for some crack in order to escape. The urge to travel to those far places, which like an insect ate into Benjamin's head, which became for him a second nature, for whose sake he discarded wife and children—precisely these travels did not let him rest for a moment, had bored, pecked into his head—it grumbled in him, and everything screamed: Benjamin, go further, go further, further!

eyner fun yene mine feygl, vos heysn vander-feygl, dos heyst azelkhe, vos zeyer teve iz ale yor sof zumer avektsufliyen un ibervintern dort in di vayte, vareme mekoymes. di teve tsu vandrevn mont aza min foygl azoy stark, az bei'm men halt im denstmol gefangen in a shtaygl, iz im nisht nikhe dos lebn, er est nisht, trinkt nisht, er drapet zikh af di glaykhe vent un zukht ergets epes a shpalt antrunen tsu vern. di nesiye ahin in yene vayte mekoymes, vos hot vi a zlidne zikh ayngegesn in binyomens kop, vos iz im gevorn di tsveyte natur, vos tsulib ir hot er avekgevorfn vayb un kinder—di dozike nesie hot im nisht gelozt ruen keyn rege, hot im geboyert, gepikt dem kop, zi hot in im geburtshet un alts geshrign: binyomen, geh vayter! geh vayter, vayter![28]

Any concern for a "holy mission" is absent from this description. What remains is the simple desire of the luftmentsh to continue his travels free

THE VICTIMS OF ADVENTURE 59

of all obligations and responsibilities, whether to family or community, to be free of the misery of his current situation, of oppression and dependencies, but not yet free to undertake anything constructive or useful.

In these final chapters of the novel, the adjective *bavaybt* (or the noun a *bavaybter*), which signifies a married man, one who has a wife, appears twice. In the first instance, Benjamin uses the term to convince Senderl to stop playing soldier and start acting like a Jew who has obligations—that is, like someone who is saddled with a wife.[29] In the second, he attempts to explain his and Senderl's family responsibilities to the military officers at the court martial hearing. In this latter instance, Benjamin alludes vaguely to their "future plans," which may very well include not taking care of their families at all but continuing their travels unimpeded by wives. Thus, after explaining to the military tribunal that they neither know nor want to know anything about war, Benjamin adds, "We are, praised be God, married men, have in mind something very different, and we absolutely cannot occupy ourselves with such things, they don't even enter our heads." *(mir zaynen, borekh hashem, bavaybte, hobn in zinen epes gor andersh, un mit azelkhe zakhenishn kenen mir lakhlutn zikh nisht opgebn, zey geyen undz afile gor in kop nisht.)*[30] The novel concludes with the release of Benjamin and Senderl from the army, but with no mention of wives, families, or community, an absence in the text that may speak louder than words. With beardless faces—not unlike Maimon's when he appears before the *beyt din*—signifying, in Jewish Orthodoxy, a complete departure from their shtetl religious practices and values, these two clean-shaven luftmentshn stride off once again into the big world. Their new, unencumbered, perhaps unmanly or "feminized" lives (at least within Jewish tradition) are announced in the heading of this final chapter: "No Longer Bride—Again a Maiden" *(Oys kale—vayter moyd)*.[31] Their wives, if abandoned, remain *agunes* as silent and invisible in the text as they would be within their communities.

Menakhem-Mendl

Although Sholem Aleykhem's *Menakhem-Mendl,* written over a period of two decades, from 1892 to 1912, consists, for the most part, of an exchange of alternating letters between Menakhem-Mendl, written as he roves the large cities of Russia (Odessa and Yehupets [Sholem Aleykhem's fictional Kiev]), and his wife Sheyne-Sheyndl ensconced in the shtetl Kasrilevke, the title of the novel bears only his name. Sheyne-Sheyndl seems relegated to a shadowy existence fixed in an archaic Eastern European hinterland and a static traditional Jewish life, and eventually to total absence when, toward the end of the novel, her letters cease to appear. In the "Preface to the Second Edition" *(tsu der tsveyter oyflage fun "Menakhem-Mendl")*—which in fact appeared after the publication of the novel and is thus a preface to the first, since no further edition of the text exists[32]—the fictional editor, Sholem Aleykhem, notes that this work may be used by merchants, speculators, brokers, matchmakers, agents, and others who need prototypes for the letters they write their wives.[33] This statement underlines the absence of husbands from their families but also, since there is no suggestion here that Sheyne-Sheyndl's letters may be considered as exemplars that wives might use to communicate with their husbands, dismisses the importance of women's writing altogether. Whereas textual evidence in the novel suggests that Sholem Aleykhem is satirizing and critiquing gender roles in the Jewish community, critics—apparently taking the text title at face value and neglecting the irony of the preface—have focused almost exclusively on the figure of Menakhem-Mendl and virtually ignored Sheyne-Sheyndl. When notice has been taken of her, she has usually been dismissed as a practical but uninteresting stereotypical small-town carping housewife, apparently unworthy of serious consideration.[34] Yet the markedly different sensibilities and interests of husband and wife reflected in their letters reinforce the dialogic structure of the epistolary novel, which highlights a personal, possibly intimate, relationship but, because of the ongoing separation of the correspondents from one another, also signals the distance and disjuncture between them.

By emulating and parodying the European epistolary novel and alluding to the *brivnshteler* of Jewish tradition, this novel draws on both genres to expose the personal, social, and cultural dislocations that arose in the nineteenth century when Eastern European shtetl Jewry gained access to urban modernity. In addition to exposing the gender differences and the relationship of adventurer to *agune,* the opening sentences of all of Menakhem-Mendl and Sheyne-Sheyndl's letters display recurring distinct formulaic forms of address presumably chosen from a *brivnshteler,*[35] and they illuminate how the intersection and parodies of various genres function in this text. Because the English translations do not distinguish between the more formal Hebrew segments and the vernacular Yiddish ones in each address, the evidence of a parodied *brivnshteler* is obscured. Menakhem-Mendl's letters begin largely in Hebrew (Yiddish words appear in italics in the English translation, and in standard typeface in the Yiddish transliteration): "To my dear, modest, wise helpmate, Mrs. Sheyne-Sheyndl, may she live. First of all, I wish to inform you, *that I am,* blessed be God, alive and well. May the Lord, blessed be His name, *grant that we always hear from one another nothing but good news* with the best, most comforting, and happiest tidings—amen. Second of all . . . " *(lezugosi hayekore hatsnue hakha-khome mores Sheyne-Sheyndl shetekhiye. reyshis, boti lehoydiekh, az ikh bin borekh ha-shem bekav hekhayim, vehasholem. hashem yisborekh zol helfn, me zol tomid horkhn eyns funem andern nor guts mit psuros toyves, yeshues venekhomes—omeyn. Vehasheynes . . .)* Thereafter, continuing in colloquial Yiddish, he usually expounds on his most recent speculative business ventures and his fantasies of becoming a millionaire. Sheyne-Sheyndl's letters begin in Hebrew: "In honor of my dear husband, the famous, illustrious, the eminent scholar, our teacher and rabbi, the Honorable Menakhem-Mendl may his light continue to shine" *(leko-ved baali hayoker hanogid hamefursem hakhokhem mufleg moyrene ve-rabyene harov reb menakhem-mendl neyre-yoer).* They continue in Yid-dish: "First of all, I come to inform you that we are all thank God in the best of health, may God grant to hear the same about you in the future nothing worse. Secondly . . . " *(ershtns, kum ikh dir tsu meldn, az mir zaynen ale got tsu danken in bestn gezunt, gib got dos nemlekhe fun dir tsu hern oyf vayter nit erger. tsveytns . . .)* This is followed very often by complaints about ailments that she and the children have suffered, the many tribulations of her difficult life, and news of family and friends.

The moderate tone of Menakhem-Mendl's address might lead one to expect a composed, temperate discourse, not his self-absorbed, tur-bulent narratives that almost always leave the important information for the postscript. Given that Menakhem-Mendl is impecunious and a bungler, certainly not a rabbi, and that he demonstrates not the slight-est interest in scholarship, the exalted form of Sheyne-Sheyndl's ad-dress is ironic and enormously humorous, designed as it is for a great scholar or holy man, not an inept mate desperately trying in vain to make something out of the nothing he has or is. The humorous effect of the formula is of course only amplified by its constant repetition in all of her letters.[36] But adopting a formula appropriate for a scholarly husband who has gone off to study Torah or Talmud may also be poi-gnant for her precisely because her form of address situates Menakhem-Mendl's departure within a long and honorable tradition of spousal abandonment for the purpose of serious religious study. Thus it may allow Sheyne-Sheyndl to experience herself in a more favorable light, not merely as the overburdened wife or the *agune* she constantly fears she will become.

The social and cultural limitations of both spouses are inscribed in the discursive personae of their letters, apparent not only in the markedly different *brivnshteler*-influenced formula that each has adopted but in their distinct epistolary discourses as well. Menakhem-Mendl details the activities and conventions of the financial and business marketplace, employing its international vocabulary, which includes such foreign words as *London, stallage, bas, haut,* terms Sheyne-Sheyndl can hardly fathom and which her husband's bungled explanations do little to clarify. She, however, retains the verbal adroitness of shtetl Yiddish, using commonplace maxims and anecdotes to support her statements and curses either to threaten her husband or to shift the onus of her struggles onto others.[37] Although her complaints are often humorous and articulated in colorful colloquialisms, they hardly conceal her distress and embarrassment: "Why do I have to be on other people's tongues," she writes, "and enemies should mutter that you have taken yourself to Odessa and have discarded me, may you not live to see that!" *(tsu vos badarf ikh lign bay yenem in moyl un sonim zoln murmeln, az du host zikh avekgelozt keyn ades un mikh host du avekgevorfn* [this term meaning "abandonment" occurs also in *Benjamin the Third*],[38] *nit derlebn zolst du dos!)*[39] Nor do her malapropisms ameliorate the effectiveness of the quotations from her mother's lore, prefaced by "How does mama say it" *(vi zogt di mame).* The discrete discursive patterns of the letters of husband and wife seem to identify two distinct worlds:[40] while his writing centers on urban Jewish life, rarely alluding to his former life in the shtetl, indeed distancing him from it, her oral folk wisdom, associated with the language and lore of shtetl women, criticizes her husband's disastrous confrontation with the evolving modern marketplace in the cities.[41] The letters reflect the tensions and dislocations that have developed between metropolis and shtetl, between the individualism or subjectivity associated with personal letter-writing in the European epistolary novel and the Jewish communal needs served by the formulaic *brivnshteler* conventions. But they also reveal changing lifestyles and values in both arenas. Thus, while Menakhem-Mendl's ineffectual and unproductive activity in the city actually mirrors, within the new context of capitalist development, the familiar behavior of shtetl residents, life in the shtetl begins increasingly to resemble that of the metropolis, where married women discard their wigs, women and men play cards together, and young people arrange their own marriages.[42]

In the preface, the fictional editor Sholem Aleykhem writes that this novel may be considered

almost a *brivnshteler*. Indeed a *brivnshteler*, divided into six distinct parts, and thereby had a purpose: a Jew a merchant, if he should want to write a letter to his wife, for instance, from Odessa—he should look in the first book "London." A speculator at the stock market for all kinds of stuff, for stocks and other such wares—will find an exemplar in the second book "Scraps of Paper," or in the third book "Millions."

kimat a brivnshteler. take a brivensteler, ayngeteylt in seks bazundere opteylungen, un derbay gehat a meyn: a yid a soykher, az er vet veln shraybn a briv tsu zayn vayb, lemoshl, fun ades—zol er zukhn inem ershtn bukh "london." a shpekulant af der berze fun yakhnehoz, fun aktsyes ukhdoyme azelkhe skhoyres—vet gefinen a muster inem tsveytn bukh "papirlekh," oder inem dritn bukh "milyonen."[43]

This novel, then, like the *brivnshteler*, is useful for men involved in the modern capitalist world of business and financial transactions. And Sholem Aleykhem seemingly expected *Menakhem-Mendl* to integrate two distinct generic forms: the traditional Jewish *brivnshteler* and the European epistolary novel, which contended with major socioeconomic transformations in the early modern period when feudal society was waning and capitalism was emerging.[44] This confluence of generic forms results in a culturally expressive form appropriate to exploring Eastern European Jewry's confrontation with historical, social, and cultural developments of Western modernity, whether in the home, the marketplace, or literature.

CONSTRUCTING A NEW IDENTITY: MENAKHEM-MENDL'S BIG "BUSYNESS" AND HIS RECEDING SHTETL

As noted above, critics of this novel focused largely on the figure of Menakhem-Mendl and virtually ignored the significance of his spouse. While Sheyne-Sheyndl and the issues her figure raises in the text deserve careful attention and should be the focal point in this study of *agunes*, it is also true that her plight and her repeated fears of becoming an *agune* do not originate in her own being or behavior but—as with all deserted wives—emerge from the activity of the husband who leaves her and their children stranded and abandoned in their shtetl home. Indeed, it is his departure from home that calls into existence this epistolary text with its two protagonists and brings to the fore its multiple tensions: tensions between women and men; between communal and familial attachments and the pursuit of individual independence; and between the countryside with its remnants of backwardness, feudal life, and folk traditions, and the city with its burgeoning mobility and volatile capitalist activity.[45] Because in this novel Menakhem-Mendl is the principal cause of his wife's predicament, it is his story that must be considered before exploring the complex matters concerning Sheyne-Sheyndl. Therefore, I discuss first the adventures of Menakhem-Mendl. It is, nonetheless, ironic and a sad but powerful commentary on the modern world of the early twentieth century that it is often virtually impossible to explore the problems of women without first scrutinizing the social roles and status of men whose positions and behavior almost always directly affect and often control the lives of women.

Possessing neither money nor skills, neither a home in Odessa or Yehupets nor even a permit to live or work there, Menakhem-Mendl appears as a quintessential luftmentsh, someone trying to create wealth and status out of nothing. Curiously, the very process of generating his persona and social identity through writing already hints at a possible underlying insubstantiality, and even his original motivation to leave the shtetl illuminates the immateriality of his existence. Indeed, his first letter reveals that he left home in a vain effort to collect dowry money owed him by a relative and soon found himself in urban money markets and stock exchanges. Thus he moved from traditional Jewish and tangible, albeit impoverished, economic practices to the elusive and unstable arena of financial speculation—from a semblance of immanence in his shtetl community to various forms of abstraction in the world of capitalist enterprise.[46] Able to obtain only a minute amount of the debt in cash and the rest in useless promissory notes, he launches a business career using not money but worthless promises on paper. And although this initial incursion into currency speculation fails badly, as do all his other economic ventures, he never again returns to his family, but instead continues unsuccessfully to pursue myriad insubstantial business endeavors in the risk-laden realms of finance, the stock market, various forms of real estate or rather "nonexistent estates," journalism, matchmaking, and insurance sales. Not unlike the continual circulation of unfulfilled desire experienced by modern erotic and economic adventurers—desire that can rarely be fulfilled but always replenished—Menakhem-Mendl's repeated business disasters only encourage him to seek ever new prospects. At the end of the novel, still penniless and no more adept at business but ever optimistic, he announces that he is about to set sail for America to continue his business dealings, leaving behind not only a string of devastating losses, including that of any self-esteem, but his wife and children as well.

In the shtetl he no doubt could have survived with little money and without significant skills and nonetheless been regarded as a respected husband, father, coreligionist, and community member, even though those roles did not seem to generate a gratifying identity for him. Indeed the flimsiest possibility of becoming a millionaire such as Brodsky and Rothschild—names that circulated in the shtetl, among the Jews scurrying around the urban financial markets, and in his epistolary discourse—was sufficient to entice Menakhem-Mendl to forsake home and hearth and to continue in vain to pursue one foolhardy economic adventure after another. It was in the big cities, at money markets and stock exchanges, in the cafes and on the boulevards, where business was conducted among men, and where a shtetl wife and family were superfluous, even an embarrassment and hindrance, that he sought to create a persona that bore no traces of his life in Kasrilevke. While cognizant of the difference between traditional Jewish values, which regarded heritage and scholarly ability as far superior to accumulation of wealth, and the new capitalistic ones in which the power of money ruled, he opted for the latter, no matter how disillusioned and depressed his business failures left him.[47] In Yehupets, for example, believing himself to be fast approaching millionaire status, he appraises the inhabitants as "truly gold and silver" *(mamesh gold un zilber)*.[48] Even after experiencing a major financial disaster and recognizing the miserable reality of his current situation, he quickly regains the confidence that—despite his lack of money, knowledge, and skills—he will yet attain greatness by making millions in other forms of speculation. "If God helps, a half a year will go by, I'll once again stand on my feet and become my own person as earlier," he writes, seemingly forgetting that he had never before been independent, "because with us in Yehupets money plays the greatest role! The person alone is mud [i.e., worthless]. About pedigree no one here wants to know. You can be whoever you want to be and every imaginable evil—as long as you have money!" *(az got helft, es geyt-avek azoy eyn halb yor, shtel ikh mikh tsurik af di fis un ver der eygener vi friyer, vorem bay undz in yehupets shpilt dos gelt di greste role! der mentsh aleyn iz blote. yikhes vil men do nisht visn. megst zikh zayn ver du vilst un vos in der kort—abi gelt!)*[49] Thus while he recognizes the fragility and questionable morality of status that is coupled with wealth, he seems not to have qualms about discarding traditional Jewish life and values for a very precarious identity of prominence founded solely on the acquisition of money in risk-ridden marketplaces.

This new capitalist valuation of the human being is, as Menakhem-Mendl learns, tenuous indeed, allowing for upward mobility when capital is available and for readily dismantling status when the money is gone. Modern petit-bourgeois adventurism certainly offered ill-equipped impoverished shtetl Jews scant opportunities for success in the volatile expanding capitalist markets. There were, after all, no Brodskys in the shtetl, and few enough in the cities. As though to underscore the futility of his incompetent business activity and yet to relieve himself of blame, Menakhem-Mendl, feeling utterly dejected after one of his many crippling financial losses, complains bitterly about the abuse he now suffers from brokers who were formerly friends and only recently had called him "the Bleichröder of Kasrilevke" *(der kasrilevker Bleykhreder)*, referring to Baron Gerson von Bleichröder, the most influential Jewish Berlin banker during Bismarck's tenure. (Both English translations read "Rothschild" instead of Bleichröder, probably because of the familiarity of Rothschild's name in the English-speaking world.) But because Menakhem-Mendl has only an ability to talk and prevaricate, which he shares with the hundreds of other luftmentshn who had drifted out of the shtetlekh and were scurrying around city streets trying to make a ruble, his prospects for change and improvement are very bleak indeed.[50] Ironically, his anxiety about creating and maintaining an identity within the context of an inherently unstable capitalist system does not permit him to discontinue his speculative business endeavors, in large part because, within that system and its bourgeois ideology, amassing wealth is absolutely necessary for establishing identity. Just as the modern adventurer affirms his status as an autonomous and powerful individual through appropriation of women or wealth and through adventurism seemingly free of social obligation or restraint, Menakhem-Mendl as modern urbanized luftmentsh—despite failures or perhaps because of them—again and again attempts to forge an identity, feeble and precarious as it may be. Thus, this ephemeral protagonist attempts also to generate a sense of self by what he resists or negates, by what he does not do, by not returning to home and community. In fact, his lack of substance and integrity mirrors the immateriality of the speculative business practices in which he participates—whether "buying" houses without money, selling nonexistent forests and estates, speculating without capital, or transforming the city of London into a monetary cipher or financial abstraction with no tangible referent.

Because Menakhem-Mendl is intent on attaining status based only on the acquisition of money, he does not, indeed cannot, leave the arena of inept small-time wheeler-dealers in the urban centers until the end of the novel, when no more business activity is possible; and then he leaves with other luftmentshn for the grand new capitalist megalopolises of America. In times of activity and hope, however, he regarded himself happily as part of the crowd, in the midst of everything (*besoykhem,* the term he repeatedly uses, literally means "among them" or "in their midst"). But persistent failures continually undermine his confidence, so that whatever sense of self he can muster arises almost solely from renewed irrational fantasies of making millions, of becoming another Brodsky, and from an absurd illusion of his own autonomy and power. Yet again and again the fictions he pursues in vain leave him feeling increasingly morose, estranged, and very much alone. At one point after failing again to make the massive fortune he had anticipated, he writes Sheyne-Sheyndl:

If there is no luck, one should rather bury oneself alive! With whatever I get involved is at the start, it seems, all good and beautiful and fine, almost-almost I grab good fortune, almost-almost good fortune is in my pocket—in the end the wheel rolls over and everything turns into nothing! Apparently it wasn't meant to be that I should rise up on brokerage, grab a pile and escape! It isn't fated that Menakhem-Mendl should rise up, like other brokers in Yehupets! Everyone makes a racket, only I alone stand and watch how the world makes business and earns money, and I wander around like a stranger. I see before me millions and can't grab them. . . . I am always somehow as if outside. . . . Apparently, I haven't yet come upon the right way? No one knows where one's good fortune is. . . . One has to look for it for a long time, and if one looks, one will find it. . . . And since I am very depressed, I shall cut this [letter] short.

az s'iz nishto keyn mazl, zol men zikh beser bagrobn a lebediker! tsu vos ikh zol mikh nisht nemen, iz lekhatkhile, dakht zikh, altsding gut un sheyn un fayn, ot-ot khap ikh dos glik, ot-ot iz dos glik bay mir in keshene—tsum sof tut zikh dos redl a drey-iber un es lozt zikh oys a nekhtiker tog! nit bashert, a ponim, az ikh zol oyfkumen fun mekleray, khapn a grobs un antloyfn! nit bashert, az Menakhem-Mendl zol oyfkumen, vi andere meklers in Yehupets! ale trasken, nor ikh eyner shtey un kuk, vi di velt makht gesheftn un fardint gelt, un ikh drey mikh arum vi a fremder. ikh ze far zikh milyonen un kon zey nisht khapn. . . . ikh bin shtendik epes vi in droy-sen. . . . a ponim, ikh hob mikh nokh nit aroyfgeshlogn afn rikhtikn veg? keyn mentsh veys nit, vu zayn mazl gefint zikh. . . . me darf es lang zukhn, un az me zukht, gefint men. . . . un makhmes ikh bin zeyer dershlogn, makh ikh dos bekitser.[51]

In the preface, the fictional editor characterizes the business practices of Menakhem-Mendl as prototypical Jewish ones. "And just as Jewish businesses are, praise God, everywhere always the same—that is, as far as beginning is concerned—they begin, it seems, not so badly, with so much confidence and splendid hopes, and as for ending, they end mostly with bad-bad luck, as with my Menakhem-Mendl, therefore one doesn't have to labor long to compose a letter." *(un azoy vi yidishe gesheftn zaynen, borekh hashem, umetum alts eyns, dos heyst, hoybn hoybn zey zikh on, dakht zikh, gants nishtkoshedik, mit azoy fil bitokhn un glentsende hofnungen, un oyslozn lozn zey zikh oys, tsum maynsten, mit shlim-shlimazl vi bay mayn Menakhem-Mendlen, lokhn bedarf men lang nisht horeven baym tsenoyf-shteln a briv.)*[52] *(Shlim-shlimazl* ["Bad-Bad Luck"] is also the title of the final book of *Menakhem-Mendl.)*

Curiously, while failure precipitates in Menakhem-Mendl a morbid sense of alienation within the business arena, it provokes an inverse re-action in relation to his family: only in times of failure does he express homesickness and concern for the well-being of those he abandoned. Thus, he concludes the passage above with greetings to his in-laws and concern for wife and children, sentiments usually absent from his let-ters: "Regards to father-in-law and mother-in-law, and write me how your health is generally, and kiss the children, may they live and be healthy, and write me what's going on with you in Kasrilevke." *(loz grisn shver un shviger un shrayb mir, vos makhst du epes in gezunt, un kush di kinder, zoln lebn un gezunt zayn, un shrayb mir, vos hert zikh epes bay aykh in kasrilevke.)*[53] This sudden concern for family, however, is as short-lived as the interval between one adventure and the next. One may wonder why, with no intention to return to Kasrilevke, he does not divorce his wife, something Sheyne-Sheyndl mentions but never actu-ally requests. There may be a clue in his repeatedly expressed fear of be-ing alone, "outside," a "stranger," a fear not unlike Sheyne-Sheyndl's fear of becoming an *agune,* a kind of "other" within her community. A complete rupture from home and family, after all, might very well leave a person like Menakhem-Mendl, whose sense of self depends, in part, on freedom from all communal obligations, with the possibility of no identity at all when the next catastrophe strikes. Such an apprehension, though unspoken, seems also to haunt Solomon Maimon's *Autobiog-raphy*—better a negative identity, one based on resisting or continually excluding social and personal commitment, than the void.

Menakhem-Mendl has adapted the attributes of immateriality associ-ated with the luftmentsh to the constantly circulating speculative busi-ness ventures of capitalism and created a life as modern economic adven-turer that is, in essence, as quintessentially Jewish as it is completely petit bourgeois. Whereas he is always on the move seeking business prospects, his concern with material existence is, as his wife reminds him, grounded in immaterial airy fictions and fantasies; Sheyne-Sheyndl remains rooted in her shtetl community. Partly because she is a woman within a male-dominated traditional culture, partly because she is so attached to the world of her mother, whose sayings are always on the tip of her tongue and pen, partly because she is burdened with responsibility for the material well-being of her family, Sheyne-Sheyndl will not, perhaps cannot, leave her home no matter how great the privation there. The disparity between Sheyne-Sheyndl and Menakhem-Mendl in this text suggests types within both traditional Jewish culture and Western European society. On the one hand, they are like many nineteenth- and early-twentieth-century Eastern European Jews who were confined to the Pale of Settlement by imperial decrees and poverty. These Jews did move around somewhat, either because they were frequently driven from their homes and towns in antisemitic riots or because peddling, one of the few trades allowed them, required that they travel from town to town, sometimes from one country to another. On the other hand, this Jewish couple also bears a remarkable resemblance to types that developed generally within Western culture during the growth of capitalist economies, when there was a significant migration from the feudal countryside and towns to evolving financial and industrial metropolitan centers.

Although Sheyne-Sheyndl is deeply dissatisfied with her life, the only change she seems to desire is the return of her husband and the reconstitution of her family. She may not be cognizant of all the ramifications of the unequal gender practices and expectations within Jewish tradition, but she does indeed recognize how differently they determine the lives of men and of women: when a man becomes a widower, she writes, "he would surely not have spilled so many tears and would perhaps right after the thirty days of mourning have brought from Berdichev a stepmother for his children. I say this really about all men, may all of you be the scapegoat for [the sins of] your wives" *(volt er gevis azoy fil trern nisht fargosn un volt mestame bald nokh shloshim gebrakht tsu firn fun barditshev a stifmame far zayne kinder. Ikh zog dos take akegn ale mansbiln, di kapore megt ir zayn far ayere vayber)*.[54] A widow with children, however, can rarely find a mate and must raise her children herself. Sheyne-Sheyndl recognizes the dangers of the outside world inscribed in her husband's letters and assesses all his efforts as "airy occupations," "airy little birds" *(luftike parnoses, luftike feygelekh)*[55] that can only bring her and her family extreme hardship.

The irreconcilability of overlapping divergent orientations that are spousal, economic, geographic, and cultural is made sufficiently clear in an exchange between husband and wife about the availability of sugar and its price. Menakhem-Mendl, speculating in the commodity market on the rising price of sugar, hopes for a sugar-beet crop failure that would send the price soaring, "because as soon as there will be no beets," he writes his wife, "there will of course be no sugar, and if there will be no sugar, sugar will be the equal of gold, the speculators will make business, the brokers will earn money, and me also included [among them]" *(vorem vi bald az es vet nit zayn keyn burikes, vet dokh nit zayn keyn tsuker, un az es vet nit zayn keyn tsuker, vet tsuker zayn mit gold glaykh, veln di "shpekulantn" makhn gesheftn, di meklers veln fardinen gelt un ikh oykh besoykhem).*[56] Sheyne-Sheyndl, however, merely mocks her husband's business acumen and all his expectations. She of course wants a bumper crop of beets because her family would suffer privation were sugar both scarce and expensive. Thus, for him, mired as he is in capitalist market practices, beets and sugar are mere quantitative abstractions, "futures" or exchange values—that is, commodities whose value consists not in their substance and utility but in their exchangeability for money or gold ("sugar will be the equal of gold"). For Sheyne-Sheyndl, sugar has a concrete qualitative value (use value) as a substance necessary for the well-being of her family and community. The discrepancy between the interests of the economic adventurer, or luftmentsh, and those of family life is manifest, as is the incompatibility of capitalist adventurism and communal solidarity.

It becomes clear from epistolary interactions such as this that Menakhem-Mendl conceives of his life activity and identity in ways that are fundamentally unrealistic or impracticable. Even though Sheyne-Sheyndl witnesses her husband's many ruinous failures and, using her "shtetl acumen," warns him of impending disasters, he apparently sees no reason to change his conduct or practices. Consider the two autobiographical sketches he composes during the course of the novel, each part of a job application: the first a written text submitted for a journalistic position;[57] and the second delivered orally for a job as an insurance broker,[58] a sketch in which he brags about the celebrity he has attained in the course of his many endeavors and failures to make millions. Curiously, he does not mention his wife and children, those backwoods family members whose presence might unsettle the text of his exciting urban life. The vitae come into play following business fiascos when, without money or future prospects, he is dejected and looking for yet another promising project. These autobiographical efforts seem in large part to be directed at substantiating an identity that may have vanished in the midst of his illusory yet, to him, momentous misfortunes. Although his overt intention is to impress future employers with his great worldliness, importance, and qualifications for the position, the vitae also function—and this may even be their primary raison d'être—to establish and confirm, through narratives of his life, his existence as an illustrious and vital, albeit unsuccessful, economic adventurer.

If the vitae actually had an underlying objective to engender for himself, in writing and in speech, an identity whose importance could be verified or affirmed by others, then Menakhem-Mendl's biographical efforts (his two vitae and a biographical profile of one of the boarders in his rooming house whose life approximates his own to an astounding degree) may have accomplished that, but perhaps not in the way he anticipated. Ultimately it is not as a Rothschild or Brodsky that he inscribes himself in this text but as the prototype of a luftmentsh, a "Menakhem-Mendl," a name that in the twentieth century became a commonplace alternate appellation for a luftmentsh. Because the persona that Menakhem-Mendl constructs in writing is both portrayed and thematized within the novel, and because the circumstances of its creation illuminate the intricate socioeconomic and gender relations that characterize the luftmentsh as deserter and the shtetl wife as *agune,* it would be valuable to traverse briefly the territory of his biographical writings to his final letter. In it, the concept of the luftmentsh—the "Menakhem-Mendl"—is identified, and the protagonist announces his departure for America.

Menakhem-Mendl's first vita, sent to the *Gazette* newspaper in pursuit of a position as journalist, is designed to impress the editor first with his ability to write and then with his capacity to write voluminously: "It is already the third day that I am writing and writing, and the writing doesn't even stop at all!" *(shoyn der driter tog, az ikh shrayb un shrayb, un se hert zikh gor nit oyf tsu shraybn!)*[59] Of course, having been apprised of the fact that the *Gazette* pays a kopeck a line, and having already calculated the large sum he will receive for lengthy essays, he now regards himself as a serious participant in a lucrative "respectable occupation like writing" (*bekovede parnose vi dos shrayberay* [*shrayberay* translates roughly as "any or all kinds of writing," not necessarily a literary or professional endeavor that requires talent and skill]).[60] Clearly, Menakhem-Mendl understands his new "respectable occupation" as yet another business enterprise whose ample monetary reward will bring the recognition he needs or desires. Thus, although he gives Sheyne-Sheyndl only a very brief outline of this first vita, he notes that the actual text covered reams of paper, the sheer quantity of text apparently designed to make evident his qualifications as writer. Not unlike his transformation of the substance and use value of beets into abstract exchangeability or exchange value, Menakhem-Mendl here transforms the qualitative and useful character of writing into a form measured in quantity and understood as exchange value:

I tell them my entire bigraphy *[sic]*. How I once was a big shot at the stock exchange in Odessa and Yehupets, how I devoted myself to all kinds of idol worship, dealt and brokered with *London* and with *stocks* [*papirlekh*, literally "scraps of paper"] and with *all sorts of stuff* into the millions, was seventy-seven times almost a rich man and almost a poor man, almost a millionaire and almost a pauper. In short, I didn't spare any effort and wrote out everything extensively, perhaps on ten little pages, and I asked them to answer me, if they liked my scribbling *[shraybekhts]*, then I'll write and write for them. . . . And if my describings are well described, they will with pleasure print my describings in their paper and will pay me by the line, a kopek a line. For this many lines, this many kopeks. Immediately I grabbed a pen, how many, for example, can I write? At the least I figure that I can write on a long summer's day a good thousand lines. Doesn't that come to a tenner [or ten rubles] a day? Then we would have no less than, that is, almost three hundred rubles a month. Not bad for a salary, what do you think?

ikh dertseyl zey oys mayn gantse begrafia [*sic*]. *vi azoy ikh hob amol geknakt af der berze, in ades un in yehupets, ibergedint kol haavoyde-zore, gehandlt un gemeklert mit* london *un mit* papirlekh *un mit* yakhnehoz *in di milyonen arayn, geven zibn un zibetsik mol ot a noged un ot a kabtsn, ot a gvir un ot an evyen. hakitser, ikh hob nisht gezhalevet mayn tirkhe un hob zey aroysgeshribn altsding barikhes, efsher af tsen zaytlekh, un gebetn hob ikh zey, zey zoln mir entfern, oyb es gefelt zey mayn shraybekhts, vel ikh zey shraybn un shraybn . . . un oyb mayne bashraybekhtsen veln zayn gut bashribn, veln zey mayne bashraybekhtsen mit fargenign opdrukn afn blat un veln mir batsoln far der shure, a kopeke a shure. vifil shures, azoy fil kopekes. hob ikh bald gegebn a khap oyf der pen, vifil, lemoshl, kon ikh opshraybn? tsum alem mindstn rekhn ikh, az ikh kon in a langn zumerdikn tog onshraybn gute toyznt shures. makht dos nit a tsenerl a tog? Hobn mir a kaymelon, heyst dos, fun kimat dray hundert rubl a khoydesh. nishkoshe fun a zhalavanye, vi meynst du?*[61]

Whereas this first vita indicates that writing is the attribute essential for the position of journalist, the second one, in support of his application for a position as an insurance agent, which required dexterity in speaking, is delivered orally. After all, Menakhem-Mendl notes, "the most important thing is—language. An agent must know language.

That is, he has to be able to talk, talk others into, talk them out of, talk over them and talk circles around them, talk so long, that the other person would already have to get himself insured against death—and that's all you need." *(der iker iz—shprakh. an agent muz konen shprach. dos heyst, er darf konen redn, tsuredn, aynredn, iberredn un farredn, azoy lang redn, biz yener zol zikh shoyn muzn shtrafirn funem toyt—un mer darf men nit.)*[62] When Menakhem-Mendl concludes the rather lengthy description of his life with a judgment that "the end was . . . not good—bad-bad luck" *(der sof iz geven . . . nisht gut—shlim-shlimazl* [*shlim-shlimazl* may refer to either his life or his person]),[63] the insurance manager replies, "You know what I'll say to you, Mr. Menakhem-Mendl? I like you. A name you have a beautiful one, and talk—praise God—you can. I prophesize that in time you will be a big agent, actually a really big one!" *(veyst ir, vos ikh vel aykh zogn, gospodin menakhem-mendl? ir gefelt mir. a nomen hot ir a sheynem, un reydn, borekh hashem, kont ir. ikh zog aykh nevies, az mit der tsayt vet ir zayn a groyser agent, take gor a groyser!)*[64] It seems relatively clear from this narrative that the applicant Menakhem-Mendl is a luftmentsh who wants desperately to be a big shot, a real "Menakhem-Mendl," which accounts for the interviewer's reference to the latter's beautiful name. This allusion to his "beautiful name" also highlights the rather pitiful, yet extremely humorous, incident described in his previous letter, in which, as matchmakers, Menakhem-Mendl and a partner inadvertently conclude a marriage contract between two women. When they realize their drastic error, the recriminations between the partners begin:

"Do you know what I'll tell you, Menakhem-Mendl? You are as much a matchmaker as I am a rabbi!" . . . I say: "And you are as much a matchmaker as I am a rabbi's wife!" . . . One word follows another—he to me: "schoolteacher [*melamed* also signifies colloquially 'an impractical dreamer']!," I to him: "liar!"; he to me: "*shlimazl!*" [here virtually synonymous with "luftmentsh"], I to him: "drunken glutton!"; he to me: "Menakhem-Mendl!," I to him: "drunkard!"

"*veyst ir, vos ikh vel aykh zogn, menakhem-mendl? ir zayt azoy a shadkhen vi ikh bin a rov!*" . . . *zog ikh:* "*un ir zayt aza shadkhen vi ikh bin a rebetsin!*" . . . *a vort far a vort—er mir:* "*melamed!*", *ikh im:* "*shakren!*"; *er mir:* "*shlimazl!*", *ikh im:* "*zoylel-vesoyvenik!*"; *er mir:* "*Menakhem-mendl!*", *ikh im:* "*shikernik!*"[65]

The identification of impractical dreamer or inept person *(shlimazl)* with the moniker *Menakhem-Mendl* is manifest: the protagonist's name is transformed into a generic appellation, a prototype, a luftmentsh, which, as the insurance manager immediately recognizes, is a person full of hot air, lots of words, nothing but talk talk talk. Menakhem-Mendl's written and oral autobiographical narratives—composed as they are after business failures, periods of unemployment, and depression—fabricate verbally an identity and life story for the narrator and may even impress someone in need of a crafty wordsmith who admits that he can "shoot off one lie after another to him and without even wincing" *(hak ikh im eyn lign nokhn andern un farkrim mikh afile nisht).*[66] In addition, the reiteration and inscription of those biographical narratives once again in his letters may seem to confirm their validity, but not only that. The narratives of the vitae plus the epistolary references to them also call attention to ways in which both oral and written language can generate a convincing social identity that may yet have scant basis in reality. Ironically, there is no evidence in the text that Sheyne-Sheyndl received or read the letters about his marriage brokering and insurance business activity.

As though both to underline and undermine Menakhem-Mendl's effort to establish the integrity of his writings in general and his life story in particular, the *Gazette* published a response, he says, and suggested that "I not invent stories out of my head" *(ikh zol ir nit oystrakhtn mayses funem kop).* He also notes, however, that the newspaper "liked my way of description, but it is a little too long" (*mayn bashreybekhts iz ir gefeln, nor es iz a bisl tsu lang* [*bashreybekhts,* a rather deprecating term, suggests something like "descriptive stuff"]).[67] "It [referring to the newspaper] wants nothing more," he explains, "but for me to *portray* (that's exactly their language) life in the city of Yehupets with all its *types.* This probably because it wants to know what is going on with us in Yehupets; otherwise why would it be literally *types?*" (*zi vil nisht mer bilti ikh zol ir* shildern *[azoy take, mit dem loshn] dos lebn fun shtot Yehupets mit ale ire* tipen. *di mashmoes, az zi vil visn, vos bay undz in yehupets tut zikh, vorem vos den iz der pshat* tipen? [emphases in the text]).[68] With this request in hand, Menakhem-Mendl undertakes a narrative about a man nicknamed Lucky *(der mutslekh,* literally "the successful or lucky person"), an important "type," a luftmentsh who is, as Menakhem-Mendl indicates, the "biggest *shlimazl*" in their rooming house, which is filled with *shlimazls.* Curiously, apart from some inconsequential biographical differences—a different shtetl abandoned, two marriages, diverse and not entirely dissimilar business ventures, plans to emigrate to America (which Menakhem-Mendl had at the time still ruled out)—the pattern of Lucky's life bears such a remarkable resemblance to Menakhem-Mendl's that the biographical profile might be viewed as a fictionalized account of the latter's own liberally invented life. The similarities notwithstanding, Menakhem-Mendl would, in some significant ways, surpass Lucky as yet a bigger *shlimazl*. With marvelous irony and humor, Menakhem-Mendl verifies this when he concludes his second vita with an open admission about his character and fate as a *shlim-shlimazl*, one step worse than a *shlimazl*. *Shlim-shlimazl* is, significantly, also the title of the concluding book of the novel, suggesting perhaps that the *shlimazl*-luftmentsh persona and its construction in the novel have finally been completed. (Sheyne-Sheyndl had earlier told her husband that "you have been a *shlimazl* and will remain a *shlimazl*" [*du bist geven a shlimazl un vest blaybn a shlimazl*].)[69]

Whereas Menakhem-Mendl's family is absent from his autobiographies, Lucky's marital status (though not his wives) finds a small, albeit rather dismissive, place in this biography ("Earlier he was a son-in-law in Ladizhin and after that in Soroki" [*an eydem iz er geven friyer a ladizhiner un nokhdem a soroker*]).[70] In addition, while Lucky suffers financial losses, they seem not to be imaginary ones; and though he makes terrible business decisions, his transactions involve actual goods and properties, such as cracked eggs, a cigarette-paper factory, a pharmacy, all of which he appears to have purchased at one time or another. If indeed Menakhem-Mendl fulfilled the editor's suggestion to "portray *types*," then his "adventure" stories about both the *shlimazl* Lucky and his own life, which was created through letters and vitae, are narrative types as well as typical narratives. Through the written word these narratives, which inscribe fanciful, even invented, lives as biography ("so much paper and ink used up, so many beautiful things invented" [*azoy fil papir un tint oysgenutst, azoy fil sheyne zakhn oysgetrakht*],[71] he confesses), generate and structure an identity of and for the writer. Furthermore, profiles or portraits that are similar, and which recur in a text, tend to attest to the actuality of such ephemeral or textualized identities. Menakhem-Mendl's exaggerated narratives of capitalist adventurism construct, perhaps unwittingly, a portrait of him as both a *shlimazl* and a writer who is, in fact, the creator of that persona. Moreover, when none of his writings are printed, he appears as either the writer as *shlimazl* or the *shlimazl* as writer, or perhaps both. Alternatively, when the writing and the written self he constructs evaporate, he emerges as an empty husk, a nullity: "I am simply in no condition," he writes his wife when there is no response from the *Gazette*, "to communicate the heartache and the depression which one feels in oneself. I cannot even get my pen to write any longer." (*ikh bin gor nit in stand dir ibergebn*

*dos agmes-nefesh, mit dem aropfaln, vos me iz bay zikh; es leygt zikh gor
nit di pen oyf tsu shraybn mer.)*[72]

By writing himself into existence in his epistolary exchange with his
wife, Menakhem-Mendl appears as a textual creation of his own making
within the fictionality of the novel. In addition, the events of his adventurous life that he relates in his letters encompass activities in a financial
marketplace that partake in neither the production nor the distribution
of goods and services, but instead wallow in abstract speculation and
exchange values that have no tangible referent. Moreover, they include
a vastly exaggerated and largely imagined participation in that capitalist
enterprise. Thus, through his epistolary discourse Menakhem-Mendl
comes into being as a character created in and for a text, and as one who
seeks an identity and status through the acquisition of great wealth.
Throughout the novel, however, he is also constantly threatened with
the erasure of identity that accompanies his business failures, which
exist principally in an imagination stimulated by desire and unrealizable dreams of glory. But to the end, even when his writings and the
writing self are virtually expunged, the desire and fantasies that fuel the
adventurer in the quest for identity remain unabated. Then once again
Menakhem-Mendl is on his way to make a grand fortune, this time to
America. His parting words to his wife at the end of the sixth book appear as an afterthought in the postscript of his final letter:

I have completely forgotten to write you where I am going. My dearest wife,
I am going to America. Not alone—a whole group is going along. That is to
say, going meaning we are actually going to Hamburg, and from there then
to America. But why to America? Because in America, they say, Jews become
happy. Gold, they say, is rolling in the streets there. Money there is reckoned in
dollars and people there are held in great esteem—a gold coin a human being!
Not to mention Jews—they are even the cream of the crop! Everyone assures
me that in America I shall, God willing, make good, really make good. The
whole world is now going to America, because here there is nothing to do.
Absolutely nothing. All businesses are finished. Today, since the world is going,
why shouldn't I also go? What have I got to lose?

*ikh hob dir gor fargesn shraybn, vuhin ikh for. zugosi hayekora, ikh for keyn
amerike. nisht aleyn—a gantse kompanye forn mir. dos heyst, forn forn mir, eygntlikh, keyn hamburg, un fun dortn shoyn keyn amerike. vos epes keyn amerike? vayl
in amerike, zogt men, vern yidn gliklekh. gold, zogt men, valgert zikh dort in di
gasn. gelt rekhnt zikh dortn af tolers un mentshn zaynen dortn bikhshives godl—a
rendl a mentsh! un ver shmuest yidn—di zaynen gor dos eybershte fun khreyn! ale
zaynen mir maftiekh, az in amerike vel ikh, im yirtse hashem, makhn gut, take vos
gut heyst. di gantse velt fort yetst keyn amerike, makhmes do iz nishto vos tsu ton.*

lakhlutn nisht. se hobn zikh oysgelozt ale gesheftn. haynt, vi bald az di velt fort, far
vos zol ikh oykh nisht forn? vos hob ikh ayntsushteln?[73]

With nothing to lose but wife, children, and other family members, none of whom apparently matter enough to him, Menakhem-Mendl prepares to set sail on a great sea adventure to that marvelous fantasyland of capitalist wealth and fulfillment, leaving Sheyne-Sheyndl like the grieving *agune* in the Talmudic midrash. In this text, however, the wailing of the woman is not even heard.

In the parting words of the final letter to her spouse at the conclusion of the fourth book, Sheyne-Sheyndl informs him that she has nothing more to write him and, once again, sends him money—this time her mother's money, she says—so that he can return home. He takes the money, of course, but not her advice and continues his business misadventures, which he details in the two ensuing letters. It may be that, because his final letters were written while traveling, no answer from his wife could reach him. Whatever the situation, Sheyne-Sheyndl's writing disappears from the text, leaving Menakhem-Mendl to pen long narcissistic letters to her; but without her response, neither he nor the reader can verify that she has read his words, that his voice is heard. What throughout the novel has been his practice of writing almost exclusively about himself to his wife evolves into writing about himself only to himself. He is finally detached, alone, having attained perhaps the only kind of autonomy (the autonomy of powerlessness) and freedom (freedom in a vacuum) that modernity and capitalism can furnish him. Sheyne-Sheyndl's complete absence from the last two books resonates on two levels: her voice, which had continuously cried out to her self-absorbed husband in his urban wilderness with barely a direct response to her words and warnings, is completely erased from the world in which writing and capital circulate; and finally, as an *agune,* she loses what little legitimacy women—as wives—might have within the shtetl community.

THE RELUCTANT WRITER SHEYNE-SHEYNDL

The primary victim of Menakhem-Mendl's adventurism is surely the wife he leaves behind, the deserted woman who must rear their children alone, who will suffer shame and degradation within the community, and who, as an *agune,* is divested of choice and chained to an irrevocable disgraced status. Unlike in the case of Benjamin the Third's wife, Zelda, who is virtually mute in the text and absent from its pages, Sheyne-Sheyndl's voice, her writing, and finally also her silence reverberate throughout this novel. Even her neglect or abuse by critics and the sly irony of the fictional editor's preface, in which her presence is barely acknowledged, cannot, however, erase the existence of her letters. Indeed, the absence of her letters from the final two books may actually alert the reader to the significance of her writing. After all, in the exchanges between husband and wife, it is more often she who listens, responds to his words, and questions his stories. Her complaints and advice, curses and adages, attempt, albeit often fretfully, to salvage an ever receding marriage to a spouse whose increasing impracticality and lack of substance result in unremitting hardship and grief for her and the family. An early sign of Sheyne-Sheyndl's dismay that her husband will not return home occurs in her first letter, where she notes her husband's estrangement. There she exhorts him to

write like a human being! What kind of goods is it that you are dealing with? How expensive is a yard of it? Or maybe it is sold by weight? I don't have the slightest idea what it is and with what one eats it! . . . And why don't you write about where you live and what you eat? Somehow like I was a stranger to you, not a wife—may it be for a hundred and twenty years—only something like a mistress, not to be said in the same breath . . . How does mama say it, may she live long? "When a cow goes off with the herd, it forgets to say good-bye."

shrayb zhe vi a mentsh! vos iz dos far a min skhoyre ot dos, vos du handlst mit dem? vi tayer leyzt men dos an arshin? tsi efsher farkoyft zikh dos af der vog? freg mir bekheyrem vos dos iz un mit vos me est dos! . . . un farvos shraybst du nit, vu du shteyst ayn un vos est du? epes glaykh vi ikh volt dir zayn a fremde, nit keyn vayb biz hundert tsvantsig yor, nor epes a polyuboavnitsa lehavdl. vi zogt di mame, zol lebn? "az a ku geyt avek in tsherede, fargest zi dem zay gezunt."[74]

Despite the many changes that Menakhem-Mendl reports—movement from city to city, on streets and boulevards, in and out of cafes, and through an exasperating series of undertakings—the changes do not seem substantial but merely constantly repeated variations of the same mistakes. This notwithstanding, throughout his letters noteworthy alterations in his character and life are articulated that reveal an intensified involvement in the petit-bourgeois business culture of the metropolis, along with an escalating detachment from family and traditional Jewish life. Indeed, it is in the context of his persistent adventurism in the capitalist marketplace that his changes of attitude—waning concern for his family, diminishing connection with religious and traditional life, and metamorphosis of pride in his honesty into overt acknowledgement of a grand ability to prevaricate—become radical; and when the values associated with his former life in the shtetl fade from his map of the contemporary scene, his wife's words disappear from the pages of this text. In other texts the prospective *agune*'s complaint, however weak, may still be heard in spite of her loss of status and social acceptability. But in this work the voices of women of the shtetl, where *mame-loshn* ("the language of the mother," that is, Yiddish) is spoken, do not merely grow silent but are covered over in the two concluding books by a barrage of Menakhem-Mendl's reports about his fantasized adventures and mishaps. Here women's voices are replaced by a male-dominated world constructed with ink on paper by illusory master hands.

Sheyne-Sheyndl's very brief final letter to her spouse concludes by cursing Yehupets and all that it signifies: "I pray to God that I shall no longer receive from you any of your little letters [*brivlekh:* a diminutive form that suggests a deprecatory view of his writing and business projects]. And as soon as you leave Yehupets, may the earth open and that city be swallowed up in the ground, just like Sodom, with all its golden businesses, good fortunes, brokers, matchmakers, rooming houses, landladies, editors, which is the wish that you may have much health and always good fortune today and forever from your truly devoted wife Sheyne-Sheyndl." *(ikh bet got, az mer zol ikh fun dir shoyn keyn brivlekh nit hobn. un vi nor du vest aroysforn fun yehupets, azoy zol zikh efenen di erd un ayngezunken zol vern di dozike shtot, azoy vi sdom, mit ale ire goldene gesheftn, glikn, meklers, shadkonim, akhsanyes, balebostes, redaktsies, vi es vinsht dir fil gezunt un imer glik haynt un ale mol. dayn baemes getraye froy Sheyne-Sheyndl.)*[75] With these words she bids farewell to Menakhem-Mendl's business ventures and disappears from the pages of a text that, however, continues with two extensive letters from him detailing at length his mishaps as matchmaker (book 5) and insurance agent (book 6). Although his wife's writing is absent from these final books, the silence is itself of great importance, for the presence of both her voice's absence and his profuse writing do in fact call attention to the effects on women of patriarchal values that inform both bourgeois society and Jewish tradition. These values permit, even facilitate, a husband's desertion of his spouse while maintaining his legal possession of her. Thus, the writings of the reluctant writer Sheyne-Sheyndl, as well as their ultimate absence, are important for an understanding of the social function and significance of the correspondence in *Menakhem-Mendl*.

What seems, in the first four books of this novel, to be an equal exchange of letters between husband and wife that suggests equality of the spouses, of the male and female correspondents, may actually conceal the marked differences in their status within the social and political system. The efficacy of the epistolary discourse in which the participants express themselves very much depends on acknowledging the distribution of social power within their particular society and body politic. Although within the polity of Eastern European society the vast majority of Jewish men were powerless, within the Jewish community they held the reins of authority and power, despite their unproductive and impecunious situation. In fact, disparities in the correspondence between Menakhem-Mendl and Sheyne-Sheyndl indicate that their status in the community is determined significantly by gender. This is especially evident in the disabilities women suffer in a patriarchal culture, where they are socially and politically powerless and, as wives, the legal possession of their husbands.

When Sheyne-Sheyndl responds to her husband's letters, she too writes herself into existence in their ensuing epistolary exchange and, like him, is adamantly concerned with identity. But while he is seeking to engender a new autonomous identity, she is desperately trying to maintain the principal one for a woman in her world, that of wife. Furthermore, because his identity is integrally connected with writing—in the autobiography that he creates through letter-writing and his journalistic pretensions—and hers is primarily dependent on his return home and the cessation of writing, each spouse's motivation for writing differs considerably, shedding light on the teachings and practices of Jewish life. Indeed, Menakhem-Mendl's conception of autonomy, one traditionally reserved for men, creates the occasion for writing letters to a wife left behind. Not unlike traditional Jewish scholars, Menakhem-Mendl, who is in fact no scholar, is nonetheless free to travel and explore the "public" sphere without the burden of family responsibilities. Tied to the domestic "private" sphere, encumbered by having to care for three small children and her parents, and hardly free to roam at will, Sheyne-Sheyndl is compelled to write not by any action or desire of her own, but by her husband's departure and her attempt to avoid the devastating eventuality of becoming an *agune*.

Beginning with the earliest letters to her husband in Odessa, two major issues inform Sheyne-Sheyndl's writing: her husband's merciless, or merely indifferent, estrangement that leaves her feeling demeaned in her own eyes and, according to her, in those of the community; and

an overriding fear that her husband will not return and she will be condemned to suffer an *agune*'s shame and social ostracism. As mentioned
earlier, in her initial letter, for example, she writes of the alienation she
senses on the part of her husband, and then quotes one of her mother's
sayings: "When a cow goes off with the herd, it forgets to say good-
bye." *(az a ku geyt avek in tsherede, fargest zi dem zay gezunt.)*[76] But
while her mother's proverb seems to refer only to Menakhem-Mendl's
herdlike thoughtlessness, Sheyne-Sheyndl, even at this early date, clearly
identifies her husband's departure as the source of her apprehension
about losing both stature in her husband's eyes and her legitimate status
as wife. In fact, in her next letter she unwittingly reveals the conditions
and characteristics of their spousal relationship that make it unlikely that
her husband will ever return home: she recognizes the questionable
nature of Menakhem-Mendl's fanciful business ventures—"airy occupations" *(luftike parnoses)*, she calls them—but because she seems not
to understand the importance of his grandiose illusions for his sense of
self-importance, her attempts to entice him to return home may actually function to keep him away. Thus, while he envisions himself as a
freewheeling big shot strolling, cane in hand, along metropolitan boulevards, she advises him to rent a small store in Kasrilevke, where her
parents will provide them with living space, and he can support their
children, who need him, all of which only emphasizes his ineptitude,
penury, and dependence on others. From her place in the shtetl, she
does not, perhaps cannot, see how fully his identity is invested in his
"airy" visions of the wealth and prominence that his business deals will
bring him. What she does recognize is what she most fears, the omi-
nous reality awaiting her: abandonment with its inevitable shame and
social stigma. "Why do I have to be on other people's tongues," she
complains, "and enemies should mutter that you have taken yourself to
Odessa and have discarded me, may you not live to see that! . . . But a
lot you care about what happens with us at home. You don't even ask
about your children, how they are. You've already forgotten that you
are a father with three small children, may they be well." *(tsu vos badarf
ikh lign bay yenem in moyl un sonim zoln murmeln, az du host zikh avekgelozt keyn ades un mikh host du avekgevorfn, nit derlebn zolst du dos! . . .
nor es geyt dir shtark on, vos bay undz in der heym tut zikh. du fregst afile
nit af di kinder, vos zey makhn. Host shoyn fargesn, az du bist a tate fun
dray kinderlekh, zoln gezunt zayn.)*[77]

It is clear from the letters of both Sheyne-Sheyndl and Menakhem-
Mendl that, in the Jewish community, deserting one's wife reflects not

so much on the husband's character as on that of his spouse, as though
she were actually to blame for his irresponsible and callous actions.
Thus, not only will she alone have to support and care for the family,
but she will also suffer the disdain and scorn of others in the community who hold her responsible for his departure. Nowhere in this text is
there an indication that men regard the conduct of a deserting husband
as inhumane, immoral, or even scandalous. Instead they see it merely
as not particularly surprising behavior. Sheyne-Sheyndl notes about one
Moyshe-Dovid that he "already long ago took a dislike to his little wife,
wanted to get rid of her, didn't know how; so off he went to America"
(*hot er zikh meyashev geven un hot shoyn lang gevorfn an umkheyn af
zayn vaybl, gevolt poter vern fun ir, nit gevust vi azoy; nemt er un fort
avek keyn amerike*).[78] There are also women who apparently do not
regard the absconding husband as immoral or callous. A sampling of
the numerous sayings of Sheyne-Sheyndl's mother suggests that, more
often than not, Menakhem-Mendl is perceived not as dastardly but
merely as foolish or oblivious ("The worm lies in the radish and thinks
there is nothing sweeter" [*der vorem ligt in khreyn un meynt, az s'iz gor
keyn ziseres nishto*]);[79] bungling and unrepentant ("When the girl [here
referring to Menakhem-Mendl] can't dance, she says—the musicians
can't play" [*az di meydl kon nit tantsen, zogt zi—di klezmer konen nit
shpiln*]);[80] shortsighted and narcissistic ("Play a bridegroom something
sad, he still only thinks about himself" [*shpilt dem khosn veynendiks, er
hot zikh zayns in zinen*]);[81] self-centered ("When a cow goes off with
the herd, it forgets to say good-bye" [*az a ku geyt avek in tsherede, fargest zi dem zay gezunt*]);[82] and certainly not mad ("A madman breaks the
windows of strangers, not his own" [*a meshugener shlogt fremde fentster,
nisht keyn eygene*]).[83] In short, he is behaving like a luftmentsh.[84] But
Sheyne-Sheyndl, whose husband has left but not yet actually deserted,
is not treated so sympathetically, not by herself, whom she blames for
not being as aggressive and demanding as other women in the shtetl,
nor by her mother, who implies that the fault lies with her daughter,
who did not keep him in tow, was too ill to pursue him, and did not
allow her mother to do so.[85]

Not only does becoming the object of gossip and mockery haunt
Sheyne-Sheyndl's life and letters, but also the dread that merely voic-
ing her true feelings could actually result in being abandoned impedes
any candid communication with others, especially her spouse. Two of
many instances in the text illustrate the magnitude of the anguish and
helplessness that result from this debilitating fear and from the power

that even a pathetic, impecunious, and inept husband wields over her life. The first instance is her reaction to Menakhem-Mendl's report that he has embarked on a new business using the money she sent for his return home. "Either one or the other," she writes him: "if you don't want me, come home and divorce me; if not, then go with all ill winds to America, like Leib-Aaron's Yossl, and at least let me not know where your bones are, if it is already fated that I remain an eternal *agune* with fresh little children! But my enemies won't live that long! It's your good luck that I can't come after you right now; I am alas punished so badly that I even have to lie in bed." *(moneshekh, vilst mikh nit, kum tsu forn un get mikh op; ele nit, for shoyn beser avek tsu aldi shvartse yor keyn amerike, vi yosl leyb-arns, un loz ikh khotsh nit visn vu dayn gebeyn iz ahingekumen, oyb s'iz mir shoyn yo bashert tsu blaybn an eybike agune mit kleyne kinder piskliates! nor azoy lang krenkn mayne sonim! dayn treyfene hatslokhe, vos ikh kon atsind tsu dir nisht forn; ikh bin, mishteyns gezogt, azoy geshtroft, az ikh muz gor lign in bet.)* Were she not ailing, she says, she would have brought him back and shown him "that a wife is a wife!" *(az a vayb iz a vayb!)* But, as though fearing the consequences of her own candor, she quickly adds, "So what if sometimes a harsh word escapes me? That is only because of vexation and doesn't last long. How does mama say it? 'A match ignites quickly and is soon extinguished.'" *(ay, vos, ikh khap zikh aroys a mol mit a harb vort? iz dos nor makhmes grizote un nit af lang. vi zogt di mame? "a shvebele tsint zikh gikh on un vert bald farloshn.")*[86] The rhetoric of this segment reveals how Sheyne-Sheyndl, facing potential abandonment, uses language both to say what she wants or needs and to rescind her words. There are the swift alternations: an ultimatum that is not really one (divorce me or go to America); wanting him out of sight while reminding him of his children; anger and aggression while seeking sympathy for her ill health; and finally, a recognition of her forthrightness and the assurance that her acrimony is harmless because it is so short-lived. This juxtaposition of candid statement and retreat may be less a display of ambivalence than the response of a powerless person confronted with someone who controls her fate—anger, resentment, and fear tempered by mollification and acquiescence.

The second instance concerns Sheyne-Sheyndl's awareness of her deteriorating image of herself in the community and of the obstacles that prevent her from conveying her rage and humiliation to her husband or, for that matter, to anyone else. Her remarks appear in a letter in which two experiences are juxtaposed: she describes her fright when she thinks her young son's life has been endangered because he swallowed (or she thought he had) a coin; and she responds to her husband's continued obsessive dealings in the stock market, with "scraps of paper" not with actual currency.[87] Here, rather than oscillating between expressing her wrath and attenuating it, she describes the intensity of her rage and her frustration at her inability, because of her husband's absence, to be candid while everyone else seems to enjoy that privilege. Not only does her husband's behavior prevent her from saying what she feels, but it also dictates, at least in her perception, the demeanor she must adopt in society, namely, a cheerful face:

If a dog were to eat my heart, it would go mad. When I look at other people and see that women also have some little say [or influence] with their husbands, sometimes put in a word, give a yell, a whoop, so that he trembles like a nine-year-old, not like me, who has to get around him with soft small talk, dares not to speak, God forbid, a crooked word, to curse sometimes because of the shame which I bear on account of you; that I still have to show a happy face for certain people. How does mama say it? "A pinch on the cheek, to bring out the color." . . . Only help, what is our life worth? I will flicker and flicker quietly, until, may it happen to the enemies of Zion, I'll be extinguished like a candle, to my enemies, or—God forbid—burst from vexation, may all your Yehupets big shots burst and burst apart, which is what is wished you today and always from the depths of my heart.

oy, a hunt zol oyfesen mayn harts, volt er meshuge gevorn. az ikh ze bay laytn, vayber hobn oykh a shtikl deye bay zeyere manen, mishn zikh arayn a mol mit a vort, tuen a geshray, a huk, az es varft mitn man dos nayn yerike, nisht azoy vi ikh darf mit im geyn mit veykhe reydelekh, nisht dervegn zikh kholile a krum vort, tsi oyssheltn a mol far di bizyoynes, vos ikh trog do iber far dir; az ikh darf nokh far itlekhn bazunder makhn a freylekh ponim. vi zogt di mame? "a knip in bak, di farb zol shteyn." . . . nor gevald, mo onu mo khayene? ikh vel azoy lang tsanken un tsanken shtilerheyt, biz ikh vel, soyne-tsion, oysgeyn vi a likht, mayne sonim, oder azoy kholile tsezetst fun grizote, tsezetst un tseshprungen zoln vern ale dayne yehupetser knakers, vi es vintsht dikh haynt un ale mol funem tifn hartsn.[88]

The images here that communicate Sheyne-Sheyndl's demoralizing fury, helplessness, and loss of control are themselves extremely compelling and disclose her ability to articulate the anguish generated by her powerlessness: from the image of the dog who would go mad from ingesting her heart to that of the seething anxiety that would cause her simply to disappear or evaporate, either silently and slowly by burning away like a candle (not like an ignited match, which would be quickly extinguished), or bombastically by being blown apart. Throughout her letters, images of burning appear in curses directed primarily at places—Odessa, Yehupets, Warsaw, Saint Petersburg, America—which she perceives as endangering her existence by supplying her husband with an array of enticing illusions he can pursue. But on occasion, she also targets people—for example, Yentele, the cousin who spread a rumor that Menakhem-Mendl had absconded to America. That she should now envision herself as soft wax burned to extinction suggests just how vulnerable and helpless she feels.

Throughout the text, Sheyne-Sheyndl compares her fate to that of a shtetl resident named Blume-Zlate, whom she characterizes as having a biting tongue and maintaining a tight grip on her husband. She writes Menakhem-Mendl that he would be back in Kasrilevke, indeed would never have been allowed to leave, if she were only as coarse and aggressive as this Blume-Zlate, though, she reminds him, she, Sheyne-Sheyndl, does not really have that in her. She is, however, openly envious of Blume-Zlate's ability to keep her family intact and covets the comfortable life that Nekhemye, the hardworking husband, has provided for his wife and family. Perhaps because she has experienced the pain of Menakhem-Mendl's male prerogative to abandon home and hearth, which has deprived her of frank expression, Sheyne-Sheyndl reserves her greatest admiration for Blume-Zlate as a woman who is so compelling that, "if she merely looks at Nekhemye, he at once loses his power of speech; he understands her already by her wink" *(az zi tut nor eyn kuk af nekhemyen, nemt im shoyn op dos loshn: er farshteyt zi shoyn afn vunk)*.[89]

While, for Sheyne-Sheyndl, Blume-Zlate is the figure who represents both the ultimate power that a woman can attain within the traditional life of the shtetl and the good life enjoyed because of that power, America looms large in her letters as the site associated with the danger of becoming an eternal *agune,* of forever losing the possibility of such power and status for herself. For Menakhem-Mendl, of course, America is the land that promises wealth, lucrative business ventures, and prominence. Their distinct differences in perception about the value of America highlight the politics of gender, of country versus city, and tradition versus modernity, all of which inform the relationship between the luftmentsh and his victim, the *agune* left behind.

From Sheyne-Sheyndl's first reference to America, in which she tells her husband that, if he no longer wants her, he should return home and divorce her or disappear in America, it is clear that, for her, America is associated with desertion; and although this statement seems forthright, all of her further allusions to America are fraught with anxiety and trepidation and suggest that her former audacity functioned largely to help her cope with the actuality of abandonment and perhaps stave off her husband's flight. Thus, when she hears a rumor that he has gone off to America, she runs panic-stricken through the town trying to verify it by tracking down its source. At other times, seemingly to discourage her husband from emigrating, she narrates tales of woe to undermine the myth of American streets lined with gold. For example, she writes him about their cousin Getsl, who had emigrated: "I am afraid, Mendl, that you will try your hand at businesses for so long that you will wind up peddling matches just like Aunt Sossi's son Getsl, who went to America, thought that there he could grab the cat by the tail. Finally he writes such notes that could move even a stone to pity. He writes that there in America each person must work his heart out, if not—if he swells up from hunger, no one will give him a piece of bread. A wonderful country, may it burn along with your Yehupets in a fire!" *(ikh hob moyre, mendl, du vest azoy lang pruvn mit gesheftn biz du vest onheybn arumtrogn shvebelekh tsu farkoyfn, azoy vi getsl der mume sosis, vos hot zikh avekgelozt keyn amerike, gemeynt, az dort khapt men dos koter, tsum sof shraybt er azelkhe brivlekh, az afile a shteyn kon dos rirn. er shraybt, az dort, in amerike, muz yeder eyntsiker arbetn mit der neshome, ele nit—meg er geshvoln vern far hunger, vet im keyner nit gebn keyn shtikl broyt. a sheyn land, brenen zol dos mit dayn yehupets af eyn fayer!)* And then, ironically but unwittingly, in a proverb that can but whet his appetite for cake, not ordinary bread, she warns him against following Getsl's example: "How does mama say it? 'If one has bread, one shouldn't hanker for sugarcake.'" *(vi zogt di mame? "az me hot broyt, zol zikh nit glustn keyn zukerlekekh.")*[90] Her final reference to America appears to be a veiled threat that she will track him down should he decide to sail away. Seemingly exhausted from urging him to return home, she tells him the story of one Moyshe-Dovid, who "already long ago took a dislike to his little wife, wanted to get rid of her, didn't know how; so off he went to America. But she nabbed him at the border and made such a scene that he will take care never to try that again. What a Litvak can do! May my troubles fall on his head!" *(hot er zikh meyashev geven un hot shoyn lang gevorfn an umkheyn af zayn vaybl, gevolt poter vern fun ir, nit gevust vi azoy; nemt er un fort avek keyn amerike. hot zi im gepakt bay der grenets un gemakht aza skandal, az er vet dos farzogn a tsentn. a litvak kon! mayne tsores af zayn kop!)*[91] Sheyne-Sheyndl tacitly admits defeat, however, when in her final letter she writes that, because she is bedridden and her father is dying, there is no one to go after him, no one to nab him at the border. Although at the time of that letter he had not yet indicated that he would emigrate, she seems already to have relinquished all hope for his return, and her writing never again appears in this text. When in his last letter Menakhem-Mendl writes that he is en route to America, it is clear that Sheyne-Sheyndl had correctly read in his letters the signs of her fate—the big country beyond the sea had indeed become the black hole into which her husband and, with him, her status as wife would disappear forever. Within the context of traditional Jewish life, the abrogation of the status as wife, which under Jewish law she cannot herself redeem, surely signifies also the erasure of the woman's voice.

For Menakhem-Mendel, however, America represents little more than another wonderful business opportunity, which, like any of his other business ventures, he seems to regard as existing completely apart from family considerations. In recounting, for example, the story of the *shlimazl* Lucky, Menakhem-Mendl notes that Lucky plans to go off to America should he, Lucky, fail to become a millionaire in Russia, and adds, "He is trying to talk me into going with him to America. He says that people like us will not get lost anywhere. But I would have to be crazy—to throw away such a respectable profession like writing and go off looking for good fortunes!" *(mikh redt er tsu, ikh zol mit im oykh forn keyn amerike. Er zogt, az azelkhe mentshn, vi mir, vern in ergets nit farfaln. nor meshuge vel ikh vern—avekvarfn aza bekovedike parnose vi dos shrayberay, un forn zukhn glikn!)*[92] Menakhem-Mendl may not consider the effect of his emigration on his family, but using the term *avekvarfn* (throw away) when rejecting the prospect of leaving his journalistic venture—the same term Sheyne-Sheyndl often uses to refer to his abandoning her and the children[93]—certainly indicates that a compelling business prospect is for him equivalent to or even more important than his wife and children, whom he is apparently not loath to discard.[94]

The self-absorption he displays here only increases in the final two books of the novel, where he continues to write about himself and his adventures but now—because of Sheyne-Sheyndl's absence as respondent—speaks only to himself. One wonders why he keeps on writing letters when he knows she cannot or will not reply. Of course, since his own existence seems to be so utterly related to his writing, ceasing to do so might call his very existence into question. In fact, his narcissism is even more glaringly conspicuous in the concluding paragraph of the novel, where, in a postscript, he announces his decision to emigrate. There Menakhem-Mendl's final words informing his wife of his intentions deviate from his earlier pronouncements only in the transparency of his completely platitudinous discourse and the elevated degree of dissociation from his family. When one reflects back on the trajectory of the text with the knowledge of his impending departure for America, one detects even in the earliest correspondence signs of the novel's outcome. Thus, when in her first letter Sheyne-Sheyndl, referring to her husband, cites her mother's saying "When a cow goes off with the herd, it forgets to say good-bye," she calls attention to two aspects of his behavior that are prominent in his parting words to her: his apparent proclivity for being a part of the herd and his indifference to those left behind. As though to corroborate the accuracy of her observation, Menakhem-Mendl begins his closing salvo with: "*Just remembered.* I have completely forgotten to write you where I am going. My dearest wife, I am going to America. Not alone—a whole group is going along. That is to say, going meaning we are actually going to Hamburg, and from there already to America." *(iker shokhakhti, ikh hob dir gor fargesn shraybn, vuhin ikh for. zugosi hayekore, ikh for keyn amerike. nisht aleyn—a gantse kompanye forn mir. dos heyst, forn forn mir, eygntlikh, keyn hamburg, un fun dortn shoyn keyn amerike.)*[95] These remarks reveal that he conceives of himself as bearing no responsibility for the support of his wife and family, and therefore any consultation with his spouse about his departure is unnecessary. In fact, this final letter written "in transit," with no forwarding address, would make it virtually impossible for her, should she so desire, to reach him. Indeed, the only indication of spousal attachment in this letter, apart from two references to his "dearest wife," is an allusion to her devotion to him, certainly not to his concern for her: "Only you shouldn't worry about me, dearest wife," he writes, "and not, God forbid, think ill of me." *(rak zolstu nor keyn yesurim nisht hobn, zugosi hayekore, un nisht ibertrakhtn af mir kholile, keyn shlekhts.)*[96] He concludes the letter and the novel with: "Only don't worry and don't take it to heart—'we have a mighty God!'" *(rak nisht gezorgt un nisht genumen zikh tsum hartsn—"mir hobn a shtarkn got!")*[97] This postscript also includes his familiar fantasies about the great future prosperity and prestige he will surely enjoy in America: "Gold, they say, is rolling in the streets there" *(gold, zogt men, valgert zikh dort in di gasn)*; people are really valued there, especially Jews, who are "considered the top of the horseradish [or cream of the crop]" *(gor dos eybershte fun khreyn)*; success will be his—"I will surely be successful, that is as sure for me as day is for the whole world" *(baglikn vel ikh ge-vis, dos iz bay mir zikher vi s'iz tog af der gantser velt)*. And he promises her to send "boat tickets for you and for the children, and [I] will take you [Sheyne-Sheyndl] there and you will live with me honorably, like the greatest lady, with the most beautiful and finest things. No speck will I let fall on you." *(vel ikh dir tsushikn shifkartn, far dir un far di kinder, un vel dir aroysnemen ahin, un vest bay mir lebn bekoved, vi di greste srorete, funem shenste un funem beste. keyn shprenkele vel ikh af dir lozn faln.)*[98] It is of course difficult to believe that Menakhem-Mendl will fulfill these promises, given that he has never kept any of the others made to his wife heretofore, whether to buy his wife watches, brooches, diamond earrings, and bracelets, or to send her money for family expenses, or to bring her and the children to Odessa and set them up in a wonderful furnished apartment. Indeed, throughout the text he recognizes that in order to be a broker or a speculator he must also be a liar, something he claims is difficult for him, although, when in book 5 he transforms himself into a matchmaker who comes from a long lineage of matchmakers, he openly admits to being an inveterate liar.[99] Perhaps because his hyperbolic fictions are present throughout the novel, they—and along with them Menakhem-Mendl, this luftmentsh constructed of words that now float without referents or response—seem by this time as jaded, lifeless, and defunct as the platitude about the "mighty God" he reaches for in the closing moment of his letters.

Although Menakhem-Mendl's writing is present throughout this text (his are the opening and closing letters), after Sheyne-Sheyndl ceases to respond to his missives the volume of his writing increases prodigiously. The final two books, which consist of one letter each, contain (in the Yiddish text) more than twenty-two and twelve pages, respectively, whereas no previous letter is longer than three and a half pages and most are considerably shorter. Curiously, when no replies are forthcoming and it is no longer clear that his letters are being read, his volubility swells formidably, almost as though excessive detail were necessary to verify not only the events he is narrating but also his own existence, which had, after all, previously been acknowledged or affirmed by his wife's responses. In the final books of the novel, Sheyne-Sheyndl's remark questioning his existence—"I no longer believe at all that you are alive!" *(es gleybt zikh mir gor nit, az du lebst!)*[100]—echoes once again in his rather boastful confessions that he is indeed alive and also an inveterate talker and liar, and his narratives suggest that he may be little more than a fantasizing mouth and a fabricating pen.

Thus, as someone who can now spin tales with little factual basis, this Menakhem-Mendl has at last evolved into a consummate luftmentsh, composed of preposterous illusory adventures narrated in increasingly vacuous phrases and clichés. Although his display of loquaciousness in the final two books seems to attest to his substantive presence, the elusiveness of the language and the fictionality of his autobiographical epistolary narratives actually reveal him to be an increasingly shadowy presence, a very tenuous being that is fast fading.

Sheyne-Sheyndl's absence from the final books may not actually signify her disappearance, however. The absence of her voice does intimate that, as an *agune,* she has lost what little legitimacy a woman has within the traditional Jewish community, and that her writing, which seemed rarely to have received a serious hearing from her spouse, has been erased from the largely masculine world in which writing and capital circulate. But these observations do not exhaust all interpretive possibilities. After all, what continues to haunt the final two books is a lingering presence, which she had earlier inscribed into the texts of her letters—not merely the emptiness of her absence but its obstinate presence. Her silence may in fact be magnified when juxtaposed with Menakhem-Mendl's verbosity. Thus, her silence may betoken something more than the absence of voice, something other than a disappearance or diminution of self: it may reflect a decisive and important step Sheyne-Sheyndl has taken in an effort to rescue her already damaged being. After all, she chooses to absent herself, chooses not to write—her final letter begins: "I am writing you, that I have nothing to write you." *(shrayb ikh dir, az ikh hob dir nit vos tsu shraybn.)*[101] Because of that decision, her continued adamant silence may be understood as neither timidity nor erasure, but as the implementation of a vow of silence taken in order to free herself from unwittingly participating in Menakhem-Mendl's "airy" adventure tales and from his endless pursuit of unachievable fantasies and exalted phantom identities. She has in effect called a halt to the charade designed by her husband to engender his status while dismantling hers and, finally, has actively written herself out of his narcissistic quest for identity that was crushing her.

Given the novel's overall structure, one may question whether this structure actually undermines its composite generic formation, which includes both the *brivnshteler* and the epistolary novel. The *brivnshteler* was a staple in the inventory of every *pakntreger* (an itinerant bookpeddler) and circulated widely among the Jewish population. Although the letters that employ the suggested *brivnshteler* formulas are individual missives, the use of standard formats and exemplars provides a communal context for epistolary communication, thereby contributing to the practice of a shared traditional life. The markedly different sensibilities reflected in the spouses' letters reinforce the dialogic structure of the epistolary novel, which highlights both a personal relationship between the writers and their separation from each other. The opening sentences of every letter of Menakhem-Mendl and Sheyne-Sheyndl display the same recurring distinct formulaic modes of address, presumably chosen from a *brivnshteler,* and illuminate how the intersection and parodies of various genres function in the text. Surely the irony and humor of their forms of address cannot be overlooked—his moderate, temperate tone and her exalted language designed to honor a great scholar or holy man. When taken at face value, however, the formulas create the impression of a stable family with a rational down-to-earth husband and a devoted wife who takes pride in her mate's scholarly prowess. Yet from the novel's beginning, the content of their letters challenges the veracity of their forms of address, but only after book 4, when Sheyne-Sheyndl has removed herself from the epistolary exchange, is the efficacy of both genres called into question. Since there is no evidence that Menakhem-Mendl's two final, very long letters are read or even received, his usual practice of writing almost exclusively about himself to his wife finally evolves into an ultimate narcissistic narrative, namely, writing about himself only to himself. He is at last detached, alone, having attained a powerless autonomy and meaningless, unproductive freedom that are perhaps all that modernity and capitalism can furnish him. It should come as no surprise that, in the two concluding books, the epistolary dialogic genres are undermined and in effect replaced by a first-person narrative form, a monologue, which may be better suited to the manipulating mouth and fabricating pen of a luftmentsh, a "Menakhem-Mendl." What has been silenced, however, is not only the world of the shtetl and its *mame-loshn* but also any interactive dialogue between the genders, between shtetl and metropolis, and between traditional communality and modern individualism.

CHAPTER 4

Agunes Disappearing in "A Gallery of Vanished Husbands"

Retrieving the Voices of Abandoned Women and Children

From the early years of the twentieth century, the New York–based Yiddish newspaper *Der Forverts (Jewish Daily Forward)* printed a feature called "A Gallery of Vanished Husbands" *(A galeriye fun farshvundene mener)* exhibiting portraits of husbands who had deserted their families, along with abbreviated descriptions of the deserters' circumstances and identifying characteristics. In an effort to locate deserters, this infamous Gallery appeared several times a week for decades, highlighting as many as thirty men in a format that, at times, covered half a page. The names and information were largely supplied by the National Desertion Bureau, a Jewish agency founded under the aegis of the National Council of Jewish Charities in 1911, and which became an independent organization in 1914. The Bureau's main mission was to locate, apprehend, and if necessary bring to justice the deserter; and though it did not provide support for the abandoned family, it apparently did counsel the family about where such assistance might be attained. The Gallery was but one venue used to accomplish the aims of the Bureau, which also contacted other agencies, as well as employers, unions, family members, and friends of deserters. But although the Gallery, appearing as it did in one of the most widely read Yiddish newspapers, brought the issue of deserting husbands compellingly into the broad public arena of the Jewish immigrant population, it did not address the predicament of the victims—the *agunes* and their children—with equal forthrightness and candor. Indeed, in the many miniature biographies of men accompanying their portraits, the wives, who are repeatedly described only as being "in great need" and seeking "help from the charities," emerge as face-less ciphers with no defining characteristics. Ironically, in their absence or shadowy presence, the wives appear as the cause of their spouses' publicized infamy, a portrayal that unwittingly reproduces the charge often levied against deserted women—including the *agune* in Glikl's story and certainly implied in the case of Senderl's wife in *Benjamin the Third*—that their behavior was in fact responsible for their husbands' departures. In order to chart the social and cultural terrain of desertion, I inquire first into the ways in which it was interpreted, administered, and presented by Jewish organizations to the community of Jews, as well as into the impact of these representations. Then, by examining two case files, I consider the ways in which the Bureau operated; and finally, through the examination of selected texts, I retrieve and explore at least fragments of the silenced voices and submerged experiences of the victimized women and children.

Charting the Terrain of Desertion: The Twentieth Century

In the closing decades of the nineteenth century, the president of the United Hebrew Charities, dismayed by the number of abandoned wives seeking charitable assistance, characterized "the wretched men" who deserted their families as "a blot on the fair name of Israel, whose sons, no less than daughters, are noted for their strong family love and domestic virtue."[1] This comment implies that family stability and communal solidarity were perceived as a reality that merely had to be protected when, in fact, there was ample evidence to the contrary. In their writings about the shtetl and Jewish ghettos, such major Eastern European Yiddish writers as S.Y. Abramovitsh, Sholem Aleykhem, I.L. Peretz, and Sholem Asch and American Jewish writers like Abraham Cahan and Henry Roth had already called into question the virtue and sanctity of the Jewish family and community. But historians of American Jewish life too often overlooked the serious dislocations that families of impoverished immigrant Jews experienced from the turn of the century to the mid-twentieth century and instead acknowledged a myth of the Jewish family as a fundamentally stable institution. This "romantically idealized image of the Jewish family as warm, supportive, and ever-nurturing" has, according to Paula E. Hyman, a long history: "In the past two centuries," she writes, "Jewish communal leaders have been quick to celebrate the virtues of

Jewish family life for purposes of self-gratification as well as apologetics, but they have been equally quick, in periods of rapid social change, to blame contemporary Jewish families for failing to live up to the standards of a noble past."[2] This myth was accepted despite the record of large numbers of desertions and scores of abandoned women so impoverished that many were forced to place their children in orphanages, become prostitutes, and commit suicide.[3] Indeed, the resulting great financial burden placed upon both Jewish and governmental charities at the end of the nineteenth century so alarmed prominent members of the established Jewish community that they turned serious attention to the problem of desertions. It is not surprising that it was the wealthy professional Jews, almost exclusively men and largely already-acculturated Central European Jews, who were alarmed by the behavior of the overwhelmingly poor recent Eastern European immigrants who were the flagrant deserters. Although the numbers of desertions among Jews did not differ significantly from those of other ethnic groups, the "uptown Jews," as the cultured and moneyed elite who lived in upper Manhattan were called, feared that this "blot on the fair name of Israel" could threaten their relatively recently acquired public stature and were, therefore, especially anxious to eradicate this embarrassment.[4] The sociologist Manheim S. Shapiro connects the "mixed motives" of these philanthropists to their concern about the social effects of antisemitism: "On the one hand, there was a sympathetic feeling for deprived fellow Jews; on the other, a fear that these alien-seeming hordes of immigrants would provoke or intensify the anti-Semitism which had been emerging in overt form since the 1880s."[5] In addition, the interest in containing and controlling desertions was focused more on protecting the public funds of taxpayers than on "the spiritual or psychic welfare of disrupted families. . . . The NDB was created after all cut costs not to increase them."[6]

Referring to the family as "the basis of social life," Charles Zunser, the counsel and director of the National Desertion Bureau, asserted that "upon its integrity rests, in the last analysis, the whole fabric of society."[7] Given this view of the relationship between family and society, it becomes clear why, in a male-centered society and Jewish community, it was considered imperative to restore the missing father in order to attack what was deemed a "social evil" of great magnitude. Consequently, all efforts were concentrated on finding the husbands who had disappeared, lobbying for criminal laws that made extradition possible, and seeking punishment for those who refused to fulfill spousal and parental responsibilities. Although these ideas had already circulated in several charitable institutions, the National Desertion Bureau wanted to facilitate the apprehension of Jewish offenders. The annual reports of the Bureau are replete with statistics about the agency's activities, almost exclusively concerned with the disposition of the male perpetrators; virtually no mention is made of the condition of the wives and children.[8] There is, in fact, evidence that some of the men who were philanthropic pioneers in the field of family welfare were so exclusively intent upon apprehending the male transgressors that they advocated subjecting the wives to even greater misery than was already their lot. In an influential work on philanthropy, Boris Bogen reports that Morris Waldman, one of the founders of the Bureau whose study of desertion in the early twentieth century was instrumental in drawing attention to the issue, proposed that, since "almost half of the deserters care for what becomes of their children," the abandoned families should be sent for charitable relief to public agencies (instead of Jewish ones), which did not provide adequate sustenance for the family. Such privation, he hoped, "might bring back the husband who has left and prevent others from leaving"; and Bogen, himself an eminent operative in one of the most important charitable undertakings (American Jewish Joint Distribution Committee), considered this to be "proper treatment from the standpoint of charitable organizations."[9] The needs of family members are thus accorded a secondary status: women and children may be exploited and victimized even further, all for the sake of apprehending the offending culprit and "restoring" an ideal entity called the family. In addition, because of the high rate of recidivism among deserters, any such successful restoration was often short-lived.[10]

Thus, underlying the magnanimous mission and strategies of agencies concerned with desertion, there appears to be an unstated and perhaps unrecognized agenda informed by gender and class. Consider, for instance, the ideological implications of a situation in which the National Desertion Bureau operates: the family is regarded as an, if not *the*, essential pillar of "the whole fabric of society," and, furthermore, men hold the commanding positions in both the family and society. Those men in positions of power and influence take upon themselves—in the capacity of philanthropists, but also acting in their own self-interest—the task of bringing into line those *other* men, the recent poor immigrants perceived to be a threat to the status of the "uptown Jews." What is occurring here seems to be primarily not a struggle for the restoration of the happy family but rather a situation in which one class of prominent and socially powerful men uses concern for family as the pretext for bringing into line another class of men, who are poor and perceived as uncultured. The victimized women and children supply the arena for the struggle between these two groups of men, the privileged and the impoverished. Moreover, wealthy established Jewish men who are designated as institutional overseers of the moral "fabric of society" might not themselves be such exemplary representatives of the solidity of the family. Desertion was, after all, often regarded as the "poor man's divorce"; men of means did not need to desert in order to leave their families, since they had ready access to other, more acceptable forms of abandonment. Although destitution was endemic among deserters, infidelity was, according the reports of the National Desertion Bureau, a primary cause of desertion; men with money, however, could comfortably care for mistresses or pay for a divorce, alimony, and child support.[11]

In 1929 Zunser noted that the Bureau handled about 2,500 cases annually, but remarkably, especially considering the increasing upward mobility of Jews, in the first half of the 1950s the numbers of cases often exceeded that figure by far. In 1953, for example, the Bureau serviced 5,777 cases, which was somewhat greater than that of previous years: in 1952—5,625; 1951—4,598; 1950—4,509; 1949—4,574; 1948—5,177.[12] In 1955 the National Desertion Bureau's name was changed to Family Location Service, although its focus remained almost exclusively on family desertions. (I have not been able to discover the reasons for the name change, but the new name surely obliterates the stigma of desertion that was prominent in the previous name; and curiously, neither agency's name indicates its Jewish affiliation.) By 1960 the caseload had diminished by almost 70 percent, to 1,646 open cases.[13] The statistics do not, of course, disclose the full dimension of the problem. There were many reasons why wives did not report abandonment: women were often not cognizant of the available options and did not know of the Bureau's existence; they were also frequently intimidated, not only by the general tendency to blame them for their husbands' reprehensible behavior, but also by the retaliation they feared from their spouses and by the shame of having to plead for charity. Zunser, noting that "four proud women waited fully thirteen years" before reporting the desertion, identified shame as one reason for their silence.[14]

PUBLIC REPRESENTATION OF DESERTION AND DESERTERS

The service performed by "A Gallery of Vanished Husbands," which appeared in the Yiddish *Forverts,* was invaluable.[15] It brought the issue graphically before the immigrant population and solicited readers' assistance in locating and apprehending perpetrators. The Gallery displayed the faces of deserters in a rogues' portrait gallery, identified specific physical characteristics, and provided only very brief personal histories, but histories nevertheless. Under the deserters' pictures one learned, albeit in abbreviated form, where they were born, where they lived or might be living, the kind of work they did, and the composition of their families. While such truncated biographies may not in themselves seem interesting, it can be argued that they were compelling not only because of the active lives recorded but also because of what was omitted—namely, any insight into the deserters' motives, intentions, and their seemingly uncanny ability to erase the realities of their pasts. The interplay of difference and similarity among the lives of those represented in the Gallery as well as the incompleteness of their portrayed lives could easily stimulate the imagination of readers and draw them to the mysteries of the men who disappeared. Following is a very small sampling of descriptions from the Gallery, which appeared in the month of January 1916. One or two examples would no doubt suffice to illustrate the format, but the sheer volume of texts as well as the variations and repetitions among these descriptions speak loudly and powerfully (as they did in the newspaper), not only about the scope of the problem, but also about the dynamics and effects of this form of representation.

January 2, 1916: Simon Wiseman, 34 years old, left his wife Yetti in Kasha, Hungary, November 1907. Mr. Wiseman was born in Odessa, Russia, and came to New York in 1907. Here in New York he married another woman, a Miss Tillie Scruss, with whom in May 1913 he had a child named Lou. Both women find themselves in great need. Wiseman is a chorus man, has sung in the Hippodrome in New York.

January 9, 1916: Joseph Grossman, 27 years old, a shoemaker by trade, disappeared from Richmond, Virginia, on November 7, 1915, leaving his wife Annie and their small baby. Mr. Grossman took everything his wife owned and left her without a penny. He was born in Russia and came to America eight years ago.

Abraham Bergsitz, 33 years old, in 1909 in New York left his wife Tillie and their two small children who are in great need. He returned later, and disappeared again in 1912. Mr. Bergsitz is a sweater knitter and a cigar maker by trade. Was born in Vilna, Russia, and came to New York in 1905.

Hyman Weissblatt or, as he calls himself, John Queen, 33 years old, disappeared from Chicago in September 1915, leaving his wife Sarah and their three small children, who find themselves in great need. Mr. Weissblatt was born

FIGURE 1. "A Gallery of Vanished Husbands," March 1920. The *Jewish Daily Forward* ran this feature several times a week for many decades.

in England and went to New York in 1892, and from New York to Chicago in 1912. He is an electrician and worked for a year for Western Electric Co. in Chicago. It is thought that he is now in New York.

Henry Jackson, 45 years old, disappeared in New York on June 14, 1911, leaving his wife Lillian and their five children who are now in great need. Mr. Jackson was born in Goldingham, Russia, and came to New York in 1897. He worked for the American Leather Goods Company in Chicago. It is thought that he is now in Chicago, where he is an agent for a large gas company.

Dave Granitz left his wife Rosa, who lives in Chicago. On October 17 she gave birth to a baby and is in a sickly condition. He was born in Kalish, Russian Poland, is 25 years old, and came to Chicago in 1911.

January 30, 1916: Emanuel Wallworth, 27 years old, left his wife Sadie in Brooklyn, New York, on the 13th of October, 1915. One day after he disappeared his wife received a letter from him, but since then she has received nothing from him. Mr. Wallworth was born in New York. He is a lawyer and had his office at 299 Broadway, New York. It is thought that he left his wife because his parents were not satisfied with his marriage. Mrs. Wallworth asks that her husband come home.

Jacob Hirsh or Joseph Sheinberg left his wife Toiba and their child Harry in New York in September 1915. Mr. Hirsh is 28 years old, a tailor by trade, born in Galicia, and came to America 14 years ago. Right after leaving his wife he wrote a letter to the Desertion Bureau that he was in Mt. Vernon living among Christians, but he did not give his address.

Morris Raymond or Joseph Stark in 1911 left his wife Dora and their small baby in New York City. In 1912 in Baltimore he married another woman, who had his child. Both women are now in New York. Mr. Raymond is 27 years old, a men's clothing tailor by trade, was born in Levintsha, District of Minsk, and came to America in 1904. It is thought that he is now in Scranton, Pa., or in Chicago, Illinois.

This Gallery of men's portraits raises important issues about the differing representations of men and women, of the victimizers and victimized. Although each man is described in his own specificity, taken as a group their profiles resemble one another to a remarkable degree: they are almost all immigrants (one exception); of the immigrants, almost all are from Eastern Europe (one exception); all are married men (some married more than once); and all have left their wives and children (one had no children). The distinct differences among the narratives do in fact underscore the similarities and also accentuate the startling gender disparity between the descriptions of husbands and wives. The portrayed renegade protagonists display, in large part, a common pattern: they are described as active people who have crossed an ocean and resettled in America, who work (sometimes at several trades), marry, father children, leave their families, and disappear into the vast expanse of their new country, sometimes to marry again, have more children, leave those families, and vanish once again into anonymity.

The acts of these men may be dastardly and irresponsible, but the biographies describe them as having accomplished something. Not so, however, with the portrayal of the wives and children, for whom there are no portraits and whose histories are not given. In the texts about their husbands, the Rosas and Annies and Yettas remain static and fixed, waiting in an eternal present for the return of their husbands, waiting for the charities. No one sees their faces, no one knows where they came from, no one knows that they too have crossed a big ocean, that they too have worked and perhaps continue to work, that they have had and still do have lives, have been and are part of communities. Their shadowy presences, articulated in a perfunctory phrase or two, contribute to their shared absence. It is surely ironic that, while their absent husbands—portraits and history—are foregrounded in the public media, the images and histories of the abandoned wives and children, though in fact very much present, are nowhere to be found. There is no "Gallery of Deserted Wives," no "Gallery of Deserted Children." "A Gallery of Vanished Husbands" reproduces discourses of patriarchy prevalent in both the dominant society and traditional Judaism. No matter how treacherous or cowardly the deserters' behavior, the men remain the dominant, important members of the society, and their stories alone are told. True, "A Gallery of Vanished Husbands" provided a vital instrument for locating deserters, but might it not have been equally important to acquaint the public with the realities of the deserted women and children? Clearly, the aims of the *Forverts,* a working-class newspaper, and agencies like the National Desertion Bureau, were principled, but those institutions were also in large part controlled by men who had power and represented the ideology that relegated women and children to shadow and silence.

THE NATIONAL DESERTION BUREAU: AIMS AND INTERESTS

The Gallery was essentially an organ of the National Desertion Bureau, which submitted the photographs and texts to the *Forverts;* and one can assume, therefore, that the Gallery represented the concerns and values of the agency. The publications and reports of the Bureau clearly indicate that its primary goal was to eliminate the embarrassing "blot on the fair name of Israel"[16] by inducing "nomad husbands"[17] to become responsible members of society, while provision for the support and care for the deserted families was left to charitable agencies. A close examination of two official Bureau documents may provide important insights into its views of desertion and deserters. The two documents, written forty years apart, reveal a remarkable confluence of values and interests, linking the founding of the agency in 1911 to that period in midcentury when its name was changed to Family Location Service. The first document, *Family Desertion*, which was the triennial report of the National Desertion Bureau for June 1912 through May 1915, was written by its secretary and counsel Monroe M. Goldstein;[18] the second, *To Rebuild the Broken Family: Family Location Service, 1905–1955*, was apparently one of the earliest documents for public consumption after the Bureau's name change. Although the earlier publication is an official report with statistical documentation and the later one an informational pamphlet for the general public, both of these texts discuss the activities of the agency and the nature of its work by citing very revealing abbreviated case histories.

Family Desertion Report (1915). The main portion of *Family Desertion* is titled "Report of the Secretary and General Counsel" and essentially concerns five major areas: (1) the Bureau's views on desertion and deserters, the scope of its operations, and the results of its activities, (2) seven case histories intended to illuminate "the psychology of desertion and how the problem is handled by the Desertion Bureau,"[19] (3) "legal aspects" of cases, (4) a brief conclusion, and finally, (5) several statistical appendices about the disposition of cases and the Bureau's finances. Of special interest here are the first two sections, which constitute the largest and most substantive portion of the document. Declaring that "from a socio-legal point of view, 'Family Desertion' may be divided into two clearly differentiated classes—(1) 'Non-support' and (2) 'Abandonment'"—the report indicates that, "in the main, the Desertion Bureau is concerned with cases of actual abandonment involving the dependency of the deserted family upon public or private charity." Although the report makes it clear that its principal and also most difficult undertaking is to locate the deserter, "to trace his whereabouts and to apply moral and legal pressure upon him to return home or provide for the maintenance of his family,"[20] it is not concerned about every deserter, only those whose families require public welfare.

Its interest in the sanctity of the family apparently did not extend to abandoned families that could fend for themselves or to cases of non-support, which could be left to the jurisdiction of the courts because the father's whereabouts were known. According to the report, the primary goal of the agency was not to provide support and care for the family but rather, as noted earlier, to eliminate the social embarrassment of desertion by inducing the "nomad husband" to rejoin the family (I discuss the significance of the term *nomad husband* later).[21]

Given this posture, it is not surprising that the three exemplary cases, which are cited in this text to illustrate the "complex and manifold causes, motives and social phases" of desertion, are concerned with the deserter's plight and his perception of his own behavior.[22] The report of the first case begins: "A deserter once stated in his own crude way, that he left his wife as a protest against the monotony of his existence; he had to work hard; troubles beset him; a child took sick; and not knowing which way to turn, he took a leap in the dark and escaped."[23] In a few impassive phrases the devastating results of his actions are given—one child was sent to a public hospital, two others to an orphanage, but not a word about the troubles that beset his wife and the agony of being forced to separate from her children. The outcome, however, was successful; for although this was the husband's second offense and, when located, he was convicted, he became contrite (especially, it seems, when faced with incarceration), a job was found for him, and "the home was completely rehabilitated."

The remaining cases illustrate alternative reactions of men—agency workers as well as deserters—to male "passions," to what were regarded as "natural" male propensities to live a nomadic life: men may either discipline themselves and become responsible citizens or, out of weakness or depravity, yield to their passion for wandering. The preamble to the second case is a diary excerpt detailing the anxiety of a man who, for the third time, wanted to desert his wife and children, but, on each occasion fearing his neighbors might see him, did not leave; instead, he states, he "went into the café where [he] played cards." Once again, the compassion articulated in the report is directed toward the predicament of the man: "Through what mental questionings, simple as they are, must a man pass on the eve of deserting. A transgression, a yielding to passion, may make him miserable, but free of the yoke."[24] Here desertion is presented not as a conscious act through which the man seeks to evade responsibility for his family. Rather the deserter's behavior is understood as resulting from desire, the fulfillment of which culminates in submission to his "passion" to be free of any obligation. The act of desertion is thus regarded not as a deliberate act undertaken for different reasons by different people who could then be held responsible for their actions but as an act of weakness, of mere surrender to instinctual male needs.

If deserters are regarded by the Bureau as either weaklings or villains, as "men who are morally weak" or "degeneratively vicious,"[25] if they are perceived as "nomad husbands" whose elemental nomadic impulses lead them to wander continuously, then one can hardly expect to hold them fully accountable for their behavior even when, by fulfilling their basic needs, they jeopardize the physical and emotional well-being of their wives and children. The Bureau's agenda is unambiguous: place deserters at center stage, rehabilitate the moral weaklings among them, imprison the degenerates, and hope that in the end the misery of the women and children in the shadows will somehow be alleviated. Indeed, in this report the plight of the women and children seems irrelevant and enters into consideration only as nebulous justification for actions taken against the perpetrator or as information necessary for documentary purposes. Consider, for instance, the final case cited, that of a "degenerately vicious" man who absolutely refused to work and support his family, who remained recalcitrant and unrepentant even though imprisoned for a year and fined one thousand dollars. After a discussion of the case lasting almost a page, the narration ends with validation for the punitive measures taken by the Bureau and not a single word about the circumstances of the wife and children during or after the period of the agency's actions. In this text, the victimized family members descend into complete oblivion, for this story of desertion apparently concerned only the transgressor and the Bureau's workers who pursued him.

The next part of the report consists of seven "typical cases" chosen from the agency files and intended to illuminate "the psychology of desertion and how the problem is handled by the Desertion Bureau."[26] The cases all involve the Bureau's attempts to locate the husbands and have them accept responsibility for supporting their families. Despite the fact that these cases are described at some length (from half a page to a page and a half), in each case the wife and children appear in the same perfunctory manner as in "A Gallery of Vanished Husbands": the differences between the brief format of the Gallery profile and the extended narrative of the case study did not alter the representation of the abandoned families. Thus, each case study exhibits formulaic overtures similar to those of the Gallery: "In 1899, Emanuel H—— left his wife

Theresa, and two children . . ." Or "Five years ago, one Elias Z—— deserted his wife, Yetta, and their eight minor children . . ." Or "N——, a waiter and portrait canvasser by trade, lived with his wife, Sarah, and two children in New York. . . . Tired of censorship [by his relatives], he deserted her in March, 1912," and so forth.

Of the three deserters among these cases who were convicted and sent to prison,[27] one remained recalcitrant to the end but was finally forced to release, for his family's support, money he had saved; another "saw the light" and returned to his wife and six children; and the third—who had abandoned his wife once before—not only returned to exploit her financially before leaving again but continued to harass her with a series of extremely "vindictive" letters (one is printed in the text). He did, however, use his epistolary skills while in prison to write a letter of apology for his behavior to the Desertion Bureau. The final sentence of this account reads: "When '64970' [Joe K.'s prison identification number] is released, his wife will be ready to receive him, for, as she has stated to the Bureau, she anxiously awaits the day of reconciliation."[28] One wonders whether anyone at the Bureau had even spoken with her about her decision to "receive" a man who had so viciously abused her verbally and financially; if they did, there is no sign of it in this case history, the report of which is by far the longest of the seven cases.

There is, however, one instance among the seven that differs significantly from the others in regard to the consideration extended to the wife and children. It is the case of N——, a waiter and canvasser who left his wife, Sarah, and two children. After N—— deserted them, the family lived with relatives who, because of financial difficulties, were soon unable to continue their support. As a result, the record states, "the wife, tortured by misery and privation, succumbed to melancholia and in consequence of brooding and despondency, committed suicide by jumping off the roof of her tenement dwelling. The home was dismembered. The little ones were taken over by the Hebrew Orphan Asylum as wards of the city."[29] This is the single instance among these typical cases where the horrible predicament of the family is recorded, albeit in appallingly mechanical terms ("The home was dismembered"). Yet, even within the context of this case history, it seems to be not the abandoned wife's suffering that drew the attention of the Bureau to her, but rather the significance of the suicide for the disposition of the case. The wife apparently had not sought assistance from the Bureau, and only after her death was a complaint filed against the husband on behalf of the children. Essentially concerned about the legal intricacies of the case, because now as a widower N—— was technically not a deserter, the Bureau sought a venue to make the man support his children. The report concludes: "Should he default in any of the conditions stated, exemplary punishment will be meted out to him."[30] There is no further mention of what happened to the children.

The conclusion to this report indicates that, while the Bureau may not have deliberately neglected the circumstances of the wives and children, the conception of its mission as the prevention of "dependency upon individuals and charitable organizations" led to operations that were restricted almost exclusively to the pursuit of vanished husbands. The Bureau's aims are described here as follows: "The Bureau is socially necessary,—as an agency to bring the abandoner to justice; to help, where practical, to rehabilitate the home on the basis of self-support, and as a deterrent to the spread of desertion." Of course, one may argue that the notion of "self-support" actually reflects the Bureau's primary interest in the well-being of the family, but there is no indication in the text that this is the case. On the contrary, the Bureau was essentially concerned with lifting the burden not from the family but from the charitable organizations. "The result of the Bureau's activities," the conclusion notes, "has prevented to a large extent the dependency upon individuals and charitable organizations caused by the abandonment of the breadwinner. The saving to the United Hebrew Charities of approximately $100,000 in a period of four years."[31] The work of the Bureau no doubt helped to alleviate the hardship of some women and children despite the fact that this objective seems not to have been its primary focus.

To Rebuild the Broken Family Pamphlet (1955). In many ways the language of the second document, *To Rebuild the Broken Family,* a pamphlet published by the Family Location Service, differs markedly from that of the 1915 report. Whereas the earlier report states unambiguously that the aim of the Bureau is "to prosecute those who willfully refuse [to support their families] or omit to do so," and that its operations are designed to be "a deterrent to the spread of desertion,"[32] the later pamphlet stresses that "there is no assignment of blame," that locating deserters is not to be viewed "as a threat to the individual missing husband or as a warning to others."[33] In addition, although this later document identifies the Family Location Service as a "social work–legal aid" organization, attention to legality is muted, while psychological rhetoric underscores the need for emotional caring and support. But an analysis of the written text, including the elucidative

FIGURE 2. Images from *To Rebuild the Broken Family,* a pamphlet published by the Family Location Service in 1955.

case studies and the illustrations interposed with the text on alternate pages, suggests that the ideology and purpose expressed in *To Rebuild the Broken Family* do not actually differ significantly from those of the *Family Desertion* report.

An examination of the gender relations in this 1955 pamphlet reflects gender differences similar to those found in the report forty years earlier. The later text emphasizes the preeminent significance of men,

primarily deserting fathers and also—peripherally, but not insignifi-
cantly—male workers for the Family Location Service. But it con-
comitantly also reveals a merely tenuous interest in the distress of
the victimized women and children. Communicated throughout this
document is a sympathetic understanding of the psychological reasons
for the deserter's behavior, not of the dire material or emotional needs
of the deserted family. Focusing mainly on the importance of men,
the text notes, for example, that some men have a suppressed desire to
return to their wives and "need only the strong, understanding voice
and helping hand of the agency to motivate their return."[34] Moreover,
of the seven drawings that accompany the pamphlet's text (see fig. 2), six
portray men: two depict only male employees; two depict male employees
with male deserters (in one picture two children stand behind the
father who appears to be delivering a payment to the administrator);
one portrays a man seemingly worried about deserting; and another
depicts two male hands locating pins on a map of North America
(perhaps identifying the locations of deserters or desertions). Only
on the final page, one that contains no written text, is a young and
vigorous woman portrayed ostensibly striding out of the pages of the
document into a happy future with a young girl by her side. These
images actually reinforce the views and principal interests of the text
and deliver a clear message about the gender values that inform the
Bureau's discourse and its practice of pursuing solutions to desertion:
the men are in charge of bringing their lapsed brethren to accept their
manly duties and paternal responsibilities, and at the end of the process the women and children will be able to stride freely (if perhaps
only alone) into the future.

One sketch that depicts an agency administrator speaking with a sailor
illustrates a case history that is discussed in the pamphlet and could be
titled "The Case of the Nomad Husband and the Wife Who Learned to
Adapt to Her Husband's Needs." Unlike the 1915 report, in which the
Bureau felt it necessary to address the nomadic desires of deserters, this
pamphlet goes one step further and counsels wives on how to adapt to
the needs of roving husbands. In this particular instance, the perception
may have been that the husband's strong need to roam provoked him
to desert, and it was the wife who had "to understand her husband and
his need to work at his own last."[35] In another case cited, a husband,
who claimed he had left his wife and three children in part because of
the interference of his mother-in-law, was located and he agreed to
return to his family. But, the text continues, "meanwhile the agency

helped Mrs. K. understand a bit better her real role as wife, mother, and daughter."[36] In both cases the underlying operative supposition is that the wife's behavior was in good part responsible for the husband's act of desertion, and therefore it is the wife's duty to adapt and cater to the requirements of her derelict spouse. But there is no indication that husbands who disappeared, without a word and without arranging for the support of wives and children, were counseled about their family's needs. The implications of this double standard are not particularly subtle: by focusing principally on the needs of men—who were, in accordance with the agency's agenda, of primary importance—the Family Location Service subscribed to the view and practice of male supremacy and female subservience that prevailed in the dominant society and Jewish community. Its male workers were, in fact, helping the deserters once again to assume their respectable patriarchal privilege not only as husbands but also as fathers; for, as *To Rebuild the Broken Family* puts it, "without a father, without even the pro forma contact of a support check, what are the chances for responsible citizenship?"[37] One cannot help but wonder what the agency thought about the role that mothers, the ones who did not abandon the family, might have had in fostering "responsible citizenship" in the family. The idea of the centrality of the father certainly provides justification for the activities of the Family Location Service's aggressive pursuit of deserters, but it also articulates very clearly the agency's proclivity to minimize the importance of women and mothers for the socialization of children, which may, of course, account for the paucity of attention accorded women in their publicized pronouncements.

A Glimpse into the National Desertion Bureau's Files

The files of the National Desertion Bureau are now housed in the YIVO storage facilities in New York City and are currently not available for examination, although the Bureau's file of applicant names and the dates of application is accessible. By a stroke of good luck, a library staff member, who had just told me that no files could be retrieved from storage at the time, noticed in his bookshelf one of the Bureau's file folders, which he allowed me to read. The folder actually contained two unrelated case files, both of which offer insights into how the Bureau's work was conducted. One of the files also contained copious documents and illuminated how complicated and difficult some cases of desertion could be.

The simpler of the two cases concerned Harry and Rose G., whose record was known to the Bureau between 1927 and 1932. Harry, who was a "pocketbook maker," an "oilcloth layer," and a gambler, left his wife and three children on July 15, 1927; the Bureau forwarded his picture and biographical information to the *Forverts* and the *Sunday World Times*, and his picture did appear in the *Forverts* on two occasions, April 17, 1927, and October 26, 1929. A tip from an informant directed the Bureau to a saloon on Rivington Street in New York's Lower East Side, where Mr. G. could often be found. He was apprehended in 1930 and sent to the workhouse, but was released, as often happened, by his wife (who did not, however, report this to the Bureau), put on probation, and ordered to pay his wife $20 a week, which he did only sporadically. He then disappeared again, was once again found and sent to the workhouse, but now had to post a bond of $1,040, which his brother, not he, supplied; the wife could withdraw $20 a week from the bond when Harry did not pay her. He was sent back to the workhouse in 1932. The file concludes with Harry's subsequent disappearance and the Bureau, with the help of Family Welfare Services, looking for him in Allentown, Pennsylvania, and Springfield, Massachusetts.

The second case in the folder was far more complex and burdened with a surfeit of documentation that included correspondence with a number of agencies and lawyers, records of interviews with the husband as well as the wife, Paul and Celia R., and a letter from their daughter to her father. The materials in this case provide insight into the enormous effort that the National Desertion Bureau made, not only to locate the deserter and to untangle the involved and thorny circumstances that came to light only during the investigative process, but also to resolve the convoluted situation. Celia and Paul, both immigrants from Russia, married in 1920 and each had a somewhat different account of their marriage and its dissolution. She claimed that he deserted her in 1921, ten months after the marriage, leaving her with an infant child. In 1927 she came to the Bureau when, she says, she first learned of its existence. She said Paul knew nine languages and had been an interpreter for the U.S. Army and also a photographer. The last address she had for him was General Delivery, Galveston, Texas. The Bureau made a concerted effort to find him, contacting the Army, Navy, Marines, and the Seamen's Union to see whether he had enlisted in the military as an interpreter. It also sent information to the *Forverts* and the *Sunday World Times* and asked the United Jewish Welfare Association for help in tracking him down. It is not clear from the record how his whereabouts were traced: it may have been by means of a man in Los Angeles who wrote about his friend's location and indicated that Paul wanted a picture of his daughter (in the file are the daughter's picture and letter, which were apparently not delivered to him), or it may have been by means of the Jewish Social Service Bureau in Los Angeles, whose 1930 letter contains information from a lengthy interview with Mr. R., who had been known to that agency since 1923.

That interview provided an account of the situation rather different from the one given by his wife. Mr. R. said that two years after the marriage they decided to get a divorce largely because of troubles stirred up by his in-laws—the father-in-law was a rabbi—who felt that he was not a good match for their daughter. He claimed that Mrs. R. obtained a *get* (Jewish divorce), that afterward he went to Philadelphia but visited his wife and child every weekend, bringing them money. When he had to change positions and could not continue his visits, he wrote to his wife but never received a reply. Thinking that with a *get* no civil divorce was required, he married again after a year, and he and his new wife had, at the time of this letter, two children, a four-year-old and an infant not yet a month old. He claimed to be heavily in debt because of the cost of the new birth and the price of cultivating his voice (he was an actor). He also said he would be happy if his daughter came to live with him and his family, and that he would do his utmost to assure her a good education. Since at the present he was heavily in debt, he suggested that, if he were sent the government insurance policy (worth $1,150), with his daughter designated to be the beneficiary when she turned twenty, he would borrow $250 to $300 on it and give the money to her, but would also replace the funds as soon as he was able. The letter from the Jewish Social Service Bureau noted that Mr. R. seemed very sincere, and it suggested to the National Desertion Bureau that his former wife obtain a civil divorce so that he could legalize his current marriage. In a 1931 interview with the Jewish Committee for Personal Social Service in Los Angeles, he claimed that, after the *get,* he had sent her $200 from a veteran's bonus and then an additional $50 a few months later.

Mrs. R. replied through a lawyer that she was very upset that her husband had married without a divorce, that she would never divorce him, would bring bigamy charges against him in California, and that his first obligation was not to his new family but to support their daughter. The case became more complicated when she, through her attorney and the Department of Public Welfare, filed to have Mr. R. extradited, and he was jailed for a period of time until California's governor refused to honor the extradition order. Mrs. R. remembered in 1931 that she had gone to a rabbi with her husband, but claimed not to remember whether or not it was for a *get,* though it seems implausible that the daughter of a rabbi would have gone to a rabbi with her husband and not remembered what that meeting was about and whether she had received a divorce. She now also stated that she did indeed receive the $200, but not the additional $50. In 1933, she finally agreed to a civil divorce, which was granted in 1935.

Mr. R. had had minor roles in several movies but was unable to find gainful employment during the years of the Great Depression, and was for a brief period supported by a temporary grant from the Motion Picture Relief Fund. Also his attempts to find work as an interpreter in the courts proved futile, and he was unable to support his second family. It is evident from the voluminous correspondence between the social agencies—the National Desertion Bureau, the Jewish Social Service Bureau of Los Angeles, the Jewish Committee for Personal Service in State Institutions of Southern California, the City of New York Department of Public Welfare, the District Attorney of King's County, Brooklyn, the Legal Aid Society—and various lawyers that there was an extensive effort not only to find Mr. R. but also to resolve the legal difficulties regarding his marriages and conditions for support. What also becomes clear from this case is that not all deserters were reprehensible scoundrels or merely weak men, nor did they all realize that they were deserters. Surely Mr. R. could have continued his attempt to locate his wife and daughter when there were no responses to his letters, but he did not. Yet it is also true that he did not leave his wife an *agune,* that he believed, as did many others, that the *get,* which his wife remembered only after being encouraged to do so, was a legal document that did not require a civil divorce decree.[38]

Retrieving Women's Voices

Not mentioned in the documents of National Desertion Bureau that I have read or, for that matter, in "A Gallery of Vanished Husbands," are the myriad problems faced by abandoned wives, including their inability to obtain a traditional Jewish divorce. In the 1915 report, however, in a segment entitled "Some Legal Aspects Met With in the Treatment of Cases," the issue of Jewish divorce is addressed, though not from the perspective of abandoned women. The Bureau's concern was to stop "the indiscriminate granting of rabbinical divorces or *'Ghets'*" by Orthodox rabbis to men who had not already obtained a civil divorce. It seems that those who had obtained a *get* often assumed they were free to remarry without the civil divorce, and the resulting bigamous marriages and the children born out of legal wedlock proved embarrassing to the community and complicated the Bureau's work.[39] No mention is made, however, of the inability of deserted women to obtain a *get* and the disabilities they suffered as a result.

One must turn to other public announcements and forums in newspapers to gain insight into the problems that confronted abandoned wives and children. Paid ads by women in the personals columns of newspapers begged husbands to return home or grant them divorces, and letters written by women and children appeared in *A bintl briv* (A Bundle of Letters), a popular daily feature in the *Forverts* in which letters were addressed to the editor but intended for the reading public. Begun in 1906, *A bintl briv* provided a forum for people to vent complaints and opinions, discuss personal and social problems, and elicit commentary and advice from the editor and, on occasion, from readers.

The texts of personals ads were usually brief, but even in their extreme brevity some of the major problems of deserted wives—such as their status as *agunes* or the welfare of their children—filtered through, as is apparent in two examples. In the first, one woman, Therez Briar, indicates that she is willing to forfeit her entire savings for a Jewish divorce; in the second, Jenny Magilevsky, resorts to a euphemism for divorce—"liberate me"—in her ad:

> William Briar! We have suffered enough already! Come home because of our child, or send me a *get* and I will give you everything I have saved—a few hundred dollars. Your wife, Therez Briar, 2387 East 37th St., Cleveland Ohio.

> I am looking for my husband, Dave Magilevsky, I assure you that I won't do anything to you. Just come home and liberate me. Just don't be afraid.—From me, Jenny.[40]

Signs of suffering and despair emerge from the few terse lines of these ads, but even given the ads' minimal format, distraught wives endeavor to comfort their transgressing mates and to entice them home. "Just don't be afraid" are the appeasing words of Jenny Magilevsky, and Ida Carnu soothingly says, "Everything will be all right" while informing her husband that their son is ill and wants his father.[41] A short news article in the January 4, 1915, *Forverts* with the caption "A Letter to Leo Feierstein from His Wife and Children" contains a wife's apology to her husband for having placed his picture in "A Gallery of Vanished Husbands"—she had no other way, she says, to tell him that she wanted him to return to her and their child. In the many apologies, pleas, and placating words that permeate these small texts, one senses not only the distress and apprehension of the women but self-condemnation and feelings of guilt as well. Yet despite the afflictions that desertion brought, almost all the women seemed prepared to receive their renegade husbands with open arms, if perhaps only to avoid remaining an *agune*.

The predicaments of abandoned wives and children are depicted somewhat more graphically and with greater specificity in the few letters about desertion printed in *A bintl briv*. Yet though the women have the opportunity to air their grievances there, desperate wives who hope for their spouses' return monitor their words so as not to antagonize or alienate their husbands. There is also the authoritative voice of the editor, Abraham Cahan, who, at times, intervenes with advice that may undermine a woman's expression of independence. Thus, even in the public forum of *A bintl briv*, women silence or muffle what they may want to communicate in response to the apparent or unapparent restraints operative in the dominant patriarchal culture.

The letters from the women communicate their anger and the pain and fear of having to cope alone with the burden of a family, but they also reveal their frightening realization that they have very little control over their lives: they are not able to provide adequate sustenance and care for their children, and their own lives seem to have come to dreadful dead ends. In a January 27, 1927, letter, a woman in Philadelphia who had been deserted years earlier addresses her husband directly, pleading with him to grant her a *get:*

> My husband! I beg you to remember your unfortunate wife and your three small children whom you deserted four and a half years ago. I don't ask for anything from you, only liberate me with a *get*. I think I have earned it that you liberate me from the iron chains in which you hold me shackled. May your conscience awaken in you and remind you of your unfortunate wife. In case you do not want to write to me directly, write through *A bintl briv*. I will do you no harm, I will be grateful to you for sending me a *get*. I hope to read your answer in *A bintl briv* that you will take pity on me and liberate me.

This is a perspective present neither in the miniature histories of men in "A Gallery of Vanished Husbands" nor in the National Desertion

Bureau's literature and agenda: a woman who has carried the burden for herself and three children for more than four years, an *agune* who experiences herself as a galley slave or prisoner, shackled and chained, begging her owner-husband to release her. Such is the overt content of her letter, but its objective, to obtain a divorce, may have also made it impossible for her to articulate the enormity of her affliction and despair for fear that she might anger her absent runaway spouse. "I will do you no harm" is no doubt a euphemism for "I will not demand child support from you" or "I will not have you arrested." Thus, even though she has the opportunity to speak of her plight, she remains a prisoner of her husband, of her status as *agune,* and has to continue the practice of self-censorship.

Other deserted women—though conscious of their *agune* status, but less concerned with obtaining a divorce than with finding support for themselves and their children—reveal more complex emotions and attitudes, albeit perhaps not always entirely consciously. An interesting and irate letter published January 17, 1908, delivers, in a few paragraphs, an ambivalent depiction of a relationship in which the woman loved her spouse but felt enslaved and servile within the marriage, perhaps even more so after her husband had abandoned the family:

> Worthy Editor of the *Forverts*!
>
> Have pity on me and my two small children and print this letter in the *Forverts*.
>
> Max! The children and I now say good-bye to you. You left us in such a terrible state. You have not a bit of compassion for us. For 6 years I loved you, loved you faithfully, took care of you like a loyal servant; for the entire 6 years I never had a happy day with you, and yet was always and am still faithful to you. Have you ever asked yourself why you left us, Max?
>
> You have always had compassion with forsaken women, used to say their terrible plight was due to the men who left them in dire need. And how did you act? You took me, a young, educated, honest girl, lived with me for six years, I bore you four children, and then finally you left me! You have made living orphans of your two children. Where is there love here? Who will raise them? Who will support us? Have you no pity for your own flesh and blood? Consider what you are doing. I want to write something more, but the tears choke me . . .
>
> Be advised, on Saturday the 18th of January I am leaving with my living orphans for Russia. We say good-bye to you and beg you to have pity on us and send us money to live.
>
> *From me your abandoned wife,*
> *Paulina Flast*
> *And your abandoned children,*
> *Sammy and Teddy*

The writer of this letter interprets her married life as a state of servitude and abuse, not, however, because she was bound to her husband by traditions of Jewish law, but rather because of the subservience to her husband. The inequality of the spouses and her vulnerability were apparently only corroborated by a husband who could simply disappear, leaving his wife with an even greater burden and with no provisions for herself or their young children. Although she does not, in this letter, call herself an *agune,* she compares her present condition of abandonment to that of forsaken women; and moreover, by describing her children as "living orphans"—parallel to the term "living widows," referring to *agunes*—she acknowledges the power of the man to enchain the woman. Thus, her decision to return to Russia is portrayed not as the beginning of a new undertaking but rather the end of a life that began with so much hope when she was "a young, educated, honest girl."

Two other letters printed were written by wives who have been forced by the circumstances of desertion to consider taking drastic measures that would further decimate their already fragmented and damaged families. In both instances the changes involve the circumstances of their children. In introductory remarks to a March 5, 1906, letter, the editor explains that a young woman named Lina Viner brought a letter into the *Forverts* office and asked that it be printed in *A bintl briv* because she knew that her husband read the feature. She had already placed an ad in the newspaper, to which her husband had responded without, however, including a forwarding address. She explained to the editor that her husband had written that he could not live with her because of her child from a former marriage. The letter to her husband announces that if he returns she is ready to give up the "foreign child," that is, her child from a former marriage (*dos fremde darf dikh nit drikn* [The foreign one need not oppress you]). The metaphor the woman uses in response to her husband's complaint—her older daughter is likened to a needle which presses or oppresses (the word *drikn* may mean either) and can be readily removed—dehumanizes the child but also the mother who, compelled by the ultimatum, uses it:

> To my husband Hymie Viner!
> I received your letter, but don't have the opportunity to answer you at your address because you did not send it to me. With only one thing have you done me a favor, that you reminded me that you read *A bintl briv* in the *Forverts.* I immediately went to the Editor's office of the *Forverts* newspaper, and the editor has been nice enough to permit my answer to you to be printed.

So I am writing you, that you don't have any reason to be afraid of me. You can choose whatever you please; I give you two alternatives: either send me a *get* or send me a letter and I will come to you with *your* child. The foreign child need not oppress you. It is very impractical of you. It presses [or oppresses] only when the needle is present. But if you remove the needle, it doesn't press [or oppress] any longer. Be a good father to your own child and forget the other one. Is it good that because of the other innocent child you should forget your own child who alas suffers so much? I have very much to write in reply to your letter, but I cannot write that to you in a letter that I have to send in such a strange way. I believe that everything that you have done is over, and in the future you can improve yourself. Regret is one of the greatest things in the world. If, however, you should have no regret, then there can be no greater murderous act in the world. Don't forget, before you take pity on me and answer me, that my whole life is now in your hands, and you must act as you wish. But I want to ask you: why are you taking such revenge on me? Write me a letter right away, and you should not start thinking that you can have any trouble because of me. Oh, no, no, I won't do that.

Your wife Lina [emphasis added]

Lina Viner's letter is fraught with ambivalence, wavering as it does between confidence and insecurity, criticism and misgivings, anger and reassurance. Although she offers her husband a resolution to his difficulty in a relatively dispassionate and confident manner, nuances of the text betray not only fear that her husband may not return despite her decision but also anger about the terrible concession she must make. The main paragraph begins and ends with comforting and reassuring words for her husband: he doesn't "have any reason to be afraid" of her, and "oh, no, no," he won't have "any trouble" because of her; and she does write that she forgives him for what he has done in the past and is confident he will improve. Yet she finds him vindictive, thinks he must experience regret for his actions, and knows that he has control over her entire existence. The incredible dilemma she faces is expressed in the oscillation between what seems to be her decision to eject the older, "foreign" child from the household, and statements which, in her effort to entice her husband to return, alternately chastise and pacify him. Even the seemingly brutal and heartless metaphor, in which her older child is likened to a needle that can easily be removed in order to alleviate her husband's discomfort, is one that establishes the kind of distance that may conceal from the husband both the inhumanity of his ultimatum and the incredible pain of her decision. Although Lina Viner has the opportunity to address her husband, both the public nature of the letter and her strong desire for her husband's return seem to prevent her from saying directly all that she wishes. Here is a woman who is strong enough to make the very grim decision to forfeit her older child when or perhaps because, in her state of abandonment, she recognizes her own powerlessness ("my whole life is now in your hands").

The second letter concerning a husband's disappearance that threatened to destroy the entire family appeared on September 15, 1910, and involved a mother of three children, the youngest of whom was an infant. Having recently emigrated from Canada with her husband, who then disappeared, and being unable to meet the residency requirements for aid from "the local Jewish charitable agencies," Mrs. Faykin was left with no means of subsistence. Because of the dire circumstances in this case and the sense of her aggravated helplessness and panic, this letter provides a less ambiguous depiction of the bitter material reality experienced by many deserted women:

> My husband, N. Faykin, deserted me and our three small children, leaving us in the most desperate need and misery, left not even a piece of bread for the children and, in addition, debts at the grocery and butcher shop, and last month's rent unpaid.
>
> I am not so much complaining about the loss of my husband as about the pain of our little children, who beg for food, and I the helpless mother am not in a position to still their hunger. I am healthy and young, I can and want to work in order to feed my dear children. But unfortunately I am tied down with my six-month-old baby. I looked for an institution that would perhaps take my little baby into its care, but my friends say that would be sure death for my child and a broken heart for me, the unfortunate mother.
>
> The local Jewish charitable agencies are allowing me and my children to die of hunger. Because my devoted husband brought me over from Canada just four months ago, I therefore do not yet deserve to eat their bread soaked with tears, and to which I am not accustomed.
>
> Therefore, I have come to the conclusion that in order to save my innocent little children from hunger and cold I would rather break my maternal heart and sell my heavenly beautiful children to those who will assure them a happy home. I don't want to sell them for money; I only want to give them away for bread, to have enough food, and for warm clothes for their little bodies. And I, the broken unfortunate young mother, agree to sign the contract with my heart's blood, so that they will belong to the good people who will treat them tenderly.
>
> Those who want to and can assure my children a happy home should apply to me at any time.
>
> *Mrs. Faykin*
> 1900 *Milwaukee Ave. Chicago, Illinois*

Unlike most of the abandoned women who, through the National Desertion Bureau and publicity in the newspapers, sought their spouses and seemed ready to reunite with them either because of or despite the adversity they had suffered, Mrs. Faykin expresses no desire for her husband's return. Perhaps because of the disastrous circumstances she faces and the fear that her family will not survive, her focus is concentrated almost solely on the needs of her young children, whose welfare was jeopardized by the charitable services she criticizes: the institution (probably an orphanage or charitable day care center) that she heard would not adequately care for her baby, and the "Jewish charitable agencies" that refused aid because of a deficient residency requirement. Indeed, the failures of the institutional resources are, according to this narrative, immediately responsible for her decision to give up her children to anyone who will provide for their basic needs and "treat them tenderly."

The reply of the editor, Abraham Cahan, does respond to the urgent circumstances outlined in Mrs. Faykin's letter, but also interprets those circumstances from the vantage point of a collective authoritative position that, in essence, undermines the personal voice and agency of the writer. Never addressing her directly, the editor speaks, as he usually does, to an audience at large:

> Is it possible that there is a person in the world whose heart would not be shattered reading this horrible offer to sell children and whose soul would not be set ablaze in a fire of holy fury against a world in which something like this is possible?!
>
> The first curse is directed toward such an inhuman father. But who can know what is happening there? Maybe he couldn't help it. Maybe he himself is unhappy. And even if he is just a scoundrel—there are some like that—the question remains, what should a mother do with little children who have the misfortune of having a scoundrel for a husband and father? Because of that should they be punished with death by starvation? Is that a human system that leaves a mother with babies in such a despairing situation that there is no other help for her than to advertise her children for sale? For heaven's sake, is that not enough to ignite in every person's heart a fire of hellish hatred for such a system?!
>
> From New York we can do no more than ask our friends and readers in Chicago that they should look into the situation of the unfortunate person and try to help her so that she herself can remain a mother to her children. She is young and healthy and it must be possible for her to get some employment that will enable her to raise her babies.
>
> What is to be said about her husband we cannot know. But no matter what happened there—if he is not a bloody tiger in a human skin, then this letter, we hope, will not remain without an effect on him.

Quite apart from the fact that this response is directed to a broad reading public and speaks not a word of solace or encouragement to the letter writer, it actually circumvents the issues raised in the letter and substitutes another agenda. While the editor exhibits his characteristic indignation and righteousness about the evils of this society and the heartlessness of the world, he evades the serious charges about the shortcomings of charitable organizations, including Jewish ones. He may avoid Mrs. Faykin's criticism because he does not want to offend the Jewish agencies—they were, after all, almost exclusively the domain of well-established men—that did not resolve this woman's terrible situation. And though he does indicate that the "first curse is directed toward such an inhuman father," he finds, even in such an extreme situation as this, at least as much sympathy for the father as he does for the distraught mother—"but who can know what is happening there? Maybe he couldn't help it. Maybe he himself is unhappy," he comments, as though this woman's letter were essentially articulating her unhappiness rather than her overwhelming concern for her children's survival. In addition, in response to this rare instance in which the woman indicates no desire for the return of her husband, the editor, who may have been either oblivious to the woman's will or found it inappropriate, seems to want the father to return—"this letter, we hope, will not remain without an effect on him." In an interesting and very disturbing 1971 sequel to Abraham Cahan's reply to this letter, the translator and editor of an English selection of letters from *A bintl briv,* Isaak Metzker, appended a curious sentence to the original, making explicit what the editor of the *Forverts* merely implies: "We hope, though, that this letter will reach him and he will return to aid them."[42] Since Mrs. Faykin's letter is atypical among those from the deserted wives—that is, it does not request the return of the husband—this editorial addition, like Cahan's response, undermines the woman's wishes, betraying either insensitivity to her will or a belief her stance is unacceptable.

The Children Speak

The concerns of deserted children are also rarely heard in public forums like *A bintl briv,* in part because children were usually not yet readers of newspapers, but also because, as the unfledged in society—even unnamed in the Gallery and the Bureau literature—they were often relegated to the margins of the adult world. Children, like women, were generally viewed merely as anonymous markers in the case histories of deserters. There are, however, a few letters from abandoned children that appeared in *A bintl briv*. Two striking ones—one from a nine-year-old boy whose father had recently deserted the family, the other from a young woman of twenty-one whose father had left when she was eight years old—reveal not only how much they share the anger, fear, and powerlessness of their abandoned mothers but also the particular vulnerability and shame of those still too young or fragile to come to terms with the devastation in the family. On January 8, 1915, there appeared in *A bintl briv* a letter from the nine-year-old boy which, the editor notes in a brief preamble, "was written in the English of a child, and we had it translated verbatim into Yiddish so that the sadness which is expressed in his naive childlike words should have a stronger effect on his father's heart":

> Please, Mr. Editor, dear sir, allow me a small place for a few words to my father. My father left the house on December 28, 1914. He left my mother sick because of her nerves. She feels very bad, crying because she wanted to take her life. Because he left, he had no reason for leaving. The small baby cries for her papa, my younger brother also cries for my father: papa, come back; and my mother cries when he says that. . . . Why didn't you ask mother about that? Come home, no one will take revenge on you. Come home, no one will say many bad words about you. Everything will be fixed in the office.[43] Apart from the office everything else will be fixed. Write mother a letter, come home and be a father to the children.
>
> I am a nine-year-old boy. I have written it in the newspaper.
> *Your devoted Philly*
>
> I also want to thank Mr. Editor. Please, Mr. Editor, write my letter in a hurry, please, because we don't have anything to eat.

The two segments—one addressed to the father and clearly intended for publication, the other written to the editor and probably not meant to be printed—are very different from one another. The first, which concludes with "Your devoted Philly," appeals to the father to return home because the mother and children all lament his absence and long for him. Like the deserted wives of the previous letters, Philly exhibits anger and despair about the condition of the family, tempered by reassurances to his father that upon returning "no one will take revenge" or malign him, and that he will suffer no legal difficulties. By addressing the father not as the breadwinner necessary to the family's material existence but as the person in the household whose presence is wanted by all, Philly underscores the central importance of the loved and desired parent. In fact, had the second portion of the letter, that addressed to the editor, not been printed, readers would have had no indication that the family was impoverished. Though perhaps not entirely intentional, the strategy to entice the father home—an appeal to the father's desire to be accepted and wanted, not needed—is in itself remarkable for a child so young; but the implicit self-censorship, the muffling of his annoyance and anger ("he had no reason for leaving," "Why didn't you ask mother about that?") betrays the afflictions of a nine-year-old who must now care for younger siblings and a distraught mother. The portion addressed to the editor, which communicates what seems to be the most urgent problem of the family—"we don't have anything to eat"—in fact highlights the extraordinary self-restraint and cautious formulation of young Philly's letter to his father. But it also reveals how difficult it is for the powerless and the dispossessed to communicate what they wish and need when confronting a person who seems to control their destiny. To attain their goal in a situation like this, powerless people apparently need to monitor their speech carefully.

The letter from the twenty-one-year-old woman—she calls herself "Rosie" within the text but signs it merely as "the oldest daughter of the father who deserted"—appeared in *A bintl briv* on April 7, 1922. Of its three parts, the initial segment addressed to the editor is the longest and explains her circumstances; the second, a short paragraph, is an appeal addressed to her father; and the third is directed to her father's compatriots from Volynia who might know of his whereabouts. It is perhaps one of the most interesting and important letters about desertion from the perspective of its victims, because it supplies information about some of the long-term devastating consequences of desertion that afflict family members; but it also reveals in rather stark terms how difficult it is for the abandoned to express themselves candidly to the absent father or husband:

Dear Mr. Editor of the *Forverts:*
I have heard much about the good that your worthy newspaper does through its *A bintl briv;* therefore I too have decided to write a letter: perhaps I will be one of the thousands who have been helped through you.

I am a twenty-one-year-old girl, born in America. As young as I am, I have already experienced a great amount of trouble. My own dear father created my suffering. I don't know whether he is entirely to blame for my unhappy life, but he is the one who directly caused my troubles. This is how it happened.

When I was eight years old, my father left my mother with their three children. I am the oldest of the three children. What kind of upbringing we had considering the conditions, anyone can easily imagine. My mother used to leave us young children alone for a whole day and would go away to earn a living. Coming home worn out from a day of hard work, she first used to start to attend to the children. One can easily imagine how much she could do for us. One can't describe what we suffered during this bitter time.

But, worthy Editor, what took place is past: it is already over. We have in any case overcome. Now I am a grown young woman and can hold my own. But the thought of my father's disappearance plagues me. I am a very capable girl, even though I grew up without a father, and one can also say without a mother: because my dear mother did not have any time to give to me. Being a capable, refined girl, there is no lack of young people who are ready to marry me. But when a boy asks about my father, I don't know what to reply. It is not comfortable to tell a lie, that my father died; and to tell the truth, that he is alive but ran away from us children and our mother, is even more uncomfortable.

Thus, worthy Editor, I would very much want to have my father, if that is only possible. We don't need him to support us: we need him only that our lives should not be miserable because of him. The thought pains me dreadfully, that when the right young man appears and will ask: "where is the father?" What will I answer then? I can find no solution as to what to do then.

Worthy Editor! I beg you to print my letter and to appeal to my father, that if he is still alive somewhere, he should return to his family. He will surely not regret it when he sees his children, how beautifully they have grown up. I also ask you, worthy Editor, to allow me to write a few words to my father.

Dear father! If you are alive and read this letter, I hope that it will awaken in your heart a spark of paternal love for us, your deserted forlorn children, and you will call us. You will enjoy seeing how your little Rosie has become a grown and beautiful young woman. You will, dear father, be proud of me.

I turn also to our compatriots born in Anapolia, Volynia, they should let us know if they see or have perhaps heard about my father. His name is Abraham Sidman. He is the son of Shaul the shoemaker. He is just 6' tall, heavy, and a little pockmarked. He is about 48 years old. Whoever knows about this man should please be so friendly as to let us know through the *Forverts*. I thank in advance all those who make the effort to help me find my father.

Very sincerely,
The oldest daughter of the father who deserted

According to this young woman's letter, her unhappiness derives principally from the consequences of her father's absence, which divested her of parental care and a loving childhood and what she considers a socially sanctioned complete family. Indeed, it is her inability to reconstitute a traditional family of two parents that haunts her adult personal relationships and propels her to write to *A bintl briv*. Her signature, "The oldest daughter of the father who deserted," indicates graphically an identity inextricably bound to the father who, she admits, "created my suffering." From Rosie's perspective, this tie to the absent parent presents her with a dilemma that can have no resolution unless, of course, the father returns, a dilemma that will persist until she is able to introduce him to her suitors. Nowhere does she entertain an alternative solution, such as, for example, the possibility that her father's absence will cease disrupting her current and future life when she can tell her friends that her father abandoned the family, and that, despite great adversity, the family thrived. Such an alternative would no doubt cause her great difficulty, because the intensity of her experience as a victim—a daughter abandoned by her father and still ashamed of that event—has apparently not enabled her to conceive of an end to her victimization apart from the recovery of the father.

The happy resolution, which Rosie anticipates from her father's return after an absence of thirteen years, rests on the prevailing ideology of the patriarch's primary significance for the well-being of the family. Although it is clear from her letter that the family did persevere without the father, albeit with great difficulty, Rosie nevertheless expects the father's very belated return to actuate family wholeness, or at least an *image* of it, which she imagines will rescue her from the shame of having been deserted. Curiously, like many victimized women and children, she has internalized the shame that rightfully belongs to the deserting father. Since shame, which persists in her life, is usually experienced within an arena of watchers or witnesses who are perceived as judgmental, Rosie opts to rid herself of shame by reconstituting a socially acceptable family with the father, instead of, let us say, identifying her own strength and dignity apart from her father and apart from the external evaluators.

The rhetorical dynamics in Rosie's letter are not unlike those found more muted in letters of other victims of desertion—that is, the articulation of anger and blame ameliorated by reassurances and loving enticements directed at the deserter. Rosie, however, does not, as others have done, practice self-censorship, but expresses with stunning forthrightness not only resentment and ire about what she has suffered but also her almost painfully deferential pleas to her father, and promises gratification should he return. On one level, the conscious effort to regulate language seems to be intended primarily to entice and not offend the deserter. But, by noting how well brought up and capable she is, it also functions to dismiss any feelings of culpability for the desertion that the deserter or victim may harbor. Thus Rosie writes, "He will surely not regret it when he sees his children, how beautifully they [she and her sisters] have grown up"; or "You will, dear father, be proud of me." What becomes agonizingly conspicuous in such remarks are the control that Rosie's father, by and in his absence, exerts over her life, as well as her apparent inability to wrest her life from this patriarchal ghost to which she has granted power. Since absence of the father does not foster adequate interchange and resolution within the family, women and children, who had already been socialized to value men and to rely upon them for material and cultural survival, are all too often left—as Rosie was—in a social vacuum when the husband or father deserts. Indeed, the rhetoric of these letters written by the abandoned disclose the lengths women and children were willing to go in order to bring back the patriarch, reconstitute the socially acceptable family (or at least its fragile image), and thereby erase the deadly and literal no-man's-land they felt that they inhabited.

Voice of the Victimizers, the Deserters

One final letter that is significant for understanding the gendered differences in perceptions of desertion and its public representation was published in *A bintl briv* on February 17, 1910, and was signed by thirty-seven men who were incarcerated for not supporting their wives and children. It is not known, of course, how many of these men failed to fulfill court-ordered obligations to wives from whom they were divorced or separated and how many were deserters, but one may assume from their threat—that they will never again return and the women will remain "eternal *agunes*"—that there were a number of married men or deserters among them:

> Worthy Editor of the *Forverts:*
> This is the voice of many unfortunate Jewish men who are buried and not covered by earth, who are bound and not chained, who are quiet and not mute; who feel their heart beat like all people and yet are not like all other people. If they looked at their striped clothing, if they looked at the dirty narrow cots on which they lie, at their fellow brothers in the cells, drunken beat-up Christians, from the lowest levels of human society—people who long ago lost their human worth, then their limbs turn to ice. They feel disheartened, downtrodden, debased, and in despair—and for what reason?

For the horrible crime—for being poor, for not being able to satisfy the crazy whims of their wives, and because of that they sit here. For that they languish here, stamped with the name "prisoner," despised by humanity, robbed of their freedom, and treated like dogs.

We ask you, Mr. Editor, to print, to publicize our letter, so that you give your readers, especially your women readers the possibility of knowing what is happening here and how we live. This letter is not written with ink, but with the blood of our hearts. We write this letter coughing and groaning because of the polluted air we breathe in these filthy cells, with broken bones from the crooked cots on which we lie, with sick stomachs from the hard leather that is given us instead of meat. We are writing you this letter, and the fear of sickness hovers over us, and therefore we ask you, Mr. Editor, not to put aside this letter for long and to publish it immediately.

Aside from all the plagues mentioned in the lists of curses *[toykhekhe]* in the Torah and all the horrors and degradations which Moses poured out on Jewish heads and all means of torment which the Inquisition thought up to torture the heretics, the non-support plague is the worst and most danger-ous torture for an unfortunate person. For the smallest foolishness they grab a person on the street or from the house, they put him in the workhouse, and they don't give him a chance to defend himself or save himself from his misfortune. In the worst times of the Russian reaction a person was not as insecure about his tomorrow as here in America because of the wives. It is as easy for a Jewish woman to place her husband in a workhouse as to try on a pair of gloves. In the whole world there is no such legal injustice for him as there is here in America, in regard to women's cases [i.e., alimony and child support]. And what do women think? If they think that good people will pity them and feed them, then they made a great big mistake. Good people can only help them to bury the men, but to give them money! . . . Why! if they, the women, think that the men will purify themselves after six months and come out good, sweet, and loving, then they have made an even greater mistake. Of the tens of Jewish men who are imprisoned here, not one of them will return to his wife when he is free again. But we believe the greatest crime is committed by the Jewish charities. The Jewish charities have sympa-thy for a miserable woman who stretches out her hand to them and asks for something to live on when her husband sits in the workhouse. They forget, however, that they are manufacturing *agunes* and living orphans. By helping the woman for a month, they drive away the husband for a year. As soon as they hand the woman a free and easy dollar, as soon as the woman knows the charities will not let her fall, the woman doesn't care that the man's life becomes miserable in the workhouse. She's got it good. She eats and drinks and amuses herself and doesn't even think about what her husband is doing in the workhouse.

It is therefore your duty, Mr. Editor, as editor of a newspaper which is read for the most part by the working class, by that class which more than all other classes delivers candidates for the workhouse and *agunes* and living orphans—-to publish this letter so as to warn all Jewish women who walk about with the horrible idea of burying their husbands in the workhouse in order to still their revenge. They harm themselves more than their husbands. That they pluck out two of their eyes for one of their husband. That they make themselves miserable for an eternity, that they drive away their husbands for their entire life, that the blood of their husbands and children falls on their heads, and they themselves are guilty of all the troubles they bring on themselves and their children.

I, the writer of these lines, am also a victim of a woman's case. My wife reads the *Forverts,* and one of our men receives the *Forverts* in the workhouse every day. We ask you to be so good and publish this letter to protect hundreds of other women and men from a similar misfortune. The women must know that the workhouse is a poor means of improving the men. This game of imprisonment is a double-edged sword and it cuts one side as well as the other, and running to the court for every triviality is a very small remedy for a man.

Above all I want to write to the women whose husbands are already in the workhouse: if they, the women, will not let their husbands out for Passover and if they let their husbands sit here in the workhouse on the greatest Jewish holiday, all the men have sworn that they are ready to sit again and again, and they will not go back to their wives, who will have to take into consideration that they will remain eternal *agunes* and will awaken not a spark of sympathy in the men's hearts. If we should see our wives die of hunger in the streets, absolutely die of hunger, we will not turn around to look at them. We are ready to suffer our entire lives, and we must show that we are human beings and not some small dogs that ladies can pet or smite as much as and when they want.

We also ask you, worthy editor, that you not hold this letter for a long time and print it as soon as possible, because we have nothing else to do here, and your paper helps to pass the lonely time.
Yours devoted,
[thirty-seven names follow]
These are all Jews who are in the workhouse for wife-cases. Those imprisoned for other things have nothing to do with this letter.

The editor replies:

What the people say about the effects of prison is completely correct. That is not the only crooked thing about the present facilities. They are almost all idiotic. They reach precisely the opposite goal that they were meant to reach.

But that is only one side of the question. There is, however, another side: the weighty crime of many men who do not want to do their duty to their family! Of course there are among the 37 some who couldn't help themselves. But the few suffer because of the rest of them. Usually it doesn't pay for the woman to have the breadwinner of her family imprisoned as soon as she sees that he is looking for a way to feed them. What they say about living it up from the charities is nonsense. What a poor way of life is such a "living it up"! When she has him jailed is when she knows for sure that he doesn't want to do anything for her and she will surely not lose anything if he remains in jail. And when the family's father does not want to support his family, that is in today's conditions the most horrible crime. We will write about this in detail another time, also about what must be done with such men. In the meantime, in any case, we advise the women to free their husbands for Passover.[44]

The rhetoric of the husbands' letter reveals much about the complex ways in which men perceived themselves, their family responsibilities, their wives, the children who, apart from a single reference, are absent from this text, and the activities of the courts and charitable organizations. The gender differential is here prominently articulated through dialectics of freedom and confinement, of power and powerlessness. The signatories are convicts who are all too conscious not only of their own confinement and former impoverished position in society but also of their lack of control over their own lives and over their wives or former wives, court rulings, and charitable support received by their abandoned families. They do not, however, reflect on the consequences of their behavior or consider the condition of their families, but cast blame on everyone else for their own offenses and threaten to enchain their wives forever in a permanent *agune* state. It is perhaps the sense of their actual powerlessness, highlighted and exacerbated by incarceration, that prompts them to perceive their wives as not only living luxuriously on very minimal welfare funds but also wielding power, as being powerful enough to have the men confined to jail and to keep them there. The powerlessness of the men notwithstanding, this letter is permeated with the language of self-aggrandizement as well as abuse and intimidation directed especially at the wives. There is not a word of concern for the welfare of their children, no sign of remorse for not having supported or not being able to support their families. Indeed, they regard their nonsupport as "the smallest foolishness," think their detention is due to the "crazy whims" of their wives, feel degraded not because of their transgressions but because of their incarceration, and berate charitable agencies for helping the women. Philanthropists Morris Waldman and Boris Bogen thought that supplying deserted families with inadequate funds for survival would encourage compassionate deserters to support their families,[45] but there is no indication that these letter writers care at all about the welfare of their families.

Although there is no suggestion in this letter that the men are willing to provide for their impoverished families, they nevertheless ask
that no aid be given them because, they claim, it helps the woman to
live happily and well without a husband. Of course, the caseload of
the National Desertion Bureau, the numbers of women seeking their
husbands through newspaper venues, and letters in *A bintl briv* testify
to the contrary: the families are indeed impoverished and desperately
want the husbands and fathers to return.

The denial of all responsibility for their behavior and for the welfare
of their families and the abusive and intimidating attacks against their
wives stand in sharp contrast to the letters of women who express anger only very reluctantly and tentatively. But the prisoners' letter also
suggests why the women and children try to mollify their spouses by
repressing the psychological and material destitution the family experiences. Even though—or perhaps because—the men are poor, generally
powerless, and imprisoned, their letter discloses that they nonetheless
know themselves to be powerful vis-à-vis women, for they can always
leave their children in the care of their wives, disappear once again, and
the women "will remain eternal *agunes*." Thus, they have the power to
flee and, in doing so, permanently enchain their wives. The men may be
to blame for denying divorces to their wives, but they hold the women
responsible for becoming *agunes* and accuse the Jewish charitable organizations of complicity in "manufacturing *agunes* and living orphans"
by helping the abandoned families.

It is also ironic that the men attempt to negotiate their release from
prison by means of a nefarious ultimatum: should they not be released in
time for Passover, the commemoration of the liberation of the Hebrews
from enslavement in Egypt, their wives would be subjected to the yoke
of being eternal *agunes*. Women in this circumstance may seem to have
power—the ability to release their husbands from imprisonment—but
they are still regarded as property that men can use as pawns to acquire
their freedom. The text reveals that, no matter how impotent or subjugated the Jewish male is, he always knows that, although he does not
possess power when confronted by the legal system or a more prominent class of Jewish men, he is nevertheless powerful in relation to the
wife whose marital destiny he owns. This letter makes it clear that the
politics of gender among traditional Jews is the politics of property and
power, which may explain why even imprisoned men are brazen in their
fulminations against women and why, in their letters, victimized wives
and children tend to reassure and placate their husbands or fathers.

The editor's response to this letter is also problematic. On the one hand, it notes "the weighty crime of many men who do not want to do their duty to their family," acknowledges that the charity women receive amounts to a pittance, and concedes that there may indeed be "among the 37 some who couldn't help themselves." On the other hand, however, it concludes by advising the women "to free their husbands for Passover," advice that closes the ranks of men—the transgressors and the powerful "worthy Editor" of a very popular working-class newspaper—against women. Nowhere in his reply does the editor ask the men to earn their release by paying alimony and child support so that their families might also commemorate Passover in an appropriate manner. Complying with the editor's advice would, of course, affirm the power of the threat-wielding transgressors and render powerless the maltreated women, whose courage and resolve in seeking justice would be undermined even further by yielding to the intimidation of their husbands.

A discourse of domination, representing men as central and predominant social actors, is subtly depicted in the pamphlets and reports of the National Desertion Bureau, in "A Gallery of Vanished Husbands," in the letter of the thirty-seven prisoners, and in the editorial responses to the letters. The few women's voices that can be retrieved from their advertisements and their letters to the *Forverts* editor are all too often muted as a result of their vulnerability within an androcentric society and Jewish community. They are also muted because of the forms of resistance and protection they have adopted in response to the discourse of domination and intimidation, namely, self-censorship, pacification, and, at times, deadly silence. Given all the obstacles they faced, it seems serendipitous or simply miraculous that the plight of these women was heard or mentioned at all in public forums.

CHAPTER 5

An Autobiography of Turmoil

Abandoned Mother, Abandoned Daughter

It was not easy to decide whether a personal biographical essay would find a comfortable and useful place in a scholarly text on representations of desertion. While such an inclusion might be discordant, the possibility was also enticing, interesting, and could prove productive. After all, if the victims of desertion are forlorn wives whose lives were shattered as a result of their husbands' behavior, then the victimization that deserted wives endure may also be the tribulation that abandoned children inherit and endure. The woes of these children can be read in the letters to *A bintl briv*, where one learns how seriously children are challenged by their struggles with poverty and social stigma, by the inability either to accept their lot in life or to change it, and by the ever-present, haunting fear of rejection. Although the effects of desertion leave their mark most noticeably on the wives who must reconfigure their lives as best they can, the ramifications do not stop there. Desertion afflicts many family members, inhabits every crevice in the household, and often contaminates friendships and communal life.

When I decided to write an account of desertion in my life, I intended to focus almost exclusively on my mother's story as an abandoned wife and only peripherally on its effects on me. For most of my life I considered my mother to be the sole victim of abandonment, because since childhood I had not perceived myself as maltreated or abused, certainly not by an invisible father's behavior. I actually thought I had completely erased from my life the man who had exited when I was just a year old, and I firmly believed that my stern refusal ever to be a victim shielded me from being tainted by the absent and unknown parent. While gathering the memories and shards of my mother's experiences for this account, however, I noticed that I often did not know what she actually thought or felt. Moreover, my presence intruded everywhere into her story: interacting, narrating, commenting, and attempting to analyze and interpret. Although my mother's story was clearly not mine to tell, I thought I could perhaps write our story—an intertwining narrative of a deserted mother and daughter—if, that is, the armor in which I had enclosed myself could be breached. My mother's story would then have to be filtered through the experiences of a daughter who refused to be, or to be seen as, a victim, and who had to come to grips with a mother who saw herself shrouded in unrelenting victimization.

In the narrative of my life that I have harbored these many years, the events of our lives and my memories of them have congealed into familiar episodic vignettes about a mother who needed to maintain complete control over her child and a resolute daughter who recognized no claims on herself, no vulnerabilities, no rejection. That a candid encounter with my mother's needs as well as my heretofore suppressed frailties and fears of rejection has come so late is probably indicative of how heavily defended were the ramparts I had constructed to protect myself from the consequences of both abandonment and an especially engulfing parent. My attempt now to explore the interlocking lives of an abandoned mother and daughter requires that I tolerate the unraveling of my standard narrative, particularly about my youth, and expose the relational areas that remained concealed from the time my father ceased to exist for me.

In childhood and for more than thirty years after, I told anyone who asked about my father that he had died, but I always knew that he was probably alive and had in fact abandoned my mother and me when I was an infant. Although all our family members knew that he had deserted us, my mother had cautioned me always to tell anyone else that he was dead. She was ashamed to admit the truth and always felt that she had lost our relatives' respect because she was "not able to keep a husband." My mother was not religious, never referred to herself as an *agune,* and seemed not to worry about getting a divorce or remarrying, but the shame that generally haunts *agunes* did not spare her. A few decades ago, while teaching a class in Yiddish literature in which some of the texts dealt with *agunes,* many of whom were deserted wives, I was confronted with students who were incredulous to learn not only that Jewish men could be deserters but also that such reprehensible conduct was portrayed as familiar behavior in the community, not as an anomaly. The students seemed never to have questioned the accepted lore about the unswerving devotion of Jewish husbands and fathers. I suggested that they read Irving Howe's recently published *World of Our Fathers,* especially the segment entitled "Boarders, Desertion, Generational Conflict," in which, referring to poor Jewish immigrant families, Howe observes that the "most severe sign of disturbance was the persistent desertion of families by immigrant husbands."[1] Howe also notes the establishment, in 1911, of the National Desertion Bureau, the Jewish organization which, until midcentury, actively pursued scofflaw husbands.

This reference to the National Desertion Bureau caused me to remember my mother taking me as a very young child to its offices to ask for help in locating my father. From early childhood I had erased from consciousness this memory, along with any concern about my father. He first deserted my mother when she was pregnant, reconciled with her when I was six months old, and finally left without a trace when I was about a year old. Although he walked away without a word and left my mother penniless, she took upon herself the shame that was rightly his. She spoke of him often to me, almost always reciting a litany of his negative characteristics and objectionable conduct; and it was his bad qualities that, when she was angered by my behavior or while trying to discipline and reform me, she found reflected in my attitude and demeanor. She never uttered a positive word about him, at least not in my presence, so I knew just what she meant when she reproached me with "You're just like your father!" This continuous accusation was not a position I could tolerate, because, although I did not want to be a victim like my mother, I certainly could not imagine myself a victimizer like my father. Yet those rebukes didn't bother me much at the time, perhaps because I had already disposed of the idea that my father had any importance in my life. Although I was told that, in accordance with New York State law, he had been declared legally dead after an absence of seven years, for me he had ceased to exist long before that.

In my youth I never understood why my mother felt shame because we were abandoned, and I developed a gamelike approach to my absent father: if anyone asked about the cause of his death, I would smite him with a different terrible disease or fatality each time. It was only when I was in my thirties and already a professor that I finally gave up the game, having decided that the secret about my father's miserable behavior could, and should, be made public, if only to free me from the onus of lying and creating new deadly ailments for his demise. I liberated myself by speaking the truth to a friend, admitting my father's desertion, burying the saga of 101 different wretched deaths, exhuming him and restoring him as a person in my life, albeit an unknown absent person. What was for me a rather rewarding or at least remunerative episode—one last winning round of the game—occurred just a few years ago when my doctor recommended a procedure for which, he said, I would have to cover the cost unless there was some history of cancer in the family, because my medical insurance would not otherwise pay for it. After I told him I didn't know my father, the doctor asked whether he might have succumbed to that ailment, I agreed that he might have and, in so doing, saved several hundred dollars—finally, after all these years, I had received a child support payment, even if it was from the insurance industry.

My mother never overcame the humiliation she felt as a deserted wife. She was born Rokhel (later Americanized to Rose) in a small shtetl in Eastern Europe, probably in the waning years of the nineteenth century—she never knew precisely when she was born, because her parents waited until there were three or more children (she was one of thirteen) to go off to the registrar in the city. Although it was not usual in her small community for a girl to receive an education, her mother insisted that Rokhel, the oldest daughter, be allowed to attend the tutorials of her two older brothers, though not actually to participate as a student. She learned to read Hebrew and to read and write Yiddish. She could also carry on a perfunctory conversation in Russian and Polish. My mother's stories about her mother led me to believe that my grandmother possessed a strong radical streak: after all, she made sure that her daughters gained as much of an education as was possible for a poor family in a backwoods shtetl. When my grandfather was absent, she not only allowed her son, who was involved in revolutionary activities, to hold political meetings in the house—in itself a very dangerous act—but also insisted that my mother be present. Never actually openly defying the authority of her husband, and ostensibly conforming to the expected behavior of a Jewish wife, she nonetheless managed to undermine his stubborn conservative and traditional demands on the family.

One of the stories my mother repeatedly told about her youth provides some insight into the sense of oppression and rejection that she felt throughout her life. She usually told this story to illustrate how she had become inured to a life in which she was harnessed to the task of survival, how in the course of living she lost a sense of herself and her abilities. When she was barely ten years old, she was sent to a town far from her home to work as a maid. She was terribly lonely, she recalled, and had to work very hard every day. When a year had passed and she had just received her annual wages, her father, whom she feared more than admired, arrived and asked her for the money she had earned. He had the opportunity to buy a cow, and a cow was a blessing for a large, impoverished family in a Polish shtetl. Without hesitating—she was only a child, after all—she gave him her year's earnings, he bought the cow, and she continued to work. A few months later a letter from her mother brought the bad news: the cow had grown sick and died. Although at times she recounted this story to acquaint me with her difficult childhood and to illustrate how a dutiful daughter behaves, I believe she really wanted me to understand how she saw herself in the world. This was for her the earliest bitter memory of repeated victimization, which later, of course, included desertion by her husband and a very precarious life raising a child alone during the Great Depression.

Throughout my mother's life, this story about her past seemed to merge with her present. Even in her very old age, when she once balked at being misused by others she nonetheless still perceived herself as someone who had been victimized. At that time she wrote in a letter to me that she had ceased to communicate with a relative who, she felt, was abusing her generosity. "The cow is dead," she wrote in Yiddish, in which the term she used for "cow" (beheyme) may also signify "fool" or "dolt." "There is no one left to milk." She had, it seems, internalized so thoroughly the helplessness and exploitation she had experienced as a very young child, identifying even with the unfortunate cow, that she could find no way out of an experience of inevitability. Conflating past and present preserved a view of her life and perhaps her world as unchanging and unchangeable, and this isolated her in a condition that seemed hopeless, in a story impervious to time, process, and progress. My mother had accomplished much in her more than eighty years: she was able to support herself from the time she was ten and to contribute to the welfare of others; alone she reared a child from infancy; she spoke and read several languages; in her sixties she learned to drive a car; in her seventies she began to weave baskets of pine needles and straw that were beautiful, useful, and valuable; in her eighties she took a course in fine tailoring; and to the very end she was jogging more than a mile a day and fighting the bureaucracies, institutions, and practices she considered unjust or unfair. These obvious abilities notwithstanding, she never realized that the frequently reiterated story about her childhood might be understood differently, that, for example, even as a ten-year-old she was someone who through her work was able to do what even adults could not, to pay for a cow. While she often enough championed and fought for her own rights and those of others, to the end of her days she also saw herself and her life mirrored in a story that had neither development nor conclusion, a story about a cow that was repeatedly sold and bought and died too soon.

My mother's two older brothers were the first family members to emigrate to the United States, and later, after settling in Detroit, they sent a ship's ticket and visa for my mother, who was not yet eighteen years old. It was probably in 1912 that she traveled alone to Hamburg, where she was to embark on the transatlantic journey. But, having no transit visa for Germany, she was arrested in Hamburg and incarcerated for weeks. She remembered being terrified and remaining in jail, not knowing what to do or to whom to turn. A local rabbi appeared at the jail, bailed her out, and allowed her to live with his family while she waited for proper travel documents. Her life in the "New World"—in Detroit, St. Louis, Boston, and New York—was very difficult, filled with a series of arduous jobs: in shoe factories, clothing shops, restaurants, ice cream parlors, and, finally, in garment factories as a seamstress or, in the demeaning parlance of the needle trade, an "operator," that is, someone who operated machines.

My mother was probably in her mid- to late thirties and had already been engaged to marry several times when she met my father in Detroit. From the few photographs I have seen of her at that age, she was very beautiful, a fashionably dressed young woman—she managed to be well dressed, she said, because she sewed her own clothes. In the only picture of my father I ever saw, a very small snapshot, he and my mother were bundled up in winter overcoats, and he looked very tall and well built, but I could hardly make out the features of his face, framed as it was between upturned collar and Stetson hat. Not long ago some cousins who had known him told me that he was indeed very handsome. They also added that, even before the wedding, they knew the marriage would not last, because, in their words, he was a "happy-go-lucky luftmentsh" (his favorite songs, I learned, were "I'm Sitting on Top of the World" and "Rosie and Me and Baby Make Three"), and my mother, a dour person, worried about everything, especially about earning a living during those years of economic depression. My mother had told me that, when she was pregnant and my father left, her relatives advised her to have an abortion; but although she was not opposed to abortion, she wanted the child. I was born in Detroit, and we lived with her brother's family until my father returned when I was six months old and the three of us went to live with his aged parents in Brooklyn. After he finally left and did not return, my mother and I moved to the southeast Bronx, but for several years we periodically visited my paternal grandparents. On one such occasion my mother took me into the bedroom to change my clothes, and I remember her pointing to a pair of very large brown shoes on the floor nearby and saying, "Your father has been here. Those are his shoes." A pair of empty shoes—like his absence—documented his existence. My mother seemed to have an amicable relationship with her in-laws, but I never asked or learned what, if anything, was discussed about my father's disappearance and whereabouts.

After we had moved to the Bronx, I was enrolled in a Jewish day care facility for the working poor, which I attended from age one, and in their after-school programs until I was in junior high school. For a fee of fifty cents a week, the day care center provided lunch and dinner, and children remained there until picked up by a parent after work. My mother worked in Manhattan's garment district, generally returning after six o'clock. We usually hurried to the market and then home, where she would quickly prepare dinner for herself and, if I hadn't already eaten, for me, bathe me, and put me to bed. Since we always had to be up early so she could drop me at day care or school before traveling to her job, the only time we spent together was during the weekend—that is, if she wasn't working overtime—and during periods of unemployment.

Until I was twelve years old, we could afford only a rented bedroom in someone's apartment, one step away from homelessness, my mother said; and because work in the garment industry was seasonal and there were weeks in the off-seasons when my mother was unemployed (this was before unemployment insurance was available), we always feared we would be unable to pay the rent and might be driven onto the street. My mother never disabused me of this fear, in part of course because she too suffered from it, but also, I now believe, because she viewed our mutual anxiety as a bond between us. I think she struggled with an *agune*'s worst fear, namely, of rejection. She had, after all, been cast off by her family when she was ten years old and deserted by her husband.

FIGURE 3. A portrait of the author and her mother,
circa 1934.

Even though I refused to acknowledge it then, I too contended with a
lifelong fear of rejection, a result of my father's abandonment, but one
that was exacerbated by my mother's frequent threats to send me to an
orphanage because of my recalcitrance.

Although when I was a child it never occurred to me that my mother
feared her daughter might also abandon her—I was too busy fending off
threats that she would leave me—in more recent times I have begun to
understand some of her remarks and behavior differently. For example,
she often told me a story about my father: he had been married before,
was widowed, and had a daughter whom my mother claimed she had

wanted to adopt, but with whom my father had wanted nothing to do. One factor that I now believe prevented me from even entertaining the idea of searching for him—I never did try to locate him—was perhaps less that he had never been a parent to me (my usual justification) and more the fear that he would reject me as he had his other daughter; and I think my mother understood my trepidation and may even have desired it. Just a few years ago, a relative who had known my father and mother before they married told me that there had never been any consideration of adopting that child, because she was severely disabled and needed constant special medical care. If indeed this is true, and I believe it is, then the intent of the often-told story about my father's discarded daughter may indeed have been to convince me not to seek out a rejecting father.

At that time it had not occurred to me that my mother feared I would leave her, even though from the age of four or five, I had run away from home many times. In the midst of one of our many arguments, when my level of frustration reached its zenith, I would pack a small doll's suitcase with a storybook, some paper and pencils, a comb and barrettes; take the two or three nickels I had saved; and then be on my way—either to visit one of several friends around the Bronx, all of them adults who seemed happy to see me, or to ride the elevated and subway trains around New York. My mother would call the police, who would check at the various friends' homes and, if I was there, bring me home. If I was riding the urban rails, discouragement would set in when I realized that it was getting late and I had no place to go but home. On one such trip, after several transfers onto different subway lines—I learned to read at age three and loved to read and figure out the subway maps—I found myself in Brooklyn at the Myrtle Avenue station and, try as I might, taking various subway trains, could not manage to find my way back to the Bronx. Frustrated and frightened, I started to cry, and a station officer asked me what was the matter, where were my parents, and what was such a young child doing there alone. I answered as best I could without revealing that I had run away from home; he calmed me and then rode with me a long way to a stop where he watched me transfer to a train that went directly to the Bronx. I dwelled on that incident for many years, in part because I did not particularly appreciate that image of me as someone vulnerable and terrified, and in part because I harbored a suspicion that I had gone to Brooklyn where my father's parents lived hoping to find him. What all my escapades brought home to me was that there was no way out of my situation. I would have to adapt, and adapt I did, but not without a relatively tenacious struggle to retain some modicum of independence and individuality while in the keep of a very needy and controlling parent.

Although for much of my life I was no doubt haunted by the possibility of rejection, I worked very hard to remove from my life anyone who might reject me. This probably accounts in some good measure for my refusal to acknowledge my absent father. My mother spoke of him often enough, wallowing, it seemed to me, in tales of his dastardliness, but I never spoke or asked about him. Thus, while my mother's stories recited her victimization and inadequacy and were silent about her capabilities, those I told even as a young child recorded my perseverance and ingenuity and little of fear or hurt. In fact, although my mother's sense of her victimization and my denial of mine were apparently opposite stances, both derived from abandonment and shared the same miserable predicament. Neither of us, however, gained comfort or resolution in this way. But I know that, had the story about her first job been mine, the power of that young person would have been clearly heard; surely the story would have concluded with: "Because I knew that my father could not afford to buy a cow, I decided to give him my money, and he bought the cow. A few months later a letter from my mother brought the bad news: the cow had become sick and died. That's the way things were in those days." And I might have added: "My father knew nothing about cows."

Although my many stories of childhood told of my daring and refusal to be intimidated or discarded, they did not obliterate the sadness and fear I knew in those years. I suppose I was very intent on protecting myself from the dangers I sensed everywhere—that I, the chubby kid who couldn't fight worth a whistle, would not make it back from school without being challenged to a bout; that when I worked in a book factory on First Avenue in Manhattan, someone would discover that I was a mere twelve years old and incarcerate me for violating child labor laws; that my only parent would die or just leave me—she often threatened to do that when she was angered by what she considered disobedient behavior—and, alone in the world, I would have to fend for myself. I somehow managed, for the most part, to disavow the reality of those fears, which had deep roots in my history of abandonment, but I could never really defeat them. They returned again and again, and a large part of my life has been beset by a constant struggle to stave off being rejected—that is, until I began to admit to myself and others that I, along with my mother, had been discarded by a man whom everyone said I resembled so closely, and that I lived in fear that my mother's threats of rejection might be realized.

My unacknowledged fears of being left alone in a forbidding world seemed to become a terrifying reality when I was thirteen years old. I came home one Saturday afternoon to find my mother hysterical, crying that she was going to die and I would be left alone. She had been to the union's health clinic that morning, and it was discovered that she had a serious lung condition she called brown lung disease—technically, byssinosis—which had an etiology (inhaling particulate matter) similar to that of black lung disease, which plagued coal miners. Like the latter, hers was an occupational ailment caused by inhaling lint in the garment factories where she worked. She told me the doctor had said she would die very soon if she continued to work there. I panicked: without work we would have no money, we would starve on the street, I would be left alone in the world. Soon thereafter my mother decided to move to Detroit, where we had relatives and, using her contacts in the garment industry, she opened a small dress shop on Twelfth Street in a relatively poor Jewish neighborhood. The store was very small, and the fixtures divided the space so that there was a tiny back room, which was used as a changing room for customers when the store was open, and which became our bedroom, living room, and kitchen during the night. My mother and I slept on a single folding bed, cooked our meals on a two-burner stovetop, used bathroom facilities in the very dark and murky basement of the building, and never had a visitor in the three years we lived there. Now, not only could we not reveal that my father had abandoned us, we could never reveal where and under what conditions we lived. Shame stalked us, and we kept our secrets.

In my teenage years, the tensions between my mother and me seemed to replicate or even surpass those of my childhood: my mother was determined to maintain her grip on her daughter, and I, feeling physically and emotionally imprisoned, constantly sought for ways to escape my stifling living conditions, my miserable life. Because of these circumstances, with no place to call home, I, who was generally gregarious, had few friends and spent most of my time studying, working in my mother's shop, and visiting relatives whenever I could. My mother was continually worried about finances and worked very hard buying, selling, and altering clothing. When the store closed for the day, we spent the evenings in the small, dimly lit back room, cooked and ate our dinner, read or listened to the radio for a while, washed up in the basement, and went to sleep. This kind of life was not what one expected in the 1940s in a major United States city, and it was certainly not what I wanted. None of our relatives lived this way; they all inhabited nicely furnished one- and two-family homes. Living in a rented bedroom in someone's apartment, as we had in New York, seemed to me infinitely preferable to this new arrangement. I think it was also very disturbing for my mother, but she was caught in a web not entirely of her own making. During the armament-manufacturing boom in Detroit during the World War II years, it was almost impossible to find apartments, especially at a reasonable price, and she worried that our finances would not cover any amount of rent. So we continued to live in squalor until the middle of my senior year in high school, when my uncle moved to Florida and left us his very pleasant three-room apartment, along with some of its ornate furnishings (my uncle was an avid antique hunter). We lived in relative comfort for a few months until my high school graduation, when my mother decided to follow my uncle to Florida. It was only then that I learned we were not as impoverished as I had been led to believe: my mother bought a rooming house in the city of Miami. All these years, while we lived in destitute conditions, she had squirreled away enough money to pay cash for that sizable house. My mother left Detroit in November, when I was in my first year of college, and while I was initially enamored of the idea of living near sunny beaches and palm trees and looked forward to joining her in Miami at the end of the semester, a week after her departure my newly found freedom and independence seemed far too precious to relinquish. My mother, feeling abandoned by me, used every means possible—including bribery and denying funds for tuition or living expenses—to coerce me to join her in Florida, but I stayed the course and remained in Michigan until going east to graduate school. It meant, of course, that to make ends meet while attending college I worked two or three difficult jobs simultaneously: selling food and drink at the zoo, working in a fur-storage facility, branding names and numbers on bowling balls, attending to toddlers in a skid row child-care home, monitoring the dormitory from midnight to 4 A.M., hawking door-to-door promotional certificates for a photography studio, and selling in a small general store, among other things.

An Uncommon Childhood

From the time I was a year old, my mother worked in dress factories, and I was almost as familiar with them as I was with playgrounds. When there was extra work available, my mother worked on weekends for reduced, nonunion wages, filling special orders (usually for bridal outfits) for upscale businesses like Bonwit-Teller and Saks Fifth Avenue. Because the day care center I attended functioned only on weekdays, I spent those weekends with her in the factory, reading books, drawing or writing, playing with my doll, or just staring out of the window. Since the garment industry is a seasonal business, and there were long hiatuses between seasons, in the off-season when there was neither work nor unemployment compensation to be had, we applied for welfare. During those fallow periods there were times, however, when my mother would be called to work perhaps one day a week to sew the sample dresses for the next season. We desperately needed the money—welfare did not cover even the bare essentials like rent and food. My mother went to work when called, but we also worried that the welfare worker would show up when she was not at home and immediately strike us from the welfare rolls, which meant no money for rent or food. I remember that we once had an African American welfare worker whom my mother thought was less callous or more understanding than others had been, someone who could imagine that a person had merely gone grocery shopping, for a walk, or perhaps even to work for a day, and my mother felt less terrified by her. When this welfare worker was moved to another district—these workers were rotated often so that they wouldn't form friendships with their clients—my mother moved into her new district, a completely Italian neighborhood near Fordham University and much too far from my friends and the child care center. Although my mother felt more secure with this social worker, I was very lonely, far from my friends, constantly abused by the neighborhood kids, who called me names like "Jew-girl" and "kike" and certainly wouldn't play with me.

My original havens were the nearby Bronx Zoo and the Bronx Botanical Garden, but after having foolishly caressed the enticing silken-looking needles of a Botanical Garden cactus with my hand, and then trying in vain to brush them away on my arms and face, I was taken to the Fordham Hospital Emergency Room to have the needles removed. Thereafter, the emergency room became my special refuge. Although welfare was discontinued when my mother returned to work, we remained in that neighborhood until our lease expired at the end of the summer, and while my mother worked, I spent long hours during the day in the hospital's waiting room, reading and talking with waiting patients. Each time my turn came to see a doctor or nurse, I gave a different name—always, however, beginning with my own initials, B. G.; once I even gave the name Betty Grable; and each time I adopted a different symptom, a new minor, usually undetectable ailment, a cough, a headache, an ingrown toenail, an assortment of elusive aches or pains. This lasted for some weeks until one day my mother returned early from work and, finding me nowhere, called the police, who had no information and told my mother to check at the hospital, where she found me listening to the complaint of a woman with a hugely swollen knee. My mother of course berated me for the worry I caused her, and I could see that she was frantic with fear that something terrible might have happened to me.

Ricocheting between the signs of my mother's anxiety at somehow losing me and her many threats to leave me or turn me over to an orphanage—after all I was an orphan—became the norm of both my life and my mother's. As a child I thought that my parental bond was exclusively with my mother because my father contributed nothing to my life. As an adult, however, I have come to realize that my father, this invisible persona, actually inhabited that arena of tension between mother and daughter, negotiating almost every negative and positive connection between the two of us. In fact, it was the reality and fear of abandonment that created a common foundation of our experience, behavior, and relationship, but because neither of us realized this we were each unable to help one another or ourselves. Each of our needs—hers to hold me fast in her grip, mine to extricate myself from her and not be crushed—derived from the effects of desertion and rejection that neither she nor I could fully comprehend or overcome.

We shared other aspects of experience and behavior that were largely rooted in the reality of my mother's immigrant condition, our poverty, and the insecurity and trepidation that derived from these circumstances. To be sure, there were good times, but they were almost always compromised by our impoverishment. Weekends when my mother wasn't working provided special occasions for me. Although I would have liked to join the neighborhood kids at the long movie matinees—a double feature, newsreel, episodes of several action serials, and cartoons—my mother wanted an educated and cultured daughter. Although she was not conversant with classical music or art, she nonetheless took me to museums, free concerts in various museums or city parks, and the planetarium. During the summer we went to beaches, parks, and the zoo, and once to Bear Mountain on an excursion by boat up the Hudson River sponsored by the Workmen's Circle, my after-school Yiddish school.

My birthdays were also special. We would go to a movie—one featuring Shirley Temple, Jane Withers, Bobby Breen, or some other child star—with a splashy stage show at Manhattan's Radio City Music Hall or the Roxy Cinema, then eat in a restaurant, usually the Automat, my favorite. We also rode on the upper deck of the Fifth Avenue bus just for the thrill. I remember my mother speaking Yiddish to me, as she generally did, but because I thought that riders on the Fifth Avenue bus were the wealthy elite who lived in the beautiful buildings along that street, I was embarrassed and would act as though I didn't know her, a source of great irritation to her. Yiddish was for me the language of those who did not live on Fifth Avenue but in the Bronx and Brooklyn ghettos, where people didn't speak English very well. Real difficulties, however, arose when we would stroll through Manhattan streets and I needed to use a bathroom. My mother would always take me up to the door of a hotel or a restaurant and, because she was afraid to accompany me, tell me to go in alone and ask for the ladies' room. She believed that if we went in together we would be told to leave—we didn't look like their clientele; we looked poor and foreign—but a child would not be denied entry. But I was afraid to go into unfamiliar posh places by myself and speak with people who were strangers to me. So I was caught between two very uncomfortable choices: suffer the need to relieve myself, at least until we reached a department store, or brace myself to approach the "other." What did I do? First I suffered, and when that was no longer possible, I braced myself.

Immigrant Sensibility, Poverty, and Food

Immigrant sensibility, poverty, and food all coalesced into unexpectedly meaningful experiences in our lives; and a brief digression into the contents and discontents of food and eating might illuminate not only our shared miserable history of abandonment but also some of the very few special, indeed delicious, moments that my mother and I shared. These aspects—an impoverished immigrant life and eating—did in fact create the ground for two rather crushing events, one in my mother's life in which she was once again discarded; the other in my life when she cautioned that she might discard me. My mother's story revolves around her sister Fradl, who lived just a few blocks from us with her husband and three daughters. Although Fradl was much younger than my mother, she had long since adopted an attitude of superiority to my mother, who in turn interpreted this posture as criticism of her as a deserted wife, as someone who could not control her husband or her life. My mother was probably correct in her assessment of her sister's view, although I didn't quite understand how she had reached this conclusion. My aunt was an extremely controlling and, in my view, cruel person who made particularly harsh demands on her children, who feared her and whom she often berated and hit.

Being extremely religious or, more accurately, observant, my aunt did not approve of my mother working on what some regarded as less important Jewish holidays or of me attending school on those days. But my mother, who was not religious and who was a socialist, needed the income, and school was a form of day care for me; besides, I liked being in school. Because the day care center was closed on all Jewish holidays, my mother would take me to a small neighborhood restaurant, where she ordered and paid for my lunch. I usually chose my favorite foods—at the time it was bacon and string beans. My mother warned me not to mention the nonkosher bacon to my relatives, but after school on one such holiday one of my cousins asked me where and what I had eaten for lunch, and, forgetting my mother's admonition, I told her. When my mother came home from work and stopped by my aunt's apartment, my aunt's screams could be heard outside on the street where I was at play. My mother emerged crying, took my hand, and we went home. She was very angry with me, and I apologized profusely. But because of the bacon, my aunt did not speak to my mother for about ten years, relenting only when I graduated from high school. I was embarrassed, even infuriated by my mother's gratitude for my aunt's "forgiveness" after a decade of punishment, a gratitude that, in my reckoning, could be explained only if one recognized my mother's anxiety about abandonment. What seemed to my mother even more painful and humiliating than Fradl's ten years of shunning her was that, during this period of silence, every Friday one of her children brought us bread and cookies baked for the Sabbath, but never a word from my aunt. I found my aunt insufferable not only for this behavior, but because of the way she terrorized her children, and I have always felt that my mother should have distanced herself from my aunt years earlier because of that inhumanity. But this probably would have been unthinkable for a person like my mother, who had so little sense of her own abilities and value.

The bacon story has a history of its own. When I was about three years old, a doctor discovered that I had rickets and, according to my mother, recommended bacon as a food that would be very helpful. Frankly, I didn't believe that the doctor had actually advised this. Buying and cooking bacon presented a big problem in a household that, while not strictly kosher, used only kosher foods. In my eyes, having to prepare bacon for a sick child activated my mother's martyr complex (ours was a family of martyrs or prospective martyrs) and provided yet another step in my mother's elevation to sainthood: she had to walk some distance to a store that sold bacon by the strip, so that she would not have to store it in the icebox; and she had to keep a special frying pan that, when not in use, was placed in a bag and stored not in the house but on the fire escape or suspended out of the window. Many years later, however, on reading a Tillie Olsen story, I was surprised to discover that bacon at one time may indeed have been a prescribed remedy for rickets, and my mother was vindicated.

Before considering the crushing event in my life, let me recount the several memories of my mother—each one associated with food—that I cherish. In each episode the seemingly eternal struggle between mother and child dissolved, primarily, I think, because we had found a way to detach ourselves from our disastrous face-to-face quotidian confrontations. One such experience was connected with my bout with rickets, as a result of which I was placed in a state-run sanitarium for children, which was a three-hour bus ride from the Bronx. The children there came from poor families, almost all from New York City, and the only visiting day was Sunday. If one had no car (no one I knew as a child drove a car, much less owned one), the only transportation was a bus that arrived just after noon when we children were still at lunch. Since visitors were not admitted until one P.M., they had to remain outside the sanitarium gate, but the children, excited and anxious to see their relatives, left their food and peered out of the dining room windows trying to catch a glimpse of a possible visitor. Only a few children had visitors, probably because the bus ride was too expensive. My mother never missed a Sunday, however, and I was always eager to see her. Visitors weren't permitted to bring food or treats for the children, but my mother, who didn't appreciate regulations that she considered unreasonable, defied the rules. Usually fashionably dressed because she sewed her own clothes, my mother wore a kind of "flapper" coat with huge cuffs, which, after the first visit, she stuffed with small, penny Hershey chocolate bars. She developed a routine: gathering the children who had no visitors in our dormitory room, she divided the candy among us, kept an eye out for any white-uniformed intruders while we ate our treats, finally packed all the paper wrappers back into her cuffs, and marched us all into the bathroom, where we washed the smell of chocolate from our breath. Even more than her concern and generosity, I admired her defiance of any system she regarded as stupid and inhumane—one of her most admirable qualities.

Another tradition of my childhood that seemed to remove us from our habitual fractiousness occurred during the summers, when we would rent an inexpensive room for a night or two near the beach in Far Rockaway. The room was called in Yiddish a *kokh aleyn,* which translated into something like "cook alone" or "cook for yourself" and meant that renters had privileges to cook their own food in a kitchen shared with all the other tenants in the house. To avoid the morning congestion in the kitchen, we would rise very early, shop at various stores for hot *bulkehs* (buns), fruit, milk, a bit of butter, and eggs, climb up onto the lifeguard's chair—he (in those days the guard was always male) didn't arrive until nine—and eat our breakfast way up high, watching the sun rise over the Atlantic Ocean (a dreamy memory from childhood that unfortunately cannot be revisited here on the West Coast). I usually did not welcome the prospect of eating meals with my mother, primarily because almost any encounter at the table was like a forced feeding event that would evolve into a stubborn standoff; which is why I would often take my food to the windowsill and eat my meals gazing out at a back alley. But perched on the lifeguard's chair, not confronting one another, and looking out in the same direction like two sedate figures in an Edward Hopper painting, it seemed so easy to talk and to feel good talking. I still have that feeling when a friend and I talk while sitting next to each other at a bar or restaurant counter.

Our feast of pomegranates, a fruit we both loved, provided another wondrous eating experience with my mother. Because she thought pomegranate juice would permanently stain everything, it was our custom to cover the kitchen table and the floor beneath it with newspaper and sit naked across from one another sharing the fruit, sucking the tangy flesh off of each kernel. Our nakedness and the newspapers somehow broke the customary household contentiousness and frustration. When we finished our exotic repast, we would gather up the inedible remains of the fruit in the newspapers, discard them, and then bathe together to erase the purple-red stains from our bodies. I always regretted that the pomegranate season was so brief, or at least seemed that way on the East Coast.

Finally, the event concerning food that really distressed me—although at the time a wall of defenses probably protected me from a panicked free fall—occurred when I was about seven years old, around the same time my aunt stopped speaking to my mother. Mary, one of my favorite cousins from Detroit, came to the Bronx to visit us. We rarely had visitors at our place because my mother was embarrassed about living in a rented bedroom. It was certainly not a place conducive to entertaining. Nonetheless, this occasion was a special treat for me. I loved my cousins, and Mary, who was on her honeymoon, was bringing her husband, a new cousin. When they arrived, my mother was in the midst of an activity that was always grueling and seemed never to end: coercing me to eat what I neither liked nor wanted. A glance at me, a healthy chubby child, would have convinced anyone that I was at least properly nourished. There were, however, a number of foods I heartily despised that my mother thought were absolutely essential for life. What seemed to make a food utterly necessary, in my mother's lore, was less its nutritional value than its repulsive characteristics. In this instance hot stewed prunes were at issue.

My mother, it must be remembered, like many deserted wives, saw herself as a failure—discarded by her husband, with no real home, very poor—and she felt respected by no one, not even by her family. She was therefore anxious to be perceived, especially by relatives, as competent and adequate to the tasks of living. Thus, in the presence of her niece, who would surely report on the visit when she returned to Detroit, it must have been particularly important to my mother that she be seen as being in control, particularly of a seven-year-old child. Although I can see this now, at the time I thought guests would protect me from doing what I did not want to do, for I was certain their presence would prevent my mother from creating a scene. But when, no matter how much I was coaxed, bribed, and threatened, I still refused to taste a morsel of hot prune, my mother lashed out at me, trying, I think, to stem her frustration and convince me to obey. She reminded me how vital she was to my survival, that she was my only parent, and that should she not be there someday, I would then be forced to fend for myself, and that, since I had no other parent, I would wander from place to place and have a hard time finding food and shelter. I remember being scared, but it was too late to change course, and I did not relent. Soon after, when my mother left the room to bring refreshments for the visitors, my cousin, eager to comfort me, assured me that I need not worry, that my many relatives in Detroit loved me and wanted me, that I would never want for food and a home. In reply I shrugged my shoulders as though to brush off the entire incident and said, "She doesn't bother me. I've got friends in Rockaway."

The incident remains vivid in my mind, but over the years I have also heard my cousins tell the story many times, and it was clear to me that they were impressed by my self-assertion, audacity, and refusal to be intimidated. This too is the way I understood the behavior of the seven-year-old. Of course, the admiration of my relatives may have influenced my unambiguous interpretation of the event. Even as a young child, I wanted to see myself, and be seen, as someone strong and self-reliant, someone who could not be rejected or discarded, which is precisely how for many years I perceived myself in that story. More recently, I have come to realize that I had not fully understood the reply I gave my cousin that day. All these years, I seemed to have attended less to my own story than to my needs. The retort, after all, spoke only peripherally of independence and self-reliance, but specifically of relying on others, on friends; and I can only believe that I as a young child knew all too well what I as an adult still had illusions about: that one could not go it alone, that one needed others in order to survive, that one needed friends.

When I reflect on my life, I believe the image of myself as confident and gutsy gave me the courage to be resourceful and persistent, to be able to survive in a world on whose good will I could not depend. For years I maintained the attitude I thought I saw reflected in the child's response: outwardly at least, I usually summarily dismissed fear and rejection and turned elsewhere when threatened by either. It is also true that I rarely took seriously my mother's intimidating threats, because she almost never carried them out, but there were a few times when I actually thought she would make good on her threat. In one instance, for example, when I was about seven years old, she became so angry with me that she went to a telephone at a neighborhood candy store and told me that she was calling the police to pick me up and take me to an orphanage. I had good reason to fear the orphanage, because on some of our walks near the Grand Concourse in the Bronx we would pass a building with bars on the windows that my mother claimed was an orphanage. (Only many years later did I learn that it was a jailhouse and court.) While my mother was telephoning, I became completely hysterical, lay down on the sidewalk and screamed, at which point my mother, looking frightened and pale, said she would call the police again and ask them not to come. For the most part, however, I don't think I could have entertained the possibility that her threats might actually be realized. Moreover, I may have stubbornly refused to be a victim as my mother had been, but I have since learned that, while salvaging some self-esteem, defending oneself against being a victim may be at least as damaging as being one. In fact, only in recent years, when I finally became aware of my suppressed fear of rejection and abandonment, did I begin to understand just how much hurt, dread, and anger my fearless retort about those "friends in Rockaway" concealed and revealed. Would it have made a difference had my cousins and others not admired my audacity but instead alerted me to the anxiety I know they recognized? I can't know that, but I think I would have resolutely held on to the story of the intrepid youngster, though I might have uncovered my vulnerabilities sooner.

It is not now clear to me—nor, I believe, has it ever been—whether my mother made a serious, determined effort to locate my father, and whether she actually wanted him to return or had even thought about what she wanted. Like many deserted wives, she was so incredibly preoccupied with warding off hunger and homelessness, as well as the sense of hurt, shame, humiliation, and despair, that she rarely seemed to consider what she actually desired or needed. She did go to the National Desertion Bureau to report her husband's disappearance, but this was necessary in order to have the state declare him dead after an absence of seven years. One reason for my suspicion is that, as far as I knew, she never sought information about his whereabouts from any of his relatives—not from his parents or his brothers and their families. When I was in college, my mother wanted to marry and could readily have done so, because her husband was deemed legally dead. But always filled with an immigrant's trepidation regarding legal matters, she feared that she would be arrested for bigamy were he actually alive. Therefore she asked my aunt to call one of my father's brothers—until then I did not know these brothers existed—who owned a business in Brooklyn. We learned that my father, Sam, was indeed alive, but instead of seeking him out, my mother placed a required ad to find him in a small local newspaper and filed for divorce. She never told me how she felt about the news that he was alive, but I was startled and experienced anger and anxiety, bewilderment and indecision: I thought about visiting him and—like the girl in the *bintl briv* who wanted her father to see what a fine young adult she had become—letting him see what an intelligent and independent daughter he had discarded. But I also feared that such a visit would greatly upset my mother, whom, despite our difficult relationship, I did not wish to cause grief. Thus, neither my mother nor I ever confronted the man who had deserted us. I think this suited my mother fine, but for a very long time as an adult I have regretted it, especially after I realized I had not confronted him primarily because I feared he would reject me once again. Anxiety about rejection, I would venture to guess, haunts almost all of us who have been abandoned, and too often it intensifies as it is transmitted to the next generation.

Epilogue

The prologue to this book may leave the impression that my involvement with the subject matter followed a rather direct trajectory, from my personal struggles with abandonment, to the experience, years later, of encountering *agunes* in the Jewish German and Yiddish literature I taught, and to inquiries into the National Desertion Bureau and "A Gallery of Vanished Husbands." Actually, my route was a far more convoluted one, encumbered by a variety of my interests intricately connected with cultural studies in general and Jewish studies in particular. On the one hand, I was drawn to multicultural concerns within Jewish studies—be they different legal systems; structures and operations of power among various groups; the social and political effects of gender, class, and status inequities; or the nexus between larger institutional constructs like the family or community and individual predicaments. On the other hand, I found it necessary to engage a broad range of interdisciplinary practices and cultural approaches—exploring various genres, analyzing literary and nonliterary texts closely, and interpreting institutional documents and media accounts. The route proved problematic because a decidedly inflexible aspect of Jewish family law was under consideration, and I found myself crossing borders between Jewish culture and the dominant society so often that, in the end, I was not always able to assess the point of origin: was the culture shaped by social structures at all, and if so, to what extent; or were the social structures shaped by the particular cultural system? In this epilogue I address some of the difficulties encountered in a cultural study concerned, in particular, with Jewish patriarchy and its implications for studying more secular women who, within the turmoil and discontinuities of modern life, increasingly were left to bear the burden of heading their families alone.

The marginality referred to in the title of this study resonates on multiple levels. It was certainly applicable to Jews living in the Diaspora, who were usually deemed socially and politically subordinate to the dominant native or nonimmigrant populations of the countries in which they resided. The traditional Jewish community, enclosed within the dominant society, did establish its own internal governance with a modicum of autonomy that included rabbinical courts, its own legal system for family law and contracts, and structures of social and political hierarchy. Gender inequality certainly governed the patriarchal economy of religious orthodoxy, with Jewish men in control, and with women, because of their legally sanctioned subaltern status, marginalized and largely confined to the domestic sphere, where, however, men could also impose their will. *Agunes,* of course, especially deserted wives, were burdened by an even more oppressive enforced marginality: their systemic exclusion from perhaps the only domain where a woman had value in her traditional community—as wife of a household. The Jewish narratives about desertion in memoirs, autobiographies, novels, and letters testify to a prevailing fear among women that an absconding husband would bring further degradation, indigence, shame, and even the erasure of any sense of self. Rarely could the abandoned family find adequate acceptance and security within either the community or an unfamiliar surrounding society.[1] Indeed, the marginality and subjection that Jews generally experienced within diasporic culture probably haunt the life of the *agune* more intensely than they do any other, for while margins are often "places where distinct domains meet, where crossings from here to there, from sameness to otherness, are constantly being negotiated," as Rachael Langford and Russell West have noted,[2] no negotiation can alter an abandoned wife's "chained" condition within traditional Judaism.

The methodological concerns and theoretical versatility of cultural studies usually focus on challenging and exposing the authority behind structures of domination, with the expectation of abolishing or at least reducing the power inequities that often lie concealed in both public and private cultural spheres. It is, therefore, ironic and more than a little disconcerting that, while these approaches to the study of abandoned Jewish wives expose the operative gender asymmetries of power, they also reveal the impossibility of altering or undoing them. The anticipation or hope that working across disciplines would provide avenues to "synergetic energies and transgressive possibilities"[3] might prove realistic for cultures more receptive to restructuring power differentials or even renouncing power, but, in a fundamentally inflexible patriarchal Jewish legal system or culture, neither of these was possible where abandoned women were concerned.

Jewish patriarchy has a long history, founded on biblical law, its legal foundation codified in the Talmud by the rabbis, and its locus of power established firmly in the androcentric social system of traditional Judaism. Thus, men controlled the privileged hegemonic center while women were relegated to a different arena and denied the rights and prerogatives men enjoyed; or, more accurately, women were excluded from the culturally most valued practice of Talmud study. Daniel Boyarin theorizes "that the exclusion of women from the study of Torah subtended the rabbinic Jewish gender hierarchy in two closely related ways, via the construction of a 'fraternity' and via the production of a social system within which a group of men (the Rabbis) held power over the actual practices and pleasures of female bodies."[4] The social and historical conditions during the exilic turmoil of the Talmudic period, however, may have made more stringent standards and practices necessary. Salo Baron notes that "the traditional moorings of the Jewish community needed considerable strengthening," and the rabbis and leaders opted for "the reconstruction of the people's life by a new emphasis upon its family and communal structure. The sexual control was now placed under the strict control of each individual and the community."[5] The emphasis on the strong family and the strict implementation of marriage and divorce laws as mechanisms to enforce community cohesiveness in a sometimes threatening diasporic situation continued well into the twentieth century, which is especially apparent in the case of oppressed Eastern European Jews.

In a discussion of the status of women in classical rabbinic Judaism, Judith Romney Wegner concludes that a "literature produced by men offers little testimony to the actual, real experience of real, historical women. . . . What we get, in the end, is the rabbinic understanding of women's nature and place in the social fabric, along with a set of rules delineating the (perhaps theoretical, perhaps actual) legal status of women in patriarchal culture."[6] Of course, there is no guarantee that literary production by women would yield the "real experience" of "real women," especially if, as Miriam Peskowitz points out, "women's voices are constructed by the same masculinist societies and discourses that construct men's voices."[7] Although a woman's voice or writings might offer a different discursive perspective—an alternate textual insight into women's lives—women within the social polity were silent or silenced and seemed to have no voice, certainly no public one. Presumably, the abandoned woman needs no voice because, according to halakha, she has no case to plead and no hope for redress. Indeed, among the texts discussed in this study, there are abundant instances where the *agune* does not speak, is not heard or heeded, or—like Sheyne-Sheyndl, finally left hopeless and helpless by failed communicative efforts—voluntarily suppresses her own voice.

The sense of being without a voice, being without vocal means of projecting into the power centers that control their lives, left Jewish women entrenched in their households. Even their economic activity in support of husband and family was regarded, within the Jewish cultural system, as part of the domestic sphere, certainly not the valued realm of male study.[8] Thus, it is not surprising that, in all the narratives in this study, the border crossings—no matter how temporary or tentative—between the Jewish community and the non-Jewish dominant society end very differently for women and for men: women return to traditional Jewish communal life, a feminized shtetl life, while the husbands are able and usually eager to "liberate" themselves from that life. In both the autobiographical and fictional texts—Glikl's story, Maimon's *Autobiography*, Abramovitsh's *Benjamin the Third,* and Sholem Aleykhem's *Menakhem-Mendl*—excursions by men into the external world ultimately lead to their disappearance from hearth and home and bring about the plight of the *agune.* In the two autobiographical texts, the women, with no intention to forsake their homes for a life outside, move into the larger society only to resolve the problem of *aginut* and, this accomplished, return to their domiciles. In fact, at the conclusion of all the narratives, the women are firmly reembedded within the boundaries of the traditional community, while—at least in the instances of Maimon, Benjamin and his companion Senderl, and Menakhem-Mendl—the husbands seem keen, even adamant, about remaining without their wives and children in the larger, more secular social world.

The European Enlightenment and expanding capitalism probably provided watershed situations for those men who—even though as Jews they continued to struggle with residence and travel restrictions—nevertheless readily availed themselves of the male prerogative to leave home and family and seek out opportunities they deemed intellectually and socially or economically more promising. The wives, long confined within the traditional shtetl household and encumbered with responsibility for the welfare of their children, certainly could not easily undertake life in an unfamiliar modern secular environment.[9] The differential of power and privilege between men and women is obvious in these narratives of Ashkenazic European culture[10] and in the thousands of cases in the United States memorialized in "A Gallery of Vanished Husbands" and the documents of the National Desertion Bureau, in which men go on the lam at will and abandoned wives can do little more than beg for the minimal assistance needed to maintain their families. The kind of impoverishment of women and children that results from spousal abandonment only further aggravates the cruelty and injustice inherent in women's subaltern status and contributes to their sense of inadequacy and powerlessness.

One of the benefits of studying a diversity of texts and a variety of approaches is that it may bring to the fore the social and political complexities of a particular culture that would not otherwise be apparent in any one text. The discussion of the National Desertion Bureau (chapter 5), for example, reveals not only overt gender inequality but also class differences among men—between the Bureau's founders and administrators, on the one hand, and the deserting husbands who were being sought, on the other. To my knowledge, no one has commented on this class issue before. Perhaps the Bureau's documents were used too perfunctorily as procedural records important primarily for their facts and figures. A closer, more careful textual reading, however, discloses the dissension between very distinct classes of Jewish men about funding the needs of women and children. The wealthy urbane German Jews who administered the Bureau had created a venue to pressure an impoverished class of recent Eastern European immigrants, who—being poor, working class, and probably not well educated—were perceived as weak or depraved, succumbing as they did to their "passion for wandering."

This disparity during the twentieth century between wealthy "uptown" Jews and poor "downtown" recent immigrants from Eastern Europe was probably related to an antagonism within Jewish patriarchy that had already become prominent in the eighteenth century, when acculturated German Jews who wanted a place, albeit often an uncomfortable one, within Western European cultural circles were anxious to call attention to the differences between themselves and the Eastern

European Jews (Ostjuden) they regarded as untutored and crude. Curiously, the language that Germans had already applied to Jews in order to distinguish "uncivilized" Jews from German Gentiles—that is, *asiatisch* and *orientalisch*—was then used by the nouveau "elite" German Jews to characterize their Eastern European brethren.[11] In fact, apart from economic differences, the fundamental distinction in status among Jewish men no doubt dates back to the valorization of the Talmudic scholar as the masculine ideal in Jewish patriarchy and the denigration of men who, because they did not or could not study Torah, were often considered "feminized" or "like women." In the late sixteenth century, the *Brantshpigl* (Burning Mirror), one of the earliest books of ethical literature not written in Hebrew but in Yiddish, notes that this "book was written in Yiddish for women and for men who are like women in not being able to learn much."[12] But of course, within Jewish law even those "feminized" men were still considered men, normative Jews who were not denied access to Torah and who were not subject to the subaltern legislation reserved for women.

For men active in both the Jewish community and the dominant society, disparate class affiliations involved an ability to fulfill very different constructions of cultural values within both domains. Hence, the particular attraction of Moses Mendelssohn, an observant Jew, who was regarded not only as a scholar of Jewish and general philosophy but also as a competent European thinker and successful businessman. Maimon, however—although very learned, intellectually brilliant, and lauded for his interpretations of the philosophical writings of Maimonides, Kant, and Fichte—had disavowed his past Orthodox religiosity while retaining such characteristics of shtetl life as an expectation to be supported financially by others while he exclusively pursued his philosophical studies. Needless to say, this expectation found little favor among his bourgeois colleagues in Enlightenment Berlin.[13] Judged by the standards of the Western cognoscenti, he was an inept Jew who, because he did not live up to the masculine expectations of either modern enlightened society or Jewish tradition, was finally shunned by the Berlin Jewish intellectuals and social elite. Indeed, Maimon himself seemed to become the battleground for a class struggle among men within enlightened modern Jewish patriarchy.

Exploring the intersection, within Jewish patriarchy, of gender inequality and the disempowerment or diminished stature of certain men may also cast some light on the connection between degraded masculinity and the treatment of women in narratives about abandonment.

In the novels of Abramovitsh and Sholem Aleykhem considered in this study, for example, gender inequality is apparent and of paramount importance, although there seem to be no very obvious class differences among the men who are actors in the texts. On closer consideration, however, a number of significant masculine figures with marked differences in class, status, and ability do hover in the fantasies or shadowy environments of the protagonists, and it is with these figures that the protagonists contend. In *Benjamin the Third* there are the fantasized powerful Red Jews and Alexander the Great, the very real Ukrainian peasant, fellow Jews who turn the protagonists over to the military, and the military officers. Menakhem-Mendl feels challenged again and again by proverbial but unseen big business magnates and by Jewish competitors at the financial markets who, unlike him, apparently manage to make money. Class issues are not only present among men but are, in fact, instrumental in spousal abandonment and the ongoing plight of the *agune*.

Consider, for example, the representations of the protagonists in both novels: inept, unproductive, impoverished Jews, certainly no scholars of Torah and Talmud, their knowledge of the world based on little more than fantastic tales and unrealizable ideals. These may be "feminized" men—even referred to as *yidenes* in the texts—but, within the construction of Jewish patriarchy, even fundamentally powerless men are powerful in relation to their wives. Some of the wives' shrewish behavior may very well further underscore the inadequacy of the men, but under the Jewish legal system these men know they can easily determine the course of their wives' lives merely by walking out on them. In fact, the only power the men maintain is exacted from the legal gender inequality operative in Jewish patriarchy. Paradoxically and unfortunately, the degraded status of these men may have encouraged them to gain a sense of their own importance by using legal male prerogatives against their wives and families. It is true, of course, that these protagonists' interest in venturing out of the shtetl for the big world is not primarily to exert control over their wives but rather to shed all familial responsibilities and seek new identities that could bring them prominence and fame within both the traditional Jewish community and the world outside the shtetl: Benjamin the Third plans to become a great hero, another Alexander the Great, but one who will bring salvation to the impoverished and oppressed shtetl denizens; and Menakhem-Mendl is sure he will become the economic tycoon of all time, another Rothschild or Brodsky. But even before the onset of their adventures, their surreptitious departures from their spouses to pursue their impossible fantasies already function as a portentous declaration of their patriarchal prerogatives.

Although these protagonists exact and wield patriarchal male privilege over women, what they seem to desire even more is to achieve class power among men. Since this is not possible given the values of Jewish tradition—they cannot become Talmud scholars—these incompetent, "feminized" men wander about the uncertain marketplaces of the capitalist world or the fantasized map of bygone heroic eras seeking in vain to attain a masculine ideal of prominence. In pursuing a new self-identity, these absconding husbands become the site of a power struggle, a terrible effort not to be excluded or marginalized, not to become or remain a degraded, feminized other. Although it is not consciously acknowledged, these men seem to understand what Judith Butler has noted about the construction of the subject: the "subject is constructed through acts of differentiation that distinguish the subject from its constitutive outside, a domain of abject alterity conventionally associated with the feminine, but clearly not exclusively."[14] By participating in the dominant society with the expectation of gaining a new identity, these men, who have already experienced the humiliation of a degraded status in traditional Judaism and now seek recognition elsewhere, are not struggling against inequality. They are rather striving, within the patriarchy of the dominant society, not merely to triumph over women and "feminized" men but to garner the spoils of dominant masculinist secular power.

But where are the abandoned wives in this narcissistic male production of self-identity? As women within the constructed system of Jewish patriarchy, their exclusion from the hegemonic center of knowledge and power[15] is the result of serious abuse: "the rapport of self-identity," Jacques Derrida reminds us, "is itself always a rapport of violence with the other."[16] But abandoned women who, along with other women, had heretofore occupied the margins of the cultural map in patriarchy are no longer just the normative excluded Other who constructs and justifies the male Jewish subject. The deserted wives in the texts under consideration here are virtually eliminated from the cultural map. The *shtetlekh,* the ghettos, the decaying tenements of the New World were abandoned by the men and erased by wily male cartographers' hands in the process of creating a new cultural map without wives and children; and the women trying to keep their families alive almost completely vanished. At the conclusion of these narratives, there are no traces of

Benjamin's wife, Zelda, and Senderl's wife; Sheyne-Sheyndl has voluntarily silenced herself after finally realizing that nothing she said to her Menakhem-Mendl mattered; and no woman's face, no woman's story, ever accompanied the hundreds of pictures and biographies of men in "A Gallery of Vanished Husbands," which appeared in the *Forverts* week after week for decades.

Fortunately, this is not the complete story, or the completed one. In the seventeenth century, Glikl's Rebekah spoke and acted for the *agunes* who could not do so for themselves and, in the process, motivated an *agune* to seek justice for herself. In the eighteenth century Maimon's wife undertook the arduous trek from Poland to Germany in order to persuade her husband to grant her the divorce she deserved. And in the twentieth century, groups of *agunes* and their supporters organized in concerted efforts to plead their case and present their cause to the public. While there is no hope for an abandoned woman to obtain a *get,* there are new possibilities open to *agunes* whose husbands refuse to grant them one. In early 2006, for example, the International Coalition for Agunah Rights, a coalition of twenty-five organizations, reported that although ten years ago an annual average of only six *agunes* were granted divorces, now 250 women—a very small portion of the women seeking them—are granted divorces each year. This problem is, of course, especially important in Israel, where only religiously sanctioned marriages and divorces are recognized, which means that even nonreligious or secular Israeli women are required to obtain a *get*. Although, through much pleading and pressure, some relief may be attained within traditional Jewish patriarchy, there can be no adequate or just solution for women within a legal and cultural system of patent inequality.

Postscript

As this book was going to press, an article appeared in the Israeli newspaper *Ha'aretz* which confirmed my sense that no acceptable moral and humane solution to the situation of *agunes* was available within Orthodox Judaism.[17]

The article, written by Amiram Barkat, concerned a conference in Israel on "chained women" that had been suddenly canceled by the organizer, Chief Sephardic Rabbi Shlomo Amar, "at the order of ultra-Orthodox Rabbi Yosef Shalom Elyashiv." This would have been the

Chief Rabbinate's first conference on this issue, and dozens of invited guests, including chief rabbis, rabbinic court heads, and rabbinic judges from around the world, were either in transit or already in Israel at the time of the cancellation.

The article appeared in *Ha'aretz* on Monday, November 6, 2006, the day before what would have been the opening session of the conference. Three months earlier, Amar had persuaded Elyashiv to approve the conference, which the latter did on the condition that women not be permitted to attend. Professor Ruth Halperin-Kaddari, head of the Rackman Center for the Advancement of Women's Status in the Faculty of Law at Bar-Ilan University, indicated that she was shocked at the cancellation, even though she thought it would probably not have been "a turning point in the rabbinical courts' treatment of women." She noted that "the conference's importance was in its existence—and canceling it indicates more than anything else the sorry state of Orthodox Judaism, which cannot deal with such a basic and humane issue."

According to *Ha'aretz*, the two Supreme Rabbinical Court judges responsible for the cancellation advocated "strengthening the husband's and rabbinical court's status in divorce cases." Indeed, one of these judges, Rabbi Hagai Izirer, "even supports canceling a divorce," an act that could retroactively turn any children born to the woman in a subsequent marriage into bastards.

Notes

Prologue

1. The Yiddish term is *agune,* pl. *agunes.* The Hebrew term is *aguna,* pl. *agunot. Aginut* is the state of being an *agune.* Since in this study the texts (apart from Solomon Maimon's German one) are in Yiddish, I shall use the Yiddish *agune* throughout. (In some citations, *agune* appears as *agunah.*) In Jewish law, only the husband can execute and deliver a divorce, or *get,* and there are essentially four reasons why a wife may be unable to obtain a Jewish divorce: the husband is mentally ill, thus legally incompetent to grant a divorce; the husband has died but there is no legally valid evidence of his death; a recalcitrant husband refuses to divorce his wife; or the husband abandons her and disappears. If the husband has truly disappeared, the wife can never obtain a Jewish divorce.

2. Myra Jehlen, "Gender," in *Critical Terms for Literary Study,* ed. Frank Lentricchia and Thomas McLaughlin (Chicago: University of Chicago Press, 1990), 265.

3. Richard Johnson, "What Is Cultural Studies Anyway?" *Social Text* 16 (Winter 1986–87): 69.

4. See n. 1 for definitions of *aginut* and *agune.*

5. See Tania Modleski, "Feminism and the Power of Interpretation," in *Feminist Studies/Critical Studies,* ed. Teresa de Lauretis (Bloomington: Indiana University Press, 1986), 130: "In my opinion, the function of feminist criticism is similarly to empower women by the force of its stories and interpretations."

6. Solomon Maimon, *Salomon Maimons Lebensgeschichte: Von ihm selbst geschrieben,* ed. Karl Philipp Moritz and newly edited by Zwi Batscha (Frankfurt am Main: Insel, 1984), 147.

7. "Gold, zogt men, valgert zikh dort in di gasn." Sholem Aleykhem, *Menakhem-Mendl,* in *Ale verk fun sholem-aleykhem* (1912; reprint, New York: Morgn-Frayhayt Ausgabe, 1937), 218.

8. Ibid., 49.

9. Morris D. Waldman, "Family Desertion," in *Proceedings of the Seventh Biennial Session of the National Conference of Jewish Charities in the United States* (St. Louis, May 17–19, 1910) (Baltimore: Kohn and Pollock, 1910), 64.

1. Abandoned Wives in Jewish Family Law

1. Khayim Grade, *Die agune: Roman* (New York: Cyco-Bicher Farlag, 1965), and Chaim Grade, *The Agunah,* trans. Curt Levant (New York: Bobbs-Merrill, 1974).

2. *Encyclopedia Judaica* (Jerusalem: Keter, 1972), 2:429.

3. In one text—Solomon Maimon's *Autobiography* (*Lebensgeschichte*)—the deserting husband, when located, becomes a recalcitrant one, thereby offering readers an unanticipated insight into the function of the rabbinical court, or *beyt din.*

4. *Tanakh: The Holy Scriptures: The New JPS Translation According to the Traditional Hebrew Text* (Philadelphia: Jewish Publication Society, 1985), 311.

5. In 1968, four decades after Conservative Judaism began its efforts to find a solution to the "plight of the *agune,*" its Committee on Jewish Law and Standards adopted a proposal for a conditional agreement to the marriage ceremony, giving its rabbis the authority to grant annulments if, after a civil divorce, the husband refused to issue a *get.* This, of course, applied only to future marriages, but in 1969 its *beyt din* granted an annulment to a woman who had been an *agune* for many years, which ended the *agune* controversy. See Pamela S. Nadell, *Conservative Judaism in America: A Biographical Dictionary and Sourcebook* (New York: Greenwood Press, 1988), 6–15, for a comprehensive history of Conservative Judaism's struggle with the problem. It should also be noted that this solution did not apply to abandoned wives whose husbands were not available to issue or refuse to issue a *get.*

6. The term *takana* (pl. *takanot*) is a transliteration from the Hebrew. In citations from other texts, there are different transliterated spellings (for example, sometimes with two *k*'s or with a final *h*), but they all refer to a directive, which, after the Talmudic period, signifies "enacted by halakhic scholars or other competent body . . . enjoying the force of law" (*Encyclopedia Judaica,* 15:713).

7. Moshe Meiselman, *Jewish Woman in Jewish Law* (New York: Ktav Publishing House, 1978), 103–4.

8. Quoted in Trude Weiss-Rosmarin, "The Unfreedom of Jewish Women," *Jewish Spectator* 35, no. 7 (October 1970): 4. According to Nadell, "Cohen had refused to allow the Committee on Jewish Law to render decisions that had the potential to affect all of the Jewish People. Thus, even though he led the committee as it wrestled with the plight of the *agunah,* he was unwilling to support any *halachic* solution that won the approval of only the Conservative rabbinate" (*Conservative Judaism in America,* 54).

9. Reuven Yaron, "The Missing Husband in Jewish Law," *Mélange à la Mémoire de Marcel-Henri Prévost* (Paris: Presses Universitaires de France, 1982), 139–40.

10. See Rivka Haut, "The *Agunah* and Divorce," in *Lifecycles: Jewish Women on Life Passages and Personal Milestones,* ed. Debra Orenstein (Woodstock, VT: Jewish Lights Publishing, 1994), 1:418n4.

11. David Golinkin, Richard Lewis, Diana Villa, and Monique Süsskind Goldberg, *Jewish Law Watch: The Agunah Dilemma,* no. 4 (Jerusalem: Schechter Institute of Jewish Studies, April 2002), 4.

12. Rachel Biale, *Women and Jewish Law: The Essential Texts, Their History, and Their Relevance for Today* (New York: Schocken, 1995), 108. See also Yaron, "The Missing Husband in Jewish Law," 139.

13. Yael V. Levy, "The Agunah and the Missing Husband: An American Solution to a Jewish Problem," *Journal of Law and Religion* 10, no. 1 (1993–94): 60.

14. Ibid., 70.

15. Ibid., 70–71.

16. Meiselman, *Jewish Woman in Jewish Law,* 104–5 passim; emphasis added.

17. Levy, "The Agunah and the Missing Husband," 62–63.

18. See Biale, *Women and Jewish Law,* 108–10; *Encyclopedia Judaica,* 2:432–33; Blu Greenberg, *On Women and Judaism: A View from Tradition* (Philadelphia: Jewish Publication Society, 1981), 135–38.

19. Biale, *Women and Jewish Law,* 112.

20. Haut notes that, although the Orthodox rabbinate had been loath to change anything in halakha, they "always managed to keep up with the times. In the area of finance, for example, nobody is disadvantaged because s/he is Orthodox. Despite the clear Toraitic prohibition against taking interest from fellow Jews (Exodus 22:24), the banking system in Israel works smoothly. . . . The organized Orthodox rabbinate is able to resolve the problem of *agunot;* it simply has chosen not to do so" ("The *Agunah* and Divorce," 197).

21. Irwin H. Haut, "'The Altar Weeps': Divorce in Jewish Law," in *Women in Chains: A Sourcebook on the Agunah,* ed. Jack Nusan Porter (Northvale, NJ: Jason Aronson, 1995), 51.

22. Shlomo Riskin, *Women and Jewish Divorce: The Rebellious Wife, the Agunah, and the Right of Women to Initiate Divorce in Jewish Law, a Halakhic Solution* (Hoboken, NJ: Ktav Publishing House, 1989), 134.

23. Ibid., 135.

24. There are three such organizations in the United States: the GET (Getting Equitable Treatment) Organization; Agunah, Inc.; and Kayama. See Adena Berkowitz, "The Prisoners of Divorce," *Lilith,* no. 18 (January 1988): 23. In the 1990s, Agunah, Inc.; GET; and a number of other organizations working for *agune* rights formed a coalition, the International Coalition for Agunah Rights (ICAR), which is active in North America and Israel. According to Rivka Haut, "The *Agunah* and Divorce," 196, "ICAR's primary goal is to influence the Israeli rabbinate to enact rabbinic legislation that will impact Jews all over the world,"

25. Levy, "The Agunah and the Missing Husband," 51.

26. Greenberg, *On Women and Judaism,* 135.

27. Ibid., 129.

2. Doubly Exiled in Germany

1. In the German and English translations, she is commonly known as Glückel because those translations have used the Germanized version of her name, Glikl (both Yiddish *glik* and German *Glück* signify either "good luck" or "happiness"). Her husband, Khayim (often transliterated as Chaim) adopted the name of his birthplace, Hameln (Yiddish *Hamel*), as a family name after he left there (in Hamburg he was called Khayim Hamel—that is, the Khayim who was from Hamel). His wife has often been referred to as Glückel *von* (of) Hameln, but when she speaks of her husband's family, she does not use *of* or *from*. Natalie Zemon Davis, "Glikl Bas Judah Leib: Arguing with God," in *Women on the Margins: Three Seventeenth-Century Lives* (Cambridge, MA: Harvard University, 1995), 8–9, argues that "Jewish names slipped and slid in the seventeenth and early eighteenth centuries," but Davis has opted to call her "Glikl bas Judah Leib, a name she [Glikl] chose among her father's names to give to her son born after his death." But since Glikl's name has been so widely connected with Khayim's birthplace, and since her writing—including its impetus—is so intimately intertwined with the life she shared with her husband, I refer to her in this study as Glikl Hamel.

2. Glikl's writings carry no title or genre designation, but the term *memoirs* (Yiddish *Zikhroynes;* German *Memoiren* or *Denkwürdigkeiten*) was given by editors, publishers, and translators of the original or translated texts. See Chava Turniansky, "Glikls Werk und die zeitgenössische jiddische Literatur," in *Die Hamburger Kauffrau Glikl: Jüdische Existenz in der frühen Neuzeit,* ed. Monika Richarz (Hamburg: Hans Christians Verlag, 2001), esp. 68–71. Following are the major texts of Glikl's manuscript. The original text, *Zikhroynes mores Glikl Hamel* (also noted in that edition on a title page as *Die Memoiren der Glückel von Hameln, 1645–1719*), ed. David Kaufmann (Frankfurt am Main: J. Kauffmann, 1896), is the publication of Glikl's writing based largely on a manuscript recorded by her son, Rabbi Moses Hamel of Baiersdorf, with emendations based on the only other extant manuscript recorded in 1799, by her grandnephew Khayim Hamel. Glikl's original writing has been lost. A good modern Yiddish translation is Glikl Hamil, *Zikhroynes,* trans. Yosef Bernfeld, ed. Shmuel Rozsansky (Buenos Aires: YIVO Literary Society, 1967). Two German translations are *Die Memoiren der Glückel von Hameln, geboren in Hamburg 1645, gestorben in Metz 19. September 1724,* trans. Bertha Pappenheim (Vienna: Meyer and Pappenheim, 1910), an excellent translation of the complete manuscript without notes; and *Denkwürdigkeiten der Glückel von Hameln,* trans. and ed. Alfred Feilchenfeld (Königstein: Jüdischer Verlag, 1980), which was originally translated and published in 1913, is a truncated and manipulated translation. There are two English translations: *The Life of Glückel von Hameln, 1646–1724, Written by Herself,* trans. Beth-Zion Abrahams (London: East and West Library, 1962), is a very good translation of almost the entire text (small omissions often include Glikl's religious entreaties, such as the homage to God that concludes the *agune* segment); and *The Memoirs of Glückel of Hameln,*

trans. Marvin Lowenthal (New York: Schocken, 1977), based almost solely on Feilchenfeld's work, is a very poorly translated and badly truncated version of the original. The translations into English in this study are, for the most part, mine, but page references to the editions mentioned above are cited after the name of the translator or editor.

Dorothy Bilik, "*The Memoirs of Glikl of Hameln:* The Archeology of the Text," *Yiddish* 8, no. 2 (1992): 6, quotes from and agrees with Hans Lamm's remark in his brief introduction to Feilchenfeld's edition about the pomposity of the term *Denkwürdigkeiten* (Memorabilia) used for its title. However, the term may be more descriptive than pompous; it is the term that Kaufmann uses most frequently in the preface and introduction to his edition; the term *Memoiren* appears even less frequently than *Aufzeichnungen* (notes or records) to refer to Glikl's writing. One may assume that *Denkwürdigkeiten* refers to the abundance of tales, anecdotes, ideas, and insights (many of which are actually omitted from Feilchenfeld's translation) not usually associated with a memoir.

3. Zwi Batscha, "Nachwort" [Afterword], in *Salomon Maimons Lebensgeschichte: Von ihm selbst geschrieben,* ed. Karl Philipp Moritz, newly edited by Zwi Batscha (Frankfurt am Main: Insel, 1984), 374, 375. The expression "leap into the alien history," which Batscha applies to Maimon, refers to a remark in Jürgen Habermas, "Der deutsche Idealismus der jüdischen Philosophen" [The German Idealism of Jewish Philosophers], in *Philosophisch-politische Profile* (Frankfurt am Main: Suhrkamp, 1981), 45, about the Jews who moved out of the ghettos into the enlightened culture of the dominant society.

4. Kaufmann, 234; Bernfeld, 258, translated as *groyse gesheyenish* (great event); Pappenheim, 221; Feilchenfeld, 210, translated as *etwas schlimmes* ("something bad"); Abrahams, 128, translated as "a wonderful incident"; Lowenthal, 184, translated as "something terrible," apparently translating Feilchenfeld's version. Only Bernfeld and Pappenheim retain the importance of the "story" in the original; the others emphasize the consequence of the event itself.

5. M. Grunwald, "Das Zeitalter der Glückel von Hameln," in *Hamburgs deutsche Juden bis zur Auflösung der Dreigemeinden, 1811* (Hamburg: Alfred Janssen, 1904), 14.

6. See Samuel ben Meir Hekscher's Hebrew account of the event taken from his notes, in Kaufmann, 394–400.

7. See, for example, N. B. Minkoff, *Glickel Hamel (1645–1724)* (New York: M. Vaxer, 1952), esp. chapters 5–8 (the chapters are not numbered; I have listed them in the order given), which are concerned with *muser* (ethical) literature and narrative representation, and chapters 9–12, which treat narrative materials and forms. This book, written in Yiddish, does not, for the most part, offer a critical discussion of Glikl's work, but rather interesting impressionistic insights by one of the founders of Yiddish Introspectivist poetry. See also Natalie Zemon Davis, "Glikl Bas Judah Leib," for a comprehensive and very interesting exploration of Glikl's life as a woman and Jew and her writings within the historical context of seventeenth-century German and European culture; and Chava Turniansky, "Glikls Werk und die zeitgenössische jiddische Literatur,"

for a meticulous account of the many complex literary, social, and historical dimensions of Glikl's writings. See also Conrad Wiedemann, "Zwei jüdische Autobiographien im Deutschland des 18. Jahrhunderts: Glückel von Hameln und Salomon Maimon," *Juden in der deutschen Literatur: Ein deutsch-israelitisches Symposium* (Frankfurt am Main: Suhrkamp, 1986), 90–91, 95–96. Bilik notes that "the incidents in Glikl's life are deeply embedded in a matrix of tales, prayers, maxims and exempla" (*"The Memoirs of Glikl of Hameln,"* 3); one might, however, also argue that, in the *agune* narrative, the exemplary tale would best be understood as embedded in a historical event. See also Robert Libeles, "Das Bild und die anderen—Das Bild der Nichtjuden in Glikls Memoiren," in *Die Hamburger Kauffrau Glikl: Jüdische Existenz in der frühen Neuzeit,* ed. Monika Richarz (Hamburg: Hans Christians Verlag, 2001), 135–46. Libeles attributes Glikl's nuanced understanding of the relationship between Christians and Jews in part to *"das Ergebnis ihres literarischen Diskurses, ihre Kreativität und Phantasie, möglicherweise, auch Folge ihrer enttäuschenden Erfahrungen mit Juden"* ("the result of her literary discourse, her creativity and fantasy, possibly also the consequence of her disappointing experiences with Jews" [145]).

8. Kaufmann, 4; Bernfeld, 21–22; Pappenheim, 3; Feilchenfeld, 13; Abrahams, 2; Lowenthal, 1.

9. Kaufmann, 6; Bernfeld, 23–24; Pappenheim, 5; Feilchenfeld omitted; Abrahams, 3; Lowenthal omitted.

10. Kaufmann, 234; Bernfeld, 258; Pappenheim, 221; Feilchenfeld, 221; Abrahams, 128; Lowenthal, 184.

11. The following translation is based largely on *The Life of Glückel of Hameln,* trans. and ed. Beth-Zion Abrahams, 128–35. I have, however, made a number of emendations and additions to the text so that it conforms more accurately to the original.

12. A small group that meets for the purpose of study, each *chevra* studying a different subject, but all dealing with the Bible and Talmud. A *chevra* is known by the name of the subject studied.

13. The term *living widow* is a translation of the Yiddish *almone khaye* (from the Hebrew *almona khaya*) and alludes to the biblical text of II Samuel 20:3, which reads, "And David came to his house in Jerusalem; and the king took the ten women as his concubines, whom he had left to keep the house, and put them in ward, and fed them, but went not unto them. So they were bound until the day of their death, in a condition of living widowhood [*almanut khayut* in the Hebrew]." This, of course, did not mean that they were in fact widows, but that they remained bound to David and because of that were not free to marry anyone else.

14. Kaufmann, 235; Bernfeld, 259; Pappenheim, 221; Feilchenfeld, 211; Abrahams, 128–29; Lowenthal, 185.

15. Grunwald, "Das Zeitalter der Glückel von Hameln," 10.

16. Kaufmann, 246; Bernfeld, 269; Pappenheim, 231; Feilchenfeld, 224–25; Abrahams, 135; Lowenthal, 197.

17. Feilchenfeld, 218n48.

18. Lowenthal, 185ff.

19. Kaufmann, 237; Bernfeld 260–61; Pappenheim, 223; Feilchenfeld, 214; Abrahams, 130; Lowenthal, 187.

20. See M. Grunwald, "Das Zeitalter der Glückel von Hameln," 5–10.

21. Kaufmann, 238–39; Bernfeld, 262; Pappenheim, 224; Feilchenfeld, 216; Abrahams, 131; Lowenthal, 189.

22. Robert Alter, *The Art of Biblical Narrative* (New York: Basic Books, 1981), 146.

23. Kaufmann, 237; Bernfeld, 261; Pappenheim, 223; Feilchenfeld, 214; Abrahams, 130; Lowenthal, 187.

24. See Solomo Aben Verga (Solomon Ibn Verga), *Shevet Jehudah,* trans. M. Wiener (Hannover: Orient-Buchhandlung Heinz Lafaire, 1924), 77–78; two *Jüdischdeutsch* (or Old Yiddish) translations of this work were available in Glikl's time, one published in Krakow in 1591, the other in Amsterdam in 1648. A version of this tale appears as part of the folktale "The Ritual Murder Charge in Constantinople," in Joseph bin Gorion, col., *Mimekor Yisrael: Classical Jewish Folktales,* trans. I. M. Lask, ed. Emanuel bin Gorion (Bloomington: Indiana University Press, 1976), 1:461–63.

25. Psalms 121:4.

26. Kaufmann, 237; Bernfeld, 261; Pappenheim, 223–24; Feilchenfeld, 214–15; Abrahams, 130; Lowenthal, 187–88. Emphasis added.

27. Kaufmann, 236; Bernfeld, 260; Pappenheim, 223; Feilchenfeld, 213; Abrahams, 130; Lowenthal, 187.

28. In 1641 Denmark occupied Altona and expanded the privileges of the Jews, among them direct access to the president of Altona, which is reflected in Glikl's account. See Heinz Mosche Graupe's introduction to *Die Statuten der drei Gemeinden Altona, Hamburg und Wandsbeck: Quellen zur jüdischen Gemeindeorganisation im 17. und 18. Jahrhundert,* ed. and trans. Heinz Mosche Graupe (Hamburg: Hans Christians Verlag, 1973), 1:17.

29. Kaufmann, 242; Bernfeld, 266; Pappenheim, 227; Feilchenfeld, 220; Abrahams, 133; Lowenthal, 192.

30. Kaufmann, 246; Bernfeld, 269; Pappenheim, 231; Feilchenfeld, 224–25; Abrahams, 135; Lowenthal, 197.

31. Many of the earlier critics of Glikl's writing, including laudatory ones, do not credit her with even a modicum of conceptual and interpretive ability; at best they praise her for actually writing a memoir, or for writing one that is personal and yet representative of her time, gender, and status. See, for example, Kaufmann's introduction to Glikl's *Zikhroynes,* esp. xii–xviii. See also Wiedemann, "Zwei jüdische Autobiographien im Deutschland des 18. Jahrhunderts," 91–92, 95–96; and L. Ysaye, "Einiges aus den Memoiren der Glückel von Hameln," *Mitteilungen der Gesellschaft für jüdische Volkskunde* (Hamburg), 7, no. 1 (1901): 4, 7, 8, 10, 16; what little praise the latter has for her diligence in doing what other women have not is consistently called into question by such condescending, sexist comments as "finally we laugh a little about the good,

talkative woman who postures before us" (1); by referring to her as "a simple Jewish woman," "the old Jewish woman," "the old Glikl" (1–3, she was forty-six when she started to write); and by noting that "she has the primitive, gullible belief of a child, she exercises no criticism" (4). There has been a marked change in the understanding of Glikl and her writing accomplishments since the rise of the feminist movement, when more careful, critical attention focused on the literary quality of her writing. See, for example, the works of Chava Turniansky and Natalie Zemon Davis and the many essays in Monika Richarz, ed., *Die Hamburger Kauffrau Glikl: Jüdische Existenz in der frühen Neuzeit* (Hamburg: Hans Christians Verlag, 2001).

32. Kaufmann, 240; Bernfeld, 264; Pappenheim, 226; Feilchenfeld, 218; Abrahams, 132; Lowenthal, 191.

33. Kaufmann, 242–43; Bernfeld, 266–67; Pappenheim, 228; Feilchenfeld, 220–21; Abrahams, 133; Lowenthal, 193.

34. Kaufmann, 245; Bernfeld, 269; Pappenheim, 230; Feilchenfeld, 223–24 passim; Abrahams, 135; Lowenthal, 196.

35. Kaufmann, 246; Bernfeld, 270; Pappenheim, 231; Feilchenfeld, 225; Abrahams omits the entire homage to God; Lowenthal omits this sentence.

36. Leviticus 26:44. Glikl quotes in Hebrew the portion of the verse from which this phrase is taken.

37. Davis's comment—"Rebecca's tenacious efforts to avenge the Jews are thus reported amid the widowed Glikl's unflagging efforts to sustain her 'orphans' against unnamed Jewish and Christian threats" ("Glikl Bas Judah Leib," 38)—seems to overlook the exemplariness of the story as well as the devastating circumstances of *agunes* in Jewish society. The avenging of the Jews seems at best to be an ancillary result of Rebekah's activity on behalf of the *agunes*.

38. Solomon Maimon, *Salomon Maimons Lebensgeschichte: Von ihm selbst geschrieben,* ed. Karl Philipp Moritz and newly edited by Zwi Batscha (Frankfurt am Main: Insel, 1984), 147. (The editors left Maimon's faulty German intact.) The English translation, *The Autobiography of Solomon Maimon,* trans. J. Clark Murray (London: East and West Library, 1954), does not include this preface. Among other things, it omits, in volume 2, ten chapters on Maimonides's works, but it does include in the appendix two omitted chapters: "Mendelssohn—A chapter devoted to the Memory of a worthy Friend," 159–65; and a chapter on the "New Chasidim" titled "On a Secret Society, and therefore a Long Chapter," 166–79. All the translations are mine; and hereafter, where possible, comparable pages in the English translation are cited.

39. Maimon, *Lebensgeschichte,* 146.

40. Ibid., 148

41. Ibid.

42. Ralph-Rainer Wuthenow, *Das erinnerte Ich: Europäische Autobiographie und Selbstdarstellung im 18. Jahrhundert* [The Remembered Self: European Autobiography and Self-Presentation in the 18th Century] (Munich: C. H. Beck, 1974), 39–42.

43. Maimon, *Lebensgeschichte*, 147; see also Batscha "Nachwort" [Afterword], 349–50.

44. Barrett J. Mandel, "Full of Life Now," in *Autobiography: Essays Theoretical and Critical*, ed. James Olney (Princeton: Princeton University Press, 1980), 64.

45. Maimon, *Lebensgeschichte*, 183; Maimon, *Autobiography*, 126.

46. Maimon, *Lebensgeschichte*, 146.

47. Ibid., 97; Maimon, *Autobiography*, 88.

48. Maimon, *Lebensgeschichte*, 198.

49. Ibid., 122; Maimon, *Autobiography*, 93.

50. Maimon, *Lebensgeschichte*, 86; Maimon, *Autobiography*, 79.

51. Maimon, *Lebensgeschichte*, 200; Maimon, *Autobiography*, 142.

52. Daniel Boyarin, "Internal Opposition in Talmudic Literature: The Case of the Married Monk," *Representations* 36 (Fall 1991): 99.

53. Maimon, *Lebensgeschichte*, 13; Maimon, *Autobiography*, 12–13.

54. Maimon, *Lebensgeschichte*, 42; Maimon, *Autobiography*, 39–40.

55. Maimon, *Lebensgeschichte*, 44, see also 29–30; Maimon, *Autobiography*, 41, see also 28.

56. Maimon, *Lebensgeschichte*, 200; Maimon, *Autobiography*, 141.

57. Maimon, *Lebensgeschichte*, 198–99; Maimon, *Autobiography*, 140.

58. Maimon, *Lebensgeschichte*, 199; Maimon, *Autobiography*, 140.

59. Maimon, *Lebensgeschichte*, 182; Maimon, *Autobiography*, 126.

60. Maimon, *Lebensgeschichte*, 186; Maimon, *Autobiography*, 129. From 1783 to 1785, Maimon attended the Christianeum Gymnasium in Altona, a city adjacent to Hamburg. Maimon mentions almost no dates, although the *Autobiography* is specific when mapping his life spatially or geographically. For more information on the Christianeum, see Franklin Kopitzsch, *Grundzüge einer Sozialgeschichte der Aufklärung in Hamburg und Altona* [Main Features of a Social History of the Enlightenment in Hamburg and Altona], pt. 2 (Hamburg: Hans Christians Verlag, 1982), 713–38.

61. Maimon, *Lebensgeschichte*, 187; Maimon, *Autobiography*, 130.

62. Maimon, *Lebensgeschichte*, 189; Maimon, *Autobiography*, 131.

63. Babylonian Talmud, Sanhedrin 7B.

64. See, for example, the chapter "Kurze Darstellung der jüdischen Religion von ihrem Ursprung bis auf die neuesten Zeiten" (in this edition of the *Lebensgeschichte* it appears in the *Anhang* [appendix], esp. 228–30), where Maimon presents the positive aspects of rabbinism and of Polish Jewish culture. This chapter is omitted from the English translation. Also note that in Maimon's written and verbal communication with the Christian pastor, mentioned above, the reasons for seeking conversion were so blatantly unacceptable that they all but guaranteed rejection, which is what in fact happened. There is more than a suggestion here that this was hardly a serious attempt at baptism. Maimon, *Lebensgeschichte*, 182–85; Maimon, *Autobiography*, 126–28.

65. Wuthenow, *Das erinnerte Ich*, 107.

66. Maimon, *Lebensgeschichte*, 199; Maimon, *Autobiography*, 140.

67. Maimon, *Lebensgeschichte*, 198; Maimon, *Autobiography*, 140.

68. Maimon, *Lebensgeschichte*, 200; Maimon, *Autobiography*, 141.

69. Maimon, *Lebensgeschichte*, 198–99; Maimon, *Autobiography*, 140.

70. Maimon, *Lebensgeschichte*, 200; Maimon, *Autobiography*, 141.

71. Maimon, *Lebensgeschichte*, 200; Maimon, *Autobiography*, 141–42.

72. Blu Greenberg, *On Women and Judaism: A View from Tradition* (Philadelphia: Jewish Publication Society of America, 1981), 129.

73. Maimon, *Lebensgeschichte*, 201; Maimon, *Autobiography*, 142.

74. If the grounds for compelling a man to divorce his wife are fulfilled and the court orders him to do so, he is legally obligated to do so; but in the Diaspora it has been virtually impossible to enforce this. In Israel, husbands may be imprisoned for contempt of court, but no such mechanism is possible outside of Israel. The Talmud states that coercion may be used until the husband states, "I want to" (Yevamot 106a), but beating, imprisoning, or otherwise harming someone living in the Diaspora usually contravenes a nation's civil law.

75. Maimon, *Lebensgeschichte*, 200; Maimon, *Autobiography*, 142.

76. Maimon, *Lebensgeschichte*, 188; *Autobiography*, 131; the English translation refers to it merely as "tribunal."

77. Maimon, *Lebensgeschichte*, 200; Maimon, *Autobiography*, 142.

78. Maimon, *Lebensgeschichte*, 63; Maimon, *Autobiography*, 31.

79. Maimon, *Lebensgeschichte*, 65; Maimon, *Autobiography*, 62.

80. Maimon, *Lebensgeschichte*, 198; Maimon, *Autobiography*, 140.

81. Wuthenow, *Das erinnerte Ich*, 103.

82. Maimon, *Lebensgeschichte*, 71; Maimon, *Autobiography*, 6.

83. Maimon, *Lebensgeschichte*, 147;

84. Maimon, *Lebensgeschichte*, 146.

85. Maimon, *Lebensgeschichte*, 154–55; Maimon, *Autobiography*, 110–11.

86. Wuthenow, *Das erinnerte Ich*, 43.

87. Maimon, *Lebensgeschichte*, 66; Maimon, *Autobiography*, 62. See also *Lebensgeschichte*, 223, not in the English translation. "The pen slips from my hand at the memory that I and others like me must pass the best years, when our powers are in their full strength, with this spirit-deadening business [Talmud studies] and stay awake nights in order to bring a meaning to what has no meaning . . . through a long chain of deductions to seize a shadow and build castles in the air." (*Die Feder entfällt meiner Hand bei der Erinnerung, daß ich und mehrere meinesgleichen die besten Jahre, wo die Kräfte in ihrer vollen Stärke sind, mit diesem geisttötenden Geschäft zubringen und Nächte durchwachen mußte, um, wo kein Sinn ist, einen Sinn hereinzubringen . . . durch eine lange Kette von Schlüssen nach einem Schatten zu haschen und Schlösser in die Luft zu bauen.*)

3. The Victims of Adventure

1. See Paul Georg Neumair, *Der Typus des Abenteurers in der neuen deutschen Dichtung* [The Prototype of the Adventurer in Modern German

Literature] (Limburg a.d. Lahm: Limburger Vereinsdrückerei, 1933), esp. chap. 4, "Versuch einer Typologie" [Attempt at a typology]. "The physical existence of the adventurer is youth. Youth is the power of all adventure, which is not conceivable without emotional or intellectual robustness and tirelessness" (104, my translation).

2. *Brivnshteler,* manuals for letter writing, which existed in various languages—Hebrew, Yiddish, English—for about four hundred years, offered to members of the Jewish community appropriate formats and exemplars of letters for professional, commercial, and personal communication. Although the letters using these formats are individual, the use of formats and exemplars creates a communal context for epistolary communication. For a brief discussion of *brivnshteler* as a genre, and of the popular Bloshteyn *brivnshteler* (Naftali Hertz Naimanovitich, *Bloshteyns briefenshteler* [Warsaw: Yakov Yitsakh Reinerman, 1924]) that appeared in either 1903 or 1904 plus a sampling of its letters in English translation, see Lewis Glinert, trans., *Mamme Dear. A Turn-of-the-Century Collection of Model Yiddish Letters* (Northvale, NJ: Jason Aronson, 1997); and Joseph Bar-El, "The Yiddish Briefenshteler (Letter Writing Manual of the 18th to 20th Century)" (master's thesis, Touro College, New York, 1970). Also see Alexander Harkavy, *Harkavis amerikanisher briefen-shteler, english un yidish* [Harkavy's American Letter Writer, with Useful Information and a Treatise on Bookkeeping; English and Yiddish] (1892; reprint, New York: Hebrew Publishing, 1902). For a comprehensive discussion of Sholem Aleykhem's use of the *brivnshteler* in *Menakhem-Mendl,* see Jennifer Sylvor's doctoral dissertation, "Literary Impersonations: On the Development of National Prose Traditions in Russian and Yiddish." PhD diss., University of California, Berkeley, 2000), 194–197.

3. "To accomplish the radical liberation of his self, the adventurer disconnects himself from everything that signifies an attachment to people: bourgeois security is his constriction *[Einengung].* Liberation begins necessarily with the destruction of all bonds of blood. . . . Especially the absence of a woman in his life is conspicuous" (Neumair, *Der Typus des Abenteurers in der neuen deutschen Dichtung,* 104–5 passim, my translation). For an interesting and illuminating analysis of adventure and adventurers, see Margaret Elizabeth Morse's doctoral dissertation, "The Works of Arthur Schnitzler as an Index of Cultural Change: Relationships Between the Sexes in Society, Ideology, and the Imagination" (PhD diss., University of California, Berkeley, 1977), especially pt. 3 ("Adventure"), chap. 4 ("The Motif of Adventure as a System of Sexual Relationships in the Imagination," 76–107).

4. See Salo W. Baron, *The Russian Jew under Tsars and Soviets* (New York: Macmillan, 1964), especially his discussion of Jewish economic structures in the nineteenth century and the pauperization of the masses (113–18). "It has been estimated that in many communities [of Eastern Europe] up to 40 percent of the entire Jewish population consisted of families of so-called *Luftmenschen,* that is persons without any particular skills, capital, or specific occupations" (114). See also the 1935 essay by Max Erik, "*Menakhem-Mendl:* A Marxist Critique,"

Prooftexts 6 (1986): 23–39. Erik regards Menakhem-Mendl as "a petty bourgeois without a set profession" in the period between the decline of feudalism and developed capitalism (28) and reads the novel as a "scathing, demolishing critique of the *luftmentsh* and of his so-called livelihoods" (23). See Sylvor's informative discussion of the luftmentsh in a segment ("Incorporating the Luftmentsh") of her dissertation, "Literary Impersonations," chap. 4, 204–16.

5. See Dan Miron, *A Traveler Disguised: A Study in the Rise of Modern Yiddish Fiction in the Nineteenth Century* (New York: Schocken, 1973), esp. chap. 5, "The Mendele Maze; 1. The Pseudonym Fallacy," 130–68. For Miron, the name Mendele Moykher Sforim "does not meet the technical criteria for a pseudonym, that is, it does not involve an attribution of authorship to a false name." Mendele does not present himself as the author of the works he delivers to the public, but as their translator or promoter or both (157). The name Mendele the Bookpeddler "conveys a host of social and economic facts": a profession and the social setting in which this profession makes sense, a specific way of life—"in short, much of what goes into the creation of a dramatic character" (158).

6. Sholem Yakov Abramovitsh, *Masoes benyomin hashlishi*, vol. 9, *Ale verk fun mendele moykher-sforim*, ed. N. Mayzl (Warsaw: Farlag Mendele, 1928) (hereafter noted as *Masoes*), 7. All citations in Yiddish refer to this text. Also included are citations to two available English translations: *The Travels and Adventures of Benjamin the Third*, trans. Moshe Spiegel (New York: Schocken, 1949) (hereafter noted as Spiegel), 15; and *The Travels of Benjamin the Third*, in *The Shtetl*, trans. and ed. Joachim Neugroschel (New York: Perigee, 1979) (hereafter noted as Neugroschel), 181. Where necessary I have translated the citations for greater accuracy, but have provided page references to the two English translations.

7. *Masoes*, 7; Spiegel, 15; Neugroschel, 181.

8. *Masoes*, 8; Spiegel, 16; Neugroschel, 182.

9. *Masoes*, 8; Spiegel, 16; Neugroschel, 182. Dan Miron and Anita Norich, "The Politics of Benjamin III: Intellectual Significance and Its Formal Correlatives in Sh. Y. Abramovitsh's *Masoes benyomin hashlishi*," in *The Field of Yiddish: Studies in Language, Folklore, and Literature*, ed. Martin Herzog, Barbara Kirshenblatt-Gimblett, Dan Miron, and Ruth Wisse, 4th collection (Philadelphia: Institute for the Study of Human Issues, 1980), 1–115. On the parody of the British parliamentary system and the importance of Benjamin Disraeli, see 49–54.

10. Daniel Boyarin, "Internal Opposition in Talmudic Literature: The Case of the Married Monk," *Representations* 36 (Fall 1991): 99; see also 107.

11. Within the androcentric system of traditional Judaism, men controlled the privileged hegemonic center while women were excluded from the most culturally valued practice of Talmud study. See Daniel Boyarin, *Unheroic Conduct: The Rise of Heterosexuality and the Invention of the Jewish Man* (Berkeley: University of California Press, 1997), 152–53; and Judith Romney Wegner, *Chattel or Person? The Status of Women in the Mishnah* (New York: Oxford University Press, 1988), chap. 6, esp. 146–48.

12. See Louis Ginzberg, *The Legends of the Jews*, vol. 1, trans. Henrietta Szold (1909; reprint, Baltimore: Johns Hopkins University Press, 1998), 286.

13. See "Shekhinah," in *Encyclopedia Judaica* (Jerusalem: Keter, 1972), 14:1349–54, esp. 1353–54.

14. *Masoes,* 28; Spiegel, 39 (this sentence omitted from this translation); Neugroschel, 198.

15. Dvora Baron, *"The First Day" and Other Stories,* ed. and trans. Naomi Seidman and Chana Kronfeld (Berkeley: University of California Press, 2001), 90–98.

16. *Masoes,* 28; Spiegel, 39; Neugroschel, 198.

17. See Miron and Norich, "The Politics of Benjamin III," 55–70, for an illuminating discussion of the complex social and political representation of the relationship between Benjamin the Third and Senderl.

18. *Masoes,* 14; Spiegel, 23; Neugroschel, 187.

19. *Masoes,* 22; Spiegel, 32; Neugroschel, 193.

20. *Masoes,* 25; Spiegel, 36; Neugroschel, 195.

21. *Masoes,* 25; Spiegel, 36 (sentence omitted from this translation); Neugroschel, 195–96.

22. *Masoes,* 50–51; Spiegel, 34–35; Neugroschel, 194.

23. *Masoes,* 31; Spiegel, 43; Neugroschel, 201.

24. *Masoes,* 35; Spiegel, 47; Neugroschel, 203.

25. *Masoes,* 35; Spiegel, 46–47; Neugroschel, 203.

26. *Masoes,* 109; Spiegel, 116; Neugroschel, 258.

27. *Masoes,* 109; Spiegel, 117; Neugroschel, 258.

28. *Masoes,* 109; Spiegel, 117; Neugroschel, 258.

29. *Masoes,* 110; Spiegel, 117; Neugroschel, 258.

30. *Masoes,* 117; Spiegel, 123; Neugroschel, 264.

31. *Masoes,* 116; Spiegel, 122; Neugroschel, 262. The Spiegel translation reads "Once a Bride, Again a Maid"; Neugroschel's is "The Wedding's Off, We're Free Again!"

32. See Chone Shmeruk, "Vegen sholem-aleykhems letzter *menakhem-mendl*-serye" [About Sholem Aleykhem's last *Menakhem-Mendl* Series], in *Die goldene keyt* [The Golden Chain], 56 (1966): 22, for an explanation of how the "Preface to the Second Edition" was actually a preface to the first and only edition of the novel. The first exchange of letters between Menakhem-Mendl and Sheyne-Sheyndl was published in 1892 in *Kol mevaser tsu der yidisher folks-bibliotek* (Voice of the Herald to the Yiddish People's Library) and appears as the first book ("London") of the novel. "At least from 1892 [the date of the earliest *menakhem-mendl* letters] to the book at the end of 1909, which Sholem Aleykhem labeled a 'second edition,' the Menakhem-Mendl figure continued to grow in a succession of letter series and of separate letters, which in 1909 remained scattered in anthologies, journals, and daily newspapers. And even though Menakhem-Mendl had already for a long time been a renowned figure in the Yiddish world, until the book-edition there had not existed a bit of the 'first edition' in the plain and direct sense of the description. When Sholem Aleykhem started to gather the Menakhem-Mendl material, he edited the book anew. He reworked the material linguistically and stylistically, intensified the

figures and made them more plastic. From the earlier divided series he artistically and consciously formed a uniform, organic work, which is considered among the greatest accomplishments of our modern literature. But Sholem Aleykhem did not want or was unable to use the entire collected Menakhem-Mendl material for this 'second edition'" (my translation).

33. Sholem Aleykhem, *Menakhem-Mendl*, in *Ale verk fun sholem-aleykhem* (1912; reprint, New York: Morgn-Frayhayt Ausgabe, 1937) (hereafter cited as *Menakhem*), i–ii. There is no English translation of the preface; the translation of the citations to the preface is mine. Where necessary I have also translated the citations from the novel for greater accuracy, but have always provided page references to the two English translations.

34. For example, Max Erik regards Sheyne-Sheyndl as a "coarse, small-town shrew," a "Kasrilevke shrew" who embodies "the fantasy of the precapitalist order, and is always the target of the author's laughter" (*"Menakhem-Mendl,"* 36–37). For Shmuel Niger, Sheyne-Sheyndl is a Kasrilevke woman who is deeply rooted in her shtetl and who "sits like a worm in the horseradish and thinks that no sweeter thing exists" (*Sholem aleykhem: Zayne vikhtikste verk, zayn humor, zayn ort in der yidisher literatur* [Sholem Aleykhem: His Most Important Works, His Humor, and His Place in Yiddish Literature] [New York: Yidisher Kultur Farlag, 1928], 95), an expression that Sheyne-Sheyndl, quoting her mother, actually applies to Menakhem-Mendl and his obsession with Odessa, or she is merely a *yente* (a busybody or vulgar woman; 98). For Y.Y. Trunk, Sheyne-Sheyndl, regarded merely as an "antithesis" to the adventuresome dreamer and fantasizer Menakhem-Mendl, is the practical housewife with no great ambitions. Since, Trunk notes, like all Jewish women she is wedded to the "children's cradle and the pot on the stove," "nature did not need to 'compensate' her with enough fantasy and provide her with the 'wings' to lift herself above boundless reality to the boundless illusion" (*Tevye un menakhem-mendel in yidishn velt-goyrl* [Tevye and Menakhem-Mendl in the Fate of the Jewish World] [New York: Bikher Farlag, 1944], 188–89; see esp. chaps. 2–4).

35. See note 2.

36. Although Max Erik speaks about "the patriarchal respect that she [Sheyne-Sheyndl] feels for her husband, the man of the house" and remarks that "his failures never shake her certainty that her Mendl is the smartest and most educated man on earth" (*"Menakhem-Mendl,"* 37), there is no indication in her letters that supports this estimation of his intellectual abilities, nor does Erik provide any evidence. In the introduction to his translation of *Menakhem-Mendl*, Hillel Halkin refers to Sheyne-Sheyndl's "love for her husband, or, more accurately, her pride in his education," but he too offers no evidence for either of these observations (*The Letters of Menakhem-Mendl and Sheyne Sheyndl*, in *The Letters of Menakhem-Mendl and Sheyne-Sheyndl and Motl, the Cantor's Son*, trans. Hillel Halkin [New Haven: Yale University, 2002] [hereafter cited as Halkin], xiv). Curiously enough, in an interesting essay, Yakov Glatshteyn does not maintain that Sheyne-Sheyndl admires or is even cognizant of her husband's intellect or scholarly ability. But he does write that she harbors for him

a "great love, a Jewish love," and "that she knows he will accomplish nothing, but is always ready to forgive him." Glatshteyn then concludes that "quietly" she is herself a Menakhem-Mendl, likes what he is doing, despite his failures, that he is "her small window into the big world," and although she may laugh at his urbanity, "she yearns for it in her heart" (*"Menakhem-Mendl,"* in *In tokh genumen: Essayn, 1945–1947* [In Essence: Essays, 1945–1947] [New York: Matones, 1947], 473). While this essay provides many interesting and illuminating insights into the language of this novel, Glatshteyn's speculations about the benefits that Menakhem-Mendl's behavior provides for his "eternally loving" wife seem more like male fantasies than critical interpretations of the text.

37. See James A. Matisoff, *Blessings, Curses, Hopes, and Fears: Psycho-Ostensive Expressions in Yiddish* (Stanford: Stanford University, 2000), esp. chap. 9, "Allo-Malo-Petition: Curses!" 71–88. Perhaps Sheyne-Sheyndl's curses may best be understood as curses having a therapeutic function, which, according to Matisoff, "are convenient, conventionalized ways of letting off steam—bursts of psychic energy that might otherwise remain hopelessly bottled up, to the detriment of the speaker's mental health" (103).

38. See, for example, *Menakhem,* 28, 35, 109; Sholom Aleichem, *The Adventures of Menahem-Mendel,* trans. Tamara Kahana (New York: G. P. Putnam's Sons, 1969; hereafter cited as Kahana), 39, 47, 117; Halkin, 198, 203, 258.

39. See, for example, *Menakhem,* 20; Kahana, 26; Halkin, 8. Hereafter, page references are given to the Yiddish text and to the two translations, Kahana and Halkin. Where necessary I have translated the citations for greater accuracy, but have provided page references to the two English translations.

40. Niger observes that Menakhem-Mendl exists between the shtetl's narrow confines and the metropolis but has not yet adapted to the demands of urban life, a position that, Niger claims, is the basis of humor in the novel (*Sholem aleykhem,* 95–99).

41. By what seems like an incredible leap of fantasy, Trunk sees Sheyne-Sheyndl's mother as a "more thoughtful antithetic type of woman" whose "practicality had crystallized into a higher more human rationality." This he concludes from the mother's sayings that Sheyne-Sheyndl quotes. He assumes from the mother's adages that she "is practical because of her great life experience and because of her large observation of life," which he characterizes as "masculine" and which make her "almost philosophic." Sheyne-Sheyndl's practicality is regarded as inferior because it is "instinctive" and the "result of her feminine lack of verve." Trunk seems not to realize that the mother's many adages are merely part of the stock of folk wisdom handed down from generation to generation and shared by the community, especially among women (*Tevye un menakhem-mendl in yidishn velt-goyrl,* 190).

42. See *Menakhem,* 95, 101–2, 134–35, 141; Kahana, 100, 106, 138–39, 144–45; Halkin, 44, 47, 63, 65–66. See also Niger on the "modern" changes taking place in Kasrilevke (*Sholem aleykhem,* 97–100). Raymond Williams argues that "capitalism, as a mode of production, is the basic process of most of what we know as the history of country and city" (*The Country and the City* [New York: Oxford,

1973], 298–302 passim). And it has both "altered our country and created our cities," which accounts for the "real social processes of alienation, separation, externality, abstraction" found in country and city alike, albeit in different degrees.

43. *Menakhem,* i–ii.

44. Ian Watt, *The Rise of the Novel: Studies in Defoe, Richardson, and Fielding* (Berkeley: University of California Press, 1957). In a chapter concerning "individualism" and the novel, Watt maintains that the concept of individualism "posits a whole society mainly governed by the idea of every individual's intrinsic independence both from other individuals and from that multifarious allegiance to past modes of thought and action denoted by the word 'tradition'—a force that is always social, not individual." Such a society, however, is based on "a special type of economic and political organization and an appropriate ideology," which he identifies as the rise of modern industrial capitalism" (60). See two essays by Lionel Trilling, "Manners, Morals, and the Novel" and "Art and Fortune," in *The Liberal Imagination: Essays on Literature and Society* (New York: Doubleday, 1950), in which he explores, at the "very heart" of the novel, the function of money and its relationship to reality, to illusion and, in a "shifting society," to matters of social class. See also the introduction to Ruth Perry, *Women, Letters, and the Novel* (New York: AMS, 1980), ix–xiii.

45. See, for example, Williams, *The Country and the City,* especially chapters 22 and 25. Although he focuses largely on the history of England and its cultural production, his insights into the separation of country and city, their changing interrelations over time, and the complex tensions between them are especially relevant for *Menakhem-Mendl.* Particularly important are Williams's discussions of mobility and immobility, isolation, and alienation that become apparent during the "metropolitan phase of development," when capitalism is the major mode of production. But he notes, "The pull of the idea of the country is toward old ways, human ways, natural ways. The pull of the ideas of the city is toward progress, modernisation, development. . . . We have really to look, in city and country alike, at the real social processes of alienation, separation, externality, abstraction" (297–98 passim).

46. See Dan Miron, "A Sampling of *Menakhem-Mendl,*" *Michigan Germanic Studies* 3, no. 2 (1977): 13–33, for a comprehensive, nuanced, and illuminating reading of the first letter of the novel.

47. Niger perceives Menakhem-Mendl as being possessed by a typically Jewish, indeed essentially Jewish, mania for buying and selling, for marketing and brokerage, even for swindling, which drives the Jew whether he wants or needs to or not (*Sholem aleykhem,* 90–91). For Miron, on the other hand, "Menakhem-Mendl is the caricature of a *homo economicus*—the man who reduces everything to its market value (although he never understands the rules of the market)," and who tries in vain to establish a sense of importance by reducing everything (including himself, of course) to exchange value ("A Sampling of *Menakhem-Mendl,* 31). This *homo economicus* does not possess an essential "marketing trait," much less an essential Jewish one, as Niger would have it, but rather one that develops under certain social, political, and economic conditions.

48. *Menakhem,* 86; Kahana, 77; Halkin, 32 (sentence omitted in this translation).

49. *Menakhem,* 99; Kahana, 91; Halkin, 39.

50. *Menakhem,* 58; Kahana, 43; Halkin, 16.

51. *Menakhem,* 150; Kahana, 153–54; Halkin, 69.

52. *Menakhem,* ii.

53. *Menakhem,* 150; Kahana, 154; Halkin, 70.

54. *Menakhem,* 133; Kahana, 137–38; Halkin, 62.

55. *Menakhem,* 160–61 passim; Kahana, 165; Halkin, 74.

56. *Menakhem,* 91; Kahana, 96; Halkin, 42.

57. *Menakhem,* 156; Kahana, 162; Halkin, 73.

58. *Menakhem,* 200–201; Kahana, 214; Halkin, 98.

59. *Menakhem,* 162–63; Kahana, 167; Halkin, 75.

60. *Menakhem,* 173; Kahana, 177; Halkin, 80.

61. *Menakhem,* 158; Kahana, 162; Halkin, 73.

62. *Menakhem,* 208–9; Kahana, 212; Halkin, 97.

63. *Menakhem,* 210–11; Kahana, 214; Halkin, 98 (Halkin translates *shlim-shlimazl* as "always a loser").

64. *Menakhem,* 211; Kahana, 214–15; Halkin, 98.

65. *Menakhem,* 203; Kahana, 206–7; Halkin, 94 (Halkin here translates *shlimazl* as "Stumblebum").

66. *Menakhem,* 194; Kahana, 198; Halkin, 90.

67. *Menakhem,* 162–63; Kahana, 166; Halkin, 75.

68. *Menakhem,* 163; Kahana, 167; Halkin, 75.

69. *Menakhem,* 129; Kahana, 133; Halkin, 60 (here Halkin translates *shlimazl* as "sucker").

70. *Menakhem,* 171; Kahana, 175; Halkin, 79.

71. *Menakhem,* 176; Kahana, 181; Halkin, 81.

72. *Menakhem,* 176–77; Kahana, 181–82; Halkin, 81.

73. *Menakhem,* 218–19; Kahana, 221; Halkin, 102.

74. *Menakhem,* 15; Kahana, 21; Halkin, 5

75. *Menakhem,* 179; Kahana, 183; Halkin, 82.

76. *Menakhem,* 15; Kahana, 21; Halkin, 5.

77. *Menakhem,* 20; Kahana, 26; Halkin, 8.

78. *Menakhem,* 161; Kahana, 165; Halkin, 74.

79. *Menakhem,* 30; Kahana, 36; Halkin, 12.

80. *Menakhem,* 113; Kahana, 117; Halkin, 52. Sheyne-Sheyndl implies that Menakhem-Mendl's irresponsible behavior is actually "feminizing" this husband and father. In the final letter of the first book ("London"), she implores him not to go on trying to make money, but instead to put his trust in God and return home: "The main point, don't be a *yidene* [Jewish woman or housewife], Mendl!" *(der iker, zolst nit zayn keyn yidene, mendl!) Menakhem,* 41; Kahana, 47; Halkin, 18.

81. *Menakhem,* 140; Kahana, 143; Halkin, 65.

82. *Menakhem,* 15; Kahana, 21; Halkin, 5.

83. *Menakhem*, 88; Kahana, 93; Halkin, 40–41.

84. Almost all the critics identify Menakhem-Mendl as a luftmentsh but do not condemn the desertion of his family. Indeed, Trunk even waxes lyrical, saying that Menakhem-Mendl, because he is a liar and lives in a world of fantasies, should be admired as "a writer, a poet, a dreamer." He absolves him of any familial or communal responsibilities because he "is like an autumn leaf, which the wind had already torn from the tree, and now he hovers in the air, the winds carry him and drive him in all the four corners, with no support, with no support" (*Tevye un menakhem-mendel in yidishn velt-goyrl*, 93, 95).

85. See *Menakhem*, 49, 179; Kahana, 55, 183; Halkin, 21, 82.

86. *Menakhem*, 49; Kahana, 55; Halkin, 21.

87. According to Lewis Mumford, "The swish and crackle of paper is the underlying sound of the metropolis. . . . What is visible and real in this world is only what has been transferred to paper." In art, business, and the academy "reputations are made—on paper"; and power and importance is measured "by the amount of paper they can command" (*The Culture of Cities* [1935; reprint, New York: Harcourt Brace Jovanovich, 1970)], 256–57 passim). Throughout *Menakhem-Mendl* the insubstantiality and abstractness of the protagonist and his numerous undertakings—from his letter writing, the worthless promissory notes received from his cousin, his currency speculations, and dealings in stocks (*papirlekh*, or "scraps of paper"), to his adventures as a matchmaker using lists of names on paper, his vitae, and writings for the *Gazette*—are connected with paper. In book 2, *Papirlekh* ("Scraps of Paper"), when he is exultant about a great imminent victory, Sheyne-Sheyndl tells him to cash in his stocks, quoting her mother: "As long as the money exists on paper, it is paper" (*kolzman dos gelt iz oyfn papir, iz dos papir; Menakhem*, 73; Kahana, 79; Halkin, 33). See also Larzer Ziff, who is interested in the importance of the "new culture of print" for the shift from a "culture of immanence to a culture of representation." This print culture made it possible to be "what one represented oneself as being" (*Writing in the New Nation: Prose, Print, and Politics in the Early United States* [New Haven: Yale University Press, 1991], 17). See also page 29 for the importance of paper currency in the move to a market economy. See Sylvor, "Literary Impersonations," 216–26.

88. *Menakhem*, 54–55; Kahana, 60–61; Halkin, 24.

89. *Menakhem*, 79; Kahana, 85; Halkin, 37.

90. *Menakhem*, 113–14; Kahana, 117–18; Halkin, 52.

91. *Menakhem*, 161; Kahana, 165; Halkin, 74.

92. *Menakhem*, 173; Kahana, 177; Halkin, 80.

93. See *Menakhem*, 20, 65, 106; Kahana, 26, 71, 110; Halkin, 8, 29, 49.

94. The same verb for "abandonment" (*avekvarfn*, or "throw away or discard"), appears in *Benjamin the Third*, where Senderl is described as sitting dejected "like a youth whose husband discarded her and went off to countries beyond the sea" (*vi a yugent, vos der man irer hot zi avekgevorfn un iz avekgegangen lemedinos hayam; Masoes*, 28; Spiegel, 39 [this sentence is omitted in the Spiegel translation]; Neugroschel, 198).

95. *Menakhem,* 218; Kahana, 221; Halkin, 102.

96. *Menakhem,* 218; Kahana, 221; Halkin, 102.

97. *Menakhem,* 219; Kahana, 222; Halkin, 102. Here, as often in this novel, Menakhem-Mendl—who seems to have long since discarded any real religious interest (along with his pawned Sabbath coat)—once again calls on God, reducing, as Miron has noted, "God to the prime mover of adventurous business" ("A Sampling of *Menakhem-Mendl,*" 26). Both Menakhem-Mendl's and Sheyne-Sheyndl's frequent entreaties to God may also be understood as efforts to invoke "the aid of a benevolent God." Matisoff notes, "One of God's guises is the Protector of mankind, the ever present help in times of trouble." Of course, even if belief in a deity has disappeared, one may still continue to use all too familiar, learned expressions, which abound in Yiddish and once served as "various techniques for the avoidance of evil." After all, it is "not hard to see why an oppressed, ghettoized people should have been so preoccupied with the precariousness of life and the ubiquitousness of evil" (*Blessings, Curses, Hopes, and Fears,* 52, 43).

98. *Menakhem,* 218–19; Kahana, 221–22; Halkin, 102.

99. *Menakhem,* 194; Kahana, 198–99 passim; Halkin, 89–90 passim.

100. *Menakhem,* 79; Kahana, 85; Halkin, 37.

101. *Menakhem,* 179; Kahana, 183; Halkin, 82.

4. *Agunes* Disappearing in "A Gallery of Vanished Husbands"

1. Family Location Service, *To Rebuild the Broken Family: Family Location Service, 1905–1955* (New York: Federation of Jewish Philanthropies of New York, n.d.), 4. This pamphlet was published by the Family Location Service, which was formerly the National Desertion Bureau.

2. Paula E. Hyman, "Introduction: Perspectives on the Evolving Jewish Family," in *The Jewish Family: Myths and Reality,* ed. Steven M. Cohen and Paula E. Hyman (New York: Holmes and Meier, 1986), 3, 4. See also Morris D. Waldman, "Family Desertion," in *Proceedings of the Sixth Biennial Session of the National Conference of Jewish Charities in the United States* (St. Louis, May 17–19, 1910), 62: "The large proportion of such cases [desertion] among Jews is alarming in the light of our pride in the decency and purity of the Jewish family life."

3. Reena Sigman Friedman, "'Send Me My Husband Who Is In New York City': Husband Desertion in the American Jewish Community, 1900–1926," *Jewish Social Studies* 44, no. 1 (Winter 1982): 7. See also Charlotte Baum, Paula Hyman, Sonya Michel, *The Jewish Woman in America* (New York: Dial Press, 1976), 115–16.

4. For the difficult relations between German and Eastern European Jews, see Baum, Hyman, and Michel, *The Jewish Woman in America,* 179–85; and Paula E. Hyman, *Gender and Assimilation: The Roles and Representation of Women* (1995; reprint, Seattle: University of Washington Press, 1997), 94–96, 106–7.

5. Manheim S. Shapiro, "Changing Life Styles, the Jewish Family, and the Jewish Community," *Congress Monthly* 42, no. 7 (1975): 16. See also Irving Howe, with the assistance of Kenneth Libo, *World of Our Fathers: The Journey of Eastern European Jews to America and the Life They Found and Made* (New York: Bantam, 1976). Howe—in different contexts—seems to project contradictory, or at least divergent, views of the relations between German and Eastern European Jews. When writing about the large influx of Eastern European Jews in the last decades of the nineteenth century, he notes that the embarrassment and social insecurity of relatively newly established German Jews explained certain philanthropic decisions they made (3–34). But when he discusses the Educational Alliance, an institution established by German Jews on the Lower East Side for the "Americanization" of recent Eastern European immigrants, Howe suggests that the motives of the German Jews were essentially pure, even though their effort "to help, to uplift, to clean up and quiet down their 'coreligionists'" was clearly in their own social self-interest (234–41). See also Jean Ulitz Mensch, "Social Pathology in Urban America: Desertion, Prostitution, Gambling, Drugs, and Crime among Eastern European Jews in New York City between 1881 and World War I" (PhD diss., Columbia University, 1983), 57.

6. Mensch, "Social Pathology in Urban America," 67–68 passim.

7. Charles Zunser, "The Domestic Relations Court," in "Legal Aid Work," special issue, *Annals of the American Academy of Political and Social Sciences* (Philadelphia), 1953 (March 1926): 1.

8. See Anna Igra, "Likely to Become a Public Charge: Deserted Women and the Family Law of the Poor in New York City, 1910–1936," *Journal of Jewish Women's History* 11, no. 4 (2000): 61–64, for a discussion of the changing treatment of abandoned wives before and during the Progressive Era in the final years of the nineteenth century and the first decade of the twentieth.

9. Boris Bogen, *Jewish Philanthropy: An Exposition of Principles and Methods of Jewish Social Service in the United States* (New York: Macmillan, 1917), 176, 178, 179.

10. Friedman, "Send Me My Husband Who Is In New York City," 5.

11. Zunser, "The Domestic Relations Court," 1. See also Charles Zunser, "Family Desertion (Report on a Study of 423 Cases)," *Annals of the American Academy of Political and Social Sciences* (Philadelphia), 2318 (September 1929): 6.

12. National Desertion Bureau, *1953 Annual Report of the National Desertion Bureau, Inc.* (New York: National Desertion Bureau [Family Location Service], 1953).

13. National Desertion Bureau, *Annual Report for 1960 Family Location Service, Inc.* (New York: National Desertion Bureau [Family Location Service], 1960), 7.

14. Zunser, "Family Desertion," 3

15. Segments of the Gallery also appeared in four other newspapers in the United States and Canada—the *Courier* in Chicago, the *Press* in Cleveland, and the *Eagle* in Montreal and Toronto.

16. Family Location Service, *To Rebuild the Broken Family,* 4.

17. Monroe M. Goldstein, *Family Desertion: Report of the Executive Committee of the National Desertion Bureau, Inc., 1912–1915* (New York City, June 1, 1915), 6.

18. Ibid. The first segment (three pages) is titled "Report of the Executive Committee"; the main text is the "Report of the Secretary and Counsel," authored by Monroe M. Goldstein.

19. Goldstein, *Family Desertion,* 10.

20. Ibid., 6.

21. Ibid., 6. Goldstein refers to the deserter as "the Nomad Husband."

22. Ibid., 9.

23. Ibid.

24. Ibid., 19.

25. Ibid., 9.

26. Ibid., 10.

27. After 1910, under the New York Criminal Code, men who abandoned their wives or children and left them with no means of support were classified as felonious "disorderly persons" subject to punishment, including imprisonment. See Igra, "Likely to Become a Public Charge," 64; Mensch, "Social Pathology in Urban America," 52–54.

28. Goldstein, *Family Desertion,* 15.

29. Ibid., 13.

30. Ibid.

31. Ibid., 17–18.

32. Ibid., 6, 17.

33. Family Location Service, *To Rebuild the Broken Family,* 1.

34. Ibid., 6.

35. Ibid., 9.

36. Ibid., 11.

37. Ibid., 2.

38. Goldstein, *Family Desertion,* 16.

39. Ibid., 16.

40. Both appeared in *Der Forverts,* January 8, 1916. All translations from the *Forverts* are mine.

41. *Der Forverts,* January 4, 1916.

42. Isaac Metzker, ed., *A Bintel Brief: Sixty Years of Letters from the Lower East Side to the Daily Forward* (New York: Ballantine, 1971), 105.

43. The term *office* probably refers to the office of a charitable organization, or perhaps the National Desertion Bureau, and suggests that the father is being told he need not worry because the charges of desertion will be dropped or stricken from the records.

44. See note 27 above, which explains that, under the New York Criminal Code (and those of many other states), men were classified as felonious criminals if they abandoned wife and children without means of support. They could be released by request of their wives, which often happened, by agreeing to

support the family, and often by posting a bond from which support payments could be paid monthly.

45. Bogen, *Jewish Philanthropy*, 176, 178, 179.

5. An Autobiography of Turmoil

1. Irving Howe, with the assistance of Kenneth Libo, *World of Our Fathers: The Journey of the Eastern European Jews to America and the Life They Found and Made* (New York: Bantam, 1976), 176.

Epilogue

1. Some deserted families at first moved in with relatives, but often this solution did not last long because of poverty and inconvenience. To protect the "taxpayer's pocketbook," family and welfare laws obligated family members to support the abandoned family: at first the laws referred to husband-wife and parent-child relationships, but later extended to grandparents and grandchildren, and finally to stepparents and stepchildren. Often these family members could not contribute, being just as destitute as the abandoned family. Unbelievably, the deserted wife was usually required to contact these extended family members and report the results of her effort. (After the National Desertion Bureau was founded, it helped Jewish women locate their spouses.) The abandoned family usually received no funds until the agencies were satisfied that all other possibilities for support had been explored, which sometimes took years. See Anna Igra, "Likely to Become a Public Charge: Deserted Women and Family Law of the Poor in New York City, 1910–1936," *Journal of Women's History* 11, no. 4 (2000): esp. 65–68.

2. Rachael Langford and Russell West, eds., *Marginal Voices, Marginal Forms: Diaries in European Literature and History* (Amsterdam: Rodopi, 1999), 7.

3. Jen Webb, "Cultural Studies and Aesthetics," in "Cultural Studies: Interdisciplinarity and Translation," ed. Stefan Herbrechter, special issue, *Critical Studies* 20 (2002): 148.

4. Daniel Boyarin, *Unheroic Conduct: The Rise of Heterosexuality and the Invention of the Jewish Man* (Berkeley: University of California Press, 1997), 154. Boyarin explains that "exclusion from the study of Torah did not, paradoxically, include the most holy book, the Bible itself, but only the culturally more valued practice of Talmud," 152–53. See also Judith Romney Wegner, *Chattel or Person? The Status of Women in the Mishnah* (New York: Oxford University Press, 1988), chap. 6, "Women and the Public Domain," especially the section "The Intrinsic Superiority of the Male" (146–48), in which she indicates that, while mishnaic Judaism was in many respects no different from other religions of antiquity regarding women's roles in the public sphere, the rabbis went further: "They barred *all* women, whatever their domestic situation and

regardless of dependent or autonomous status, from participating in public religious exercises" (146).

5. Salo W. Baron, *A Social and Religious History of the Jews,* vol. 2, pt. 2 (New York: Columbia University Press, 1952), 290.

6. Judith Romney Wegner, "The Image and Status of Women in Classical Rabbinic Judaism," in *Jewish Women in Historical Perspective,* ed. Judith R. Baskin (Detroit: Wayne State Press, 1991), 88.

7. Miriam Peskowitz, "Engendering Jewish Religious History," *Shofar* 14, no. 1 (Fall 1995): 28–29.

8. Women, in the traditional Jewish community, had for centuries worked to support their families (including, of course, those husbands who were often occupied almost exclusively with the most valued activity of Torah study), but their work was not viewed as participation in the "public" sphere where the men studied. Rather their work was regarded as part of that devalued economic or business realm that also contained the domestic household. See also Boyarin, *Unheroic Conduct,* 160–63. This created a paradoxical situation, especially within a capitalist context, where both the marketplace and the arena where ideas and information were exchanged were clearly understood as public spaces. In addition, the Enlightenment's understanding of "truth" (also Maimon's perception) as constructed within the realm of "privacy"—that is, as something at odds with public interest or necessity—seems to coincide with the value of Torah study in Jewish Orthodoxy. In this construction, therefore, women, domestic space, and women's work are deemed part of the degraded "public" realm.

9. Iris Parush maintains that women who were excluded from Talmudic studies were used by Maskilim (advocates of the Jewish Enlightenment) as "agents who would spread [to the masses] the spirit of modernity and enlightenment," the ideas women acquired through reading secular Yiddish novels. Girls were permitted a secular education that also included the study of foreign languages. According to Parush, "The marginal place in society that these women occupied created special opportunities and pathways for their influence." Parush also notes that most of the women were "agents of enlightenment," but she offers scant evidence of the actual effects of this female "agency" (*Reading Women: Marginality and Modernization in Nineteenth-Century Eastern European Jewish Society,* trans. Saadya Sternberg [Waltham, MA: Brandeis University Press, 2004], 83, 96, 160). Other questions not answered by this text are: which women and what percentage of women received this secular education; what foreign languages did they study and what did they read in those languages; and which Enlightenment ideas did they spread to the masses and how did they do so? There is, of course, evidence in a number of literary texts (for example, Sholem Aleykhem's *Tevye der Milkhiger* [Tevye the Dairyman]) of modern ideas appearing in traditional communities—ideas such as young people choosing their own mates rather than relying on matchmakers, or joining progressive social and political movements. But while Parush does maintain that "women had a substantial role in advancing the processes of secularization and modernization of Jewish society of the time" (154), she does

not indicate, as I have noted, which views were disseminated to the masses or how this was accomplished.

10. Ashkenaz, the Hebrew name for Germany, had referred to the cultural complex of the Jews of northwestern Europe and was used to distinguish that culture from Sepharad, the Jewish cultural complex that originated in Spain and spread throughout the Mediterranean area. The term *Ashkenazi* came to refer to the large majority of world Jewry who, from the sixteenth century, lived in the Kingdom of Poland and the Duchy of Lithuania and had adopted recognizable Ashkenazic cultural aspects, including religious rites and the Yiddish language. See Benjamin Harshav, *The Meaning of Yiddish* (Berkeley: University of California Press, 1990), esp. chap. 1; and his *Language in Time of Revolution* (Berkeley: University of California Press, 1993), esp. chap. 4.

11. See my chapter "A Politics and Poetics of Diaspora: Heine's 'Hebräische Melodien,'" in *Diasporas and Exiles: Varieties of Jewish Identity,* ed. Howard Wettstein (Berkeley: University of California Press, 2002), 61–63.

12. See Chava Weissler, "'For Women and for Men Who Are Like Women': The Construction of Gender in Jewish Devotional Literature," *Journal of Feminist Studies in Religion* 5, no. 2 (Fall 1989): 9–10.

13. Curiously, Maimon's expectations of complete devotion to scholarly studies were not inconsistent with Enlightenment ideas, but in the Enlightenment tradition the scholar was apparently not expected to leave wife and family bereft of support. See Geoffrey Galt Harpham, "So . . . What *Is* Enlightenment? An Inquisition into Modernity," *Critical Inquiry* 20 (Spring 1994): 554: "In the Enlightenment ethos, truth is achieved by Kantian men of learning who undertake patient, exacting, scholarly work in a spirit of free inquiry—free, that is, of coercive external pressures or distracting desires."

14. Judith Butler, "Contingent Foundations: Feminism and the Question of 'Postmodernism,'" in *Feminists Theorize the Political,* ed. Judith Butler and Joan W. Scott (New York: Routledge, 1992), 12. Also noteworthy here is her discussion of "autonomy" that results from the exclusion of the other and harbors the illusion that it does not conceal a "disavowed dependency."

15. See Peskowitz, "Engendering Jewish Religious History," esp. 14–22, on the importance of understanding the relation of knowledge and power when considering gender as a category in history.

16. Jacques Derrida, "Deconstruction and the Other," in *Debates in Continental Philosophy: Conversations with Contemporary Thinkers,* ed. Richard Kearney (New York: Fordham University Press, 2004), 148–49.

17. Amiram Barkat, "Rabbis Cancel Conference on 'Chained Women,'" *Ha'aretz,* November 6, 2006, www.haaretz.com/hasen/spages/783697.html.

Bibliography

Abramovitsh, Sholem Yakov (Mendele Moykher Sforim). *Masoes benyomin hashlishi.* Vol. 9 of *Ale verk fun mendele moykher-sforim.* Ed. N. Mayzl. Warsaw: Farlag Mendele, 1928.

———. *The Travels and Adventures of Benjamin the Third.* Trans. Moshe Spiegel. New York: Schocken, 1949.

———. *The Travels of Benjamin the Third.* In *The Shtetl.* Trans. and ed. Joachim Neugroschel, 179–264. New York: Perigee, 1979.

Agnon, S. Y. "Agunot (1908)." In *Modern Hebrew Literature,* ed. Robert Alter and trans. Baruch Hochman, 199–213. New York: Behrman House, 1975.

Alter, Robert. *The Art of Biblical Narrative.* New York: Basic Books, 1981.

Altman, Janet Gurkin. "The Letter Book as a Literary Institution: Toward a Cultural History of Published Correspondence in France." *Yale French Studies* 71 (1986): 17–62.

Aschheim, Steven E. "The East European Jew and German Jewish Identity." In *Studies in Contemporary Jewry.* Ed. Jonathan Frankel, 1: 3–25. Bloomington: Indiana University Press, 1984.

Ayrenschmalz, Armin. "Stirbt der Abenteuerroman Aus?" *Welt und Wort* 8, no. 1 (1963): 1–6.

Baker, Mark. "The Voice of Deserted Jewish Women, 1867–1870." *Jewish Social Studies* 2, no. 1 (Fall 1995): 98–123.

Bakhtin, M. M. *The Dialogic Imagination: Four Essays by M. M. Bakhtin.* Ed. Michael Holquist. Austin: University of Texas Press, 1981.

Bakshi-Doron, Eliahu, Ysrael Meir Lau, and Shlomo Dichovsky. *Jewish Law Watch: The Agunah Problem,* no. 5. Jerusalem: Schechter Institute of Jewish Studies, August 2002.

Bammer, Angelika, ed. *Displacements: Cultural Identities in Question.* Bloomington: Indiana University Press, 1994.

————. "Mother Tongues and Other Strangers: Writing 'Family' across Cultural Divides." In *Displacements: Cultural Identities in Question,* ed. Angelika Bammer, 90–109. Bloomington: Indiana University Press, 1994.

Bar-El, Joseph. "The Yiddish Briefenshteler (Letter Writing Manual of the 18th to 20th Century)." Master's thesis, Touro College, New York, 1970.

Barkat, Amiram. "Rabbis Cancel Conference on 'Chained Women.'" *Ha'aretz,* November 6, 2006, www.haaretz.com/hasen/spages/783697.html.

Baron, Dvora. *"The First Day" and Other Stories.* Ed. and trans. Naomi Seidman and Chana Kronfeld. Berkeley: University of California Press, 2001.

Baron, Salo W. *The Russian Jew under Tsars and Soviets.* New York: Macmillan, 1964.

————. *A Social and Religious History of the Jews.* Vol. 2, pt. 2. New York: Columbia University Press, 1952.

Baron, Salo W., Arcadius Kahan, Nachum Gross, and others, eds. *Economic History of the Jews.* Jerusalem: Keter, 1995.

Baskin, Judith R., ed. *Jewish Women in Historical Perspective.* Detroit: Wayne State University Press, 1991.

Batscha, Zwi. "Zur Aufklärungsproblematik in Salomon Maimons *Lebensgeschichte.*" *Internationales Symposium, Dezember 1979* (Tel-Aviv) (1979): 91–117.

————. "Nachwort." In *Salomon Maimons Lebensgeschichte: Von ihm selbst geschrieben,* ed. Karl Philipp Moritz; newly edited by Zwi Batscha, 329–92. Frankfurt am Main: Insel, 1984.

Baum, Charlotte, Paula Hyman, and Sonya Michel. *The Jewish Woman in America.* New York: Dial Press, 1976.

Bendavid, Lazarius. "Salomon Maimon." *Nationalzeitschrift für Wissenschaft, Kunst und Gewerbe in den preußischen Staaten, nebst einem Korrespondenz-Blatte* (Berlin), 1 (1901): 88–103.

Berkowitz, Adena. "The Prisoners of Divorce." *Lilith,* no. 18 (January 1988): 18–23.

Bérubé, Michael. *Marginal Forces/Cultural Centers: Tolson, Pynchon, and the Politics of the Canon.* Ithaca: Cornell University Press, 1992.

Biale, Rachel. *Women and Jewish Law: The Essential Texts, Their History, and Their Relevance for Today.* New York: Schocken, 1995.

Bilik, Dorothy. "*The Memoirs of Glikl of Hameln:* The Archeology of the Text." *Yiddish* 8, no. 2 (1992): 5–22.

bin Gorion, Joseph, col. *Mimekor Yisrael: Classical Jewish Folktales.* Trans. I. M. Lask, ed. Emanuel bin Gorion. 2 vols. Bloomington: Indiana University Press, 1976.

Bogen, Boris. *Jewish Philanthropy: An Exposition of Principles and Methods of Jewish Social Service in the United States.* New York: Macmillan, 1917.

Boyarin, Daniel. "Internal Opposition in Talmudic Literature: The Case of the Married Monk." *Representations* 36 (Fall 1991): 87–113.

————. *Unheroic Conduct: The Rise of Heterosexuality and the Invention of the Jewish Man.* Berkeley: University of California Press, 1997.

Boyarin, Jonathan. "The Other Within and the Other Without." In *The Other in Jewish Thought and History: Constructions of Jewish Culture and Identity*, ed. Lawrence J. Silberstein and Richard L. Cohn, 424–52. New York: New York University Press, 1994.

Breitowitz, Irving A. *Between Civil and Religious Law: The Plight of the Agunah in American Society.* Westport: Greenwood, 1993.

———. "The Plight of the *Agunah:* A Study in *Halacha,* Contract, and the First Amendment." *Maryland Law Review* 51 (1992): 312–421.

Butler, Judith. "Contingent Foundations: Feminism and the Question of 'Postmodernism.'" In *Feminists Theorize the Political,* ed. Judith Butler and Joan W. Scott, 3–21. New York: Routledge, 1992.

———. *Gender Trouble: Feminism and the Subversion of Identity.* New York: Routledge, 1990.

Butler, Judith, and Joan W. Scott, eds. *Feminists Theorize the Political.* New York: Routledge, 1992.

Cantor, Aviva. *Jewish Women, Jewish Men: The Legacy of Patriarchy in Jewish Life.* New York: Harper Collins, 1995.

Carson, James. "Narrative Cross-Dressing and the Authorship in the Novels of Richardson." In *Writing the Female Voice: Essays on Epistolary Literature,* ed. Elizabeth C. Goldsmith, 95–113. Boston: Northeastern University Press, 1989.

Chigier, M. "Ruminations over the Agunah Problem." *Jewish Law Annual* 4 (1981): 207–25.

Cohen, Boaz. *Jewish and Roman Law: A Comparative Study.* Vol. 1. New York: Jewish Theological Seminary of America, 1966.

Cohen, Steven M., and Paula E. Hyman, eds. *The Jewish Family: Myths and Reality.* New York: Holmes and Meier, 1986.

Cornell, Drucilla L. "Gender, Sex, and Equivalent Rights." In *Feminists Theorize the Political,* ed. Judith Butler and Joan W. Scott, 280–96. New York: Routledge, 1992.

Davis, Lennard J. *Factual Fictions: The Origins of the English Novel.* New York: Columbia University Press, 1983.

Davis, Natalie Zemon. "Glikl Bas Judah Leib: Arguing with God." In *Women on the Margins: Three Seventeenth-Century Lives,* 5–62. Cambridge, MA: Harvard University Press, 1995.

de Lauretis, Teresa, ed. *Feminist Studies/Critical Studies.* Bloomington: Indiana University Press, 1986.

Der Forverts (Jewish Daily Forward). New York.

Derrida, Jacques. "Deconstruction and the Other." In *Debates in Continental Philosophy: Conversations with Contemporary Thinkers,* ed. Richard Kearney, 139–56. New York: Fordham University Press, 2004.

Dick, Judah. "Is an Agreement to Deliver or Accept a *Get* in the Event of a Civil Divorce Halakhically Feasible?" *Tradition* 21 (Summer 1983): 91–106.

Dinse, Helmut. *Die Entwicklung des jiddischen Schrifttums im deutschen Sprachgebiet.* Stuttgart: J. B. Metzlerische Verlagsbuchhandlung, 1974.

Dominguez, Virginia R. *People as Subject, People as Object: Selfhood and People-hood in Contemporary Israel.* Madison: University of Wisconsin Press, 1989.

Dubnov, Shmuel. *Fun "zhargon" tsu Yidish un andere artikeln: Literarische zikhroynes.* Vilna: N. Kletzkin, 1929.

During, Simon, ed. *The Cultural Studies Reader.* 2nd ed. London: Routledge, 1999.

Eagleton, Terry. *The Rape of Clarissa: Writing, Sexuality, and Class Struggle in Samuel Richardson.* Oxford: Basil Blackwell, 1982.

Edgar, Andrew, and Peter Sedgwick, eds. *Key Conceptes in Cultural Theory.* London, Routledge, 1999.

Encyclopedia Judaica. Jerusalem: Keter, 1972.

Erik, Max. "*Menakhem-Mendl:* A Marxist Critique." *Prooftexts* 6 (1986): 23–39.

Etkes, Immanuel. "Marriage and Torah Study among the *Lomdim* in Lithuania in the Nineteenth Century." In *The Jewish Family: Metaphor and Memory,* ed. David Kraemer, 153–78. New York: Oxford University Press, 1989.

Family Location Service (formerly the National Desertion Bureau). *To Rebuild the Broken Family: Family Location Service, 1905–1955.* New York: Federation of Jewish Philanthropies of New York, n.d.

Fein, Richard J. "Satire and the Travels of Benjamin III." *Yiddish* 7, no. 1 (1987): 30–37.

Fleck, Jeffrey. "Mendele in Pieces." *Prooftexts* 3, no. 2 (1983): 169–88.

Fridkis, Ari Lloyd. "Desertion in the American Jewish Immigrant Family: The Work of the National Desertion Bureau in Cooperation with the Indus-trial Removal Office." *American Jewish History* 71, no. 2 (December 1981): 285–99.

Frieden, Ken. *Classic Yiddish Fiction.* Albany: State University of New York Press, 1995.

Friedman, Reena Sigman. "'Send Me My Husband Who Is In New York City': Husband Desertion in the American Jewish Community, 1900–1926." *Jewish Social Studies* 44, no. 1 (Winter 1982): 1–18.

Frisby, David. *Fragments of Modernity: Theories of Modernity in the Work of Sim-mel, Kracauer, and Benjamin.* Cambridge, MA: MIT Press, 1986.

Frow, John. *Cultural Studies and Cultural Values.* Oxford: Clarendon Press, 1995.

Gallagher, Catherine. *Nobody's Story: The Vanishing Acts of Women Writers in the Marketplace.* Berkeley: University of California Press, 1994.

Gatens, Moira. "Power, Bodies, and Difference." In *Destabilizing Theory: Con-temporary Feminist Debates,* ed. Michèle Barrett and Anne Phillips, 220–37. Stanford: Stanford University Press, 1992.

Gilman, Sander L. *Inscribing the Other.* Lincoln: University of Nebraska Press, 1991.

———. *Jewish Self-Hatred, Anti-Semitism, and the Hidden Language of the Jews.* Baltimore: Johns Hopkins University Press, 1986.

Ginzberg, Louis. *The Legends of the Jews.* Vol. 1. Trans. Henrietta Szold. 1909. Reprint, Baltimore: Johns Hopkins University Press, 1998.

Glanz, Rudolf. *The Jewish Woman in America: Two Female Immigrant Generations, 1820–1929*. Vols. 1 and 2. New York: Ktav Publishing House, 1976.

Glatshteyn, Yakov. *Menakhem-Mendl*. In *In tokh genumen: eseyn, 1945–1947*, 469–84. New York: Matones, 1947.

Glen, Susan A. *Daughters of the Shtetl: Life and Labor in the Immigrant Generation*. Ithaca: Cornell University Press, 1990.

Glick, Shanah D. "The Agunah in the American Legal System: Problems and Solutions." *Journal of Family Law* 31 (1992–93): 885–914.

Glinert, Lewis, trans. *Mamme Dear: A Turn-of-the-Century Collection of Model Yiddish Letters*. Northvale, NJ: Jason Aronson, 1997.

Goldsmith, Elizabeth C., ed. *Writing the Female Voice: Essays on Epistolary Literature*. Boston: Northeastern University Press, 1989.

Goldstein, Bluma. "A Politics and Poetics of Diaspora: Heine's 'Hebräische Melodien.'" In *Diasporas and Exiles: Varieties of Jewish Identity*, ed. Howard Wettstein, 60–77. Berkeley: University of California Press, 2002.

Goldstein, Monroe M. *Family Desertion: Report of the Executive Committee of the National Desertion Bureau, Inc., 1912–1915*. New York City, June 1, 1915.

Golinkin, David, Richard Lewis, Diana Villa, and Monique Süsskind Goldberg. *Jewish Law Watch: The Agunah Dilemma*, no. 4. Jerusalem: Schechter Institute of Jewish Studies, April 2002.

Grade, Chaim. *The Agunah*. Trans. Curt Levant. New York: Bobbs-Merrill, 1974.

Grade, Khayim. *Die agune: Roman*. New York: Cyco-Bicher Farlag, 1965.

Graupe, Heinz Mosche, ed. and trans. *Die Statuten der drei Gemeinden Altona, Hamburg und Wandsbeck: Quellen zur jüdischen Gemeindeorganisation im 17. und 18. jüdischen*. Hamburg: Hans Christians Verlag, 1973.

Greenberg, Blu. *On Women and Judaism: A View from Tradition*. Philadelphia: Jewish Publication Society of America, 1981.

Grossberg, Lawrence, Cary Nelson, and Paula Treichler, eds. *Cultural Studies*. New York: Routledge, 1992.

Grunwald, M. "Beiträge zu den Memoiren der Glückel von Hameln." *Mitteilungen zür jüdischen Volkskunde* (Hamburg), 18: no. 1–2 (1915): 63–70.

———. "Das Zeitalter der Glückel von Hameln." In *Hamburgs deutsche Juden bis zur Auflösung der Dreigemeinden, 1811*. Hamburg: Alfred Janssen, 1904.

Habermas, Jürgen. *Philosophisch-politische Profile*. Frankfurt am Main: Suhrkamp, 1981.

Halkin, Hillel. "Adventures in Translating Mendele." *Prooftexts* 10, no. 1 (1990): 69–89.

Hamel, Glikl. *Die Memoiren der Glückel von Hameln, geboren in Hamburg 1645, gestorben in Metz 19. September 1724*. Trans. Bertha Pappenheim. Vienna: Meyer and Pappenheim, 1910.

———. *Denkwürdigkeiten der Glückel von Hameln*. Trans. and ed. Alfred Feilchenfeld. 1913. Reprint, Königstein: Jüdischer Verlag, 1980.

———. *The Life of Glückel von Hameln, 1646–1724, Written by Herself*. Trans. Beth-Zion Abrahams. London: East and West Library, 1962.

————. *The Memoirs of Glückel of Hameln*. Trans. Marvin Lowenthal. New York: Schocken, 1977.

————. *Zikhroynes*. Trans. Yosef Bernfeld, ed. Shmuel Rozsansky. Buenos Aires: YIVO Literary Society, 1967.

————. *Zikhroynes mores Glikl Hamel*. Ed. David Kaufmann. Frankfurt am Main: J. Kauffmann, 1896.

Harkavy, Alexander. *Harkavis amerikanisher briefen-shteler, english un yidish* [Harkavy's American Letter Writer, with Useful Information and a Treatise on Bookkeeping; English and Yiddish]. 1892. Reprint, New York: Hebrew Publishing, 1902.

Harpham, Geoffrey Galt. "So . . . What *Is* Enlightenment? An Inquisition into Modernity." *Critical Inquiry* 20 (Spring 1994): 524–56.

Harshav, Benjamin. *Language in Time of Revolution*. Berkeley: University of California Press, 1993.

————. *The Meaning of Yiddish*. Berkeley: University of California Press, 1990.

Haut, Irwin H. "'The Altar Weeps': Divorce in Jewish Law." In *Women in Chains: A Sourcebook on the Agunah*, ed. Jack Nusan Porter, 45–59. Northvale, NJ: Jason Aronson, 1995.

Haut, Rivka. "The *Agunah* and Divorce." In *Lifecycles: Jewish Women on Life Passages and Personal Milestones*, ed. Debra Orenstein, 188–200. Vol. 1. Woodstock, VT: Jewish Lights Publishing, 1994.

Hekscher, Samuel ben Meir. "Aus Samuel ben Meir Hekschers Notizen." In *Zikhroynes mores Glikel Hamel, 1645–1719*, ed. David Kaufmann, 394–400. Frankfurt am Main: J. Kauffmann, 1896.

Herbrechter, Stefan, ed. "Cultural Studies: Interdisciplinarity and Translation." Special issue, *Critical Studies* 20 (2002).

Herzog, Martin, Barbara Kirshenblatt-Gimblett, Dan Miron, and Ruth Wisse, eds. *The Field of Yiddish: Studies in Language, Folklore, and Literature*. 4th collection. Philadelphia: Institute for the Study of Human Issues, 1980.

Heschel, Susannah, ed. *On Being a Jewish Feminist: A Reader*. New York: Schocken, 1983.

Howe, Irving, with the assistance of Kenneth Libo. *World of Our Fathers: The Journey of Eastern European Jews to America and the Life They Found and Made*. New York: Bantam, 1976.

Hyman, Paula E. *Gender and Assimilation: The Roles and Representation of Women*. 1995. Reprint, Seattle: University of Washington Press, 1997.

————. "Gender and the Immigrant Experience in the United States." In *Jewish Women in Historical Perspective*, ed. Judith R. Baskin, 222–42. Detroit: Wayne State University Press, 1991.

————. "Introduction: Perspectives on the Evolving Jewish Family." In *The Jewish Family: Myths and Reality*, ed. Steven M. Cohen and Paula E. Hyman, 3–13. New York: Holmes and Meier, 1986.

————. "The Jewish Family: Looking for a Usable Past." In *On Being a Jewish Feminist: A Reader*, ed. Susannah Heschel, 19–26. New York: Schocken, 1983.

Igra, Anna. "Likely to Become a Public Charge: Deserted Women and the Family Law of the Poor in New York City, 1910–1936." *Journal of Jewish Women's History* 11, no. 4 (2000): 59–81.

Jehlen, Myra. "Gender." In *Critical Terms for Literary Study,* ed. Frank Lentricchia and Thomas McLaughlin, 263–73. Chicago: University of Chicago Press, 1990.

Johnson, Richard. "What Is Cultural Studies Anyway?" *Social Text* 16 (Winter 1986–87): 38–80.

Kaufman, Michael. *The Woman in Jewish Law and Tradition.* Northvale, NJ: Jason Aronson, 1993.

Kearney, Richard, ed. *Debates in Continental Philosophy: Conversations with Contemporary Thinkers.* New York: Fordham University Press, 2004.

Klein, Isaac. *A Guide to Jewish Religious Practice.* New York: Jewish Theological Union of America, 1979.

Kopitzch, Franklin. *Grundzüge einer Sozialgeschichte der Aufklärung in Hamburg und Altona.* Vols. 1, 2. Hamburg: Hans Christians Verlag, 1982.

Landau, A. "Die Sprache der Memoiren Glückel von Hameln." *Mitteilungen der Gesellschaft für jüdische Volkskunde* 7, no. 1 (1901): 20–68.

Landy, Marcia. "The Silent Woman: Towards a Feminist Critique." In *The Authority of Experience: Essays in Feminist Criticism,* ed. Arlyn Diamond and Lee R. Edwards, 16–27. Amherst: University of Massachusetts Press, 1977.

Langford, Rachael, and Russell West, eds. *Marginal Voices, Marginal Forms: Diaries in European Literature and History.* Amsterdam: Rodopi, 1999.

Lask, Beth-Zion. "Memoirs of a Matriarch: Glückel of Hameln." *Menorah Journal* 20, no. 4 (Spring 1932): 35–38.

Lentricchia, Frank, and Thomas McLaughlin, eds. *Critical Terms for Literary Study.* Chicago: University of Chicago Press, 1990.

Levy, Yael V. "The Agunah and the Missing Husband: An American Solution to a Jewish Problem. *Journal of Law and Religion* 10, no. 1 (1993–94): 49–71.

Libeles, Robert. "Das Bild und die anderen—Das Bild der Nichtjuden in Glikls Memoiren." In *Die Hamburger Kauffrau Glikl: Jüdische Existenz in der frühen Neuzeit,* ed. Monika Richarz, 135–46. Hamburg: Hans Christians Verlag, 2001.

Lipking, Lawrence. *Abandoned Women and Poetic Tradition.* Chicago: University of Chicago Press, 1988.

Maimon, Solomon. *The Autobiography of Solomon Maimon.* Trans. J. Clark Murray. London: East and West Library, 1954.

———. *Salomon Maimons Lebensgeschichte, Von ihm selbst geschrieben.* Ed. Karl Philipp Moritz and newly edited by Zwi Batscha. Frankfurt am Main: Insel, 1984.

Maimoniana oder Rhapsodien zur Charakteristik Salomon Maimon's. Ed. Sabattia Joseph Wolff. Berlin: G. Hahn, 1813.

Maitlis, J. "London Yiddish Letters of the Early Eighteenth Century." Pts. 1, 2. *Journal of Jewish Studies* 6 (1955): 153–65, 237–52.

Mandel, Barrett J. "Full of Life Now." In *Autobiography: Essays Theoretical and Critical,* ed. James Olney, 49–72. Princeton: Princeton University Press, 1980.

Matisoff, James A. *Blessings, Curses, Hopes, and Fears: Psycho-Ostensive Expressions in Yiddish*. Stanford: Stanford University Press, 2000.

Meiselman, Moshe. *Jewish Woman in Jewish Law*. New York: Ktav Publishing House, 1978.

Mensch, Jean Ulitz. "Social Pathology in Urban America: Desertion, Prostitution, Gambling, Drugs, and Crime among Eastern European Jews in New York City between 1881 and World War I." PhD diss., Columbia University, 1983.

Metzker, Isaac, ed. *A Bintel Brief: Sixty Years of Letters from the Lower East Side to the Daily Forward*. New York: Ballantine, 1971.

Michaels, Walter Benn. *The Gold Standard and the Logic of Naturalism*. Berkeley: University of California Press, 1987.

Minkoff, N. B. *Glickel Hamel (1645–1724)*. New York: M. Vaxer, 1952.

Miron, Dan. *The Image of the Shtetl and Other Studies of Modern Jewish Literary Imagination*. Syracuse: Syracuse University Press, 2000.

———. "A Sampling of *Menakhem-Mendl*." *Michigan Germanic Studies* 3, no. 2 (1977): 13–33.

———. *A Traveler Disguised: A Study in the Rise of Modern Yiddish Fiction in the Nineteenth Century*. New York: Schocken, 1973.

Miron, Dan, and Anita Norich. "The Politics of Benjamin III: Intellectual Significance and Its Formal Correlatives in Sh. Y. Abramovitsh's *Masoes benyomin hashlishi*." In *The Field of Yiddish: Studies in Language, Folklore, and Literature*, ed. Martin Herzog, Barbara Kirshenblatt-Gimblett, Dan Miron, and Ruth Wisse, 1–115. 4th collection. Philadelphia: Institute for the Study of Human Issues, 1980.

Modena, Leon. *The Autobiography of a Seventeenth-Century Venetian Rabbi: Leon Modena's Life of Judah*. Trans. and ed. Mark R. Cohen. Princeton: Princeton University Press, 1988.

Modleski, Tania. "Feminism and the Power of Interpretation." In *Feminist Studies/Critical Studies*, ed. Teresa de Lauretis, 121–37. Bloomington: Indiana University Press, 1986.

Moladovski, Kadya. "Di shlislen fun sholem aleykhems shtil." *Di tsukunft* 62 (June 1957): 225–27.

Moritz, Karl Philipp, ed. *Salomon Maimons Lebensgeschichte: Von ihm selbst geschrieben*. Newly edited by Zwi Batscha. Frankfurt am Main: Insel, 1984.

Morse, Margaret Elizabeth. "The Works of Arthur Schnitzler as an Index of Cultural Change: Relationships between the Sexes in Society, Ideology, and the Imagination." PhD diss., University of California, Berkeley, 1977.

Mumford, Lewis. *The Culture of Cities*. 1935. Reprint, New York: Harcourt Brace Jovanovich, 1970.

Nabokov, Vladimir. *Lectures on Don Quixote*, ed. Fredson Bowers. San Diego: Harcourt Brace Jovanovich, 1983.

Nadell, Pamela S. *Conservative Judaism in America: A Biographical Dictionary and Sourcebook*. New York: Greenwood Press, 1988.

National Desertion Bureau. *1953 Annual Report of the National Desertion Bureau, Inc.* New York: National Desertion Bureau [Family Location Service], 1953.

———. *Annual Report for 1960 Family Location Service, Inc.* New York: National Desertion Bureau [Family Location Service], 1960.

Neumair, Paul Georg. *Der Typus des Abenteurers in der neuen deutschen Dichtung* [The Prototype of the Adventurer in Modern German Literature]. Limburg a.d. Lahm: Limburger Vereinsdrückerei, 1933.

Niger, Shmuel. *Sholem aleykhem: Zayne vikhtikste verk, zayn humor, zayn ort in der yidisher literatur.* New York: Yidisher Kultur Farlag, 1928.

Niggl, Günter. *Geschichte der deutschen Autobiographie im 18. Jahrhundert: Theoretische Grundlegung und literarische Entfaltung.* Stuttgart: J. B. Metzler, 1977.

Nochlin, Linda, and Tamar Garb, eds. *The Jew in the Text: Modernity and the Construction of Identity.* London: Thames and Hudson, 1995.

Olney, James, ed. *Autobiography: Essays Theoretical and Critical.* Princeton, NJ: Princeton University Press, 1980.

Orenstein, Debra. *Lifecycles: Jewish Women on Life Passages and Personal Milestones.* Vol. 1. Woodstock, VT: Jewish Lights Publishing, 1994.

Parush, Iris. *Reading Jewish Women: Marginality and Modernization in Nineteenth-Century Eastern European Jewish Society.* Trans. Saadya Sternberg. Waltham, MA: Brandeis University Press, 2004.

Penslar, Derek J. *Shylock's Children: Economics and Jewish Identity in Modern Europe.* Berkeley: University of California Press, 2001.

Perry, Menakhem. "Thematic and Structural Shifts in Autotranslations by Bilingual Hebrew-Yiddish Writers: The Case of Mendele Mokher Sforim." *Poetics Today* 2, no. 4 (Autumn 1981): 181–92.

Perry, Ruth. *Women, Letters, and the Novel.* New York: AMS, 1980.

Peskowitz, Miriam. "Engendering Jewish Religious History." *Shofar* 14, no. 1 (Fall 1995): 8–34.

Peskowitz, Miriam, and Laura Levitt, eds. *Judaism Since Gender.* New York: Routledge, 1997.

Plaskow, Judith. "Jewish Feminism: 'The Year of the Agunah.'" *Tikkun* 8, no. 5 (1993–94): 52–54.

———. *Standing Again at Sinai: Judaism from a Feminist Perspective.* San Francisco: Harper and Row, 1990.

Porter, Jack Nusan, ed. *Women in Chains: A Sourcebook on the Agunah.* Northvale, NJ: Jason Aronson, 1995.

Richarz, Monika, ed. *Die Hamburger Kauffrau Glikl: Jüdische Existenz in der frühen Neuzeit.* Hamburg: Hans Christians Verlag, 2001.

Riskin, Shlomo. *Women and Jewish Divorce: The Rebellious Wife, the Agunah, and the Right of Women to Initiate Divorce in Jewish Law, a Halakhic Solution.* Hoboken, NJ: Ktav Publishing House, 1989.

Roskies, David G. *A Bridge of Longing: The Lost Art of Yiddish Storytelling.* Cambridge, MA: Harvard University Press, 1995.

Rothbell, Gladys. "The Jewish Mother: Social Construction of a Popular Image." In *The Jewish Family: Myths and Reality,* 118–128. ed. Steven M. Cohen and Paula E. Hyman. New York: Holmes and Meier, 1986.

Ruthven, K.K. *Feminist Literary Studies: An Introduction.* Cambridge: Cambridge University Press, 1990.

Said, Edward. "On Repetition." In *The Literature of Fact: Selected Papers from the English Institute,* ed. Angus Fletcher, 135–58. New York: Columbia University Press, 1976.

Sarna, Jonathan D. "A Great Awakening: The Transformation That Shaped Twentieth-Century American Judaism." In *American Jewish Women's History: A Reader,* ed. Pamela S. Nadell, 43–63. New York: New York University Press, 2003.

Schechter, Solomon. *Studies in Judaism.* 2nd series. Philadelphia: Jewish Publication Society of America, 1908.

Schoeps, Julius H. "Aufklärung, Judentum und Emanzipation." In *Judentum im Zeitalter der Aufklärung,* ed. Günter Schulz, 2:75–102. Wolfenbüttel: Jacobi Verlag, 1977.

Seidman, Naomi. "Carnal Knowledge: Sex and the Body in Jewish Studies." *Jewish Social Studies* 1, no. 1 (Fall 1994): 115–46.

———. *A Marriage Made in Heaven: The Sexual Politics of Hebrew and Yiddish.* Berkeley: University of California Press, 1997.

———. "Theorizing Jewish Patriarchy *in Extremis.*" In *Judaism Since Gender,* ed. Miriam Peskowitz and Laura Levitt, 40–48. New York: Routledge, 1997.

Shaked, Gershon. "Midrash and Narrative: Agnon's 'Agunot.'" In *Midrash and Literature,* ed. Geoffrey H. Hartman and Sanford Budick, 285–303. New Haven: Yale University Press, 1986.

Shapiro, Manheim S. "Changing Life Styles, the Jewish Family, and the Jewish Community." *Congress Monthly* 42, no. 7 (1975): 14–21.

Shapiro, Susan E. "Écriture judaïque: Where are the Jews in Western Discourse?" In *Displacements: Cultural Identities in Question,* ed. Angelika Bammer, 182–200. Bloomington: Indiana University Press, 1994.

Shapiro, Sylvia. "Women and Divorce in the Jewish Community." *Jewish Social Work Forum* 24 (Spring 1988): 45–54.

Shmeruk, Chone. "Vegen sholem-aleykhems letzter *menakhem-mendl*-serye." In *Die goldene keyt,* 56 (1966): 22–27.

Sholem Aleichem. *The Letters of Menakhem-Mendl and Sheyne-Sheyndl.* In *The Letters of Menakhem-Mendl and Sheyne-Sheyndl and Motl, the Cantor's Son.* Trans. Hillel Halkin. New Haven: Yale University, 2002.

Sholem Aleykhem. *Menakhem-Mendl.* In *Ale verk fun sholem-aleykhem.* 1912. Reprint, New York: Morgn-Frayhayt Ausgabe, 1937.

Sholem Aleichem. *The Adventures of Menahem-Mendl.* Trans. Tamara Kahana. New York: G.P. Putnam's Sons, 1969.

Silberstein, Laurence J. "Others Within and Others Without: Rethinking Jewish Identity and Culture." In *The Other in Jewish Thought and History:*

Constructions of Jewish Culture and Identity, ed. Laurence J. Silberstein and Robert L. Cohn, 1–34. New York: New York University Press, 1994.

Silberstein, Laurence J., and Robert L. Cohn, eds. *The Other in Jewish Thought and History: Constructions of Jewish Culture and Identity.* New York: New York University Press, 1994.

Slack, Jennifer Daryl, and Laurie Anne Whitt. "Ethics and Cultural Studies." In *Cultural Studies,* ed. Lawrence Grossberg, Cary Nelson, and Paula A. Treichler, 571–92. New York: Routledge, 1992.

Sreter, Debbie Eis. "Nothing to Lose but Their Chains: A Survey of the *Aguna* Problem in Jewish Law." *Journal of Family Law* 28 (1989–90): 703–27.

Swidler, Leonard. *Women in Judaism: The Status of Women in Formative Judaism.* Metuchen, NJ: Scarecrow Press, 1976.

Sylvor, Jennifer. "Literary Impersonations: On the Development of National Prose Traditions in Russian and Yiddish." PhD diss., University of California, Berkeley, 2000.

Tanakh: The Holy Scriptures: The New JPS Translation According to the Traditional Hebrew Text. Philadelphia: Jewish Publication Society, 1985.

Trilling, Lionel. *The Liberal Imagination: Essays on Literature and Society.* New York: Doubleday, 1950.

Trunk, Y. Y. *Tevye un menakhem-mendel in yidishn velt-goyrl.* New York: Bikher Farlag, 1944.

Turniansky, Chava. "Glikls Werk und die zeitgenössische jiddische Literatur." In *Die Hamburger Kauffrau Glikl: Jüdische Existenz in der frühen Neuzeit,* ed. Monika Richarz, 68–90. Hamburg: Hans Christians Verlag, 2001.

———. "Tsu vuser literarishn zhaner gehert glikl hamels shafung?" *Proceedings of the Eleventh World Congress of Jewish Studies, Div. C:3* (Jerusalem), (1994): 283–90.

Verga, Solomo Aben (Solomon Ibn Verga). *Shevet Jehudah.* Trans. M. Wiener. Hannover: Orient-Buchhandlung Heinz Lafaire, 1924.

Waldman, Morris D. "Family Desertion." In *Proceedings of the Seventh Biennial Session of the National Conference of Jewish Charities in the United States* (Cleveland, June 9–12, 1912), 51–123. Baltimore: Kohn and Pollock, 1912.

———. "Family Desertion." In *Proceedings of the Sixth Biennial Session of the National Conference of Jewish Charities in the United States* (St. Louis, May 17–19, 1910), 54–111. Baltimore: Kohn and Pollock, 1910.

Watt, Ian. *The Rise of the Novel: Studies in Defoe, Richardson, and Fielding.* Berkeley: University of California Press, 1957.

Waxman, Meyer. *A History of Jewish Literature.* Vol. 2 (1933). Vol. 3 (1936). Reprint, New York: Thomas Yoseloff, 1960.

Webb, Jen. "Cultural Studies and Aesthetics." In "Cultural Studies: Interdisciplinarity and Translation," ed. Stefan Herbrechter. Special issue, *Critical Studies* 20 (2002): 147–57.

Wegner, Judith Romney. *Chattel or Person? The Status of Women in the Mishnah.* New York: Oxford University Press, 1988.

———. "The Image and Status of Women in Classical Rabbinic Judaism." In *Jewish Women in Historical Perspective,* ed. Judith R. Baskin, 68–93. Detroit: Wayne State University Press, 1991.

Weinberg, Sydney Stahl. *The World of Our Mothers: The Lives of Jewish Immigrant Women.* Chapel Hill: University of North Carolina Press, 1988.

Weiss-Rosmarin, Trude. "The Unfreedom of Jewish Women." *Jewish Spectator* 35, no. 7 (October 1970): 2–7, 31–32.

Weissler, Chava. "'For Women and for Men Who Are Like Women': The Construction of Gender in Jewish Devotional Literature." *Journal of Feminist Studies in Religion* 5, no. 2 (Fall 1989): 7–24.

Wettstein, Howard, ed. *Diasporas and Exiles: Varieties of Jewish Identity.* Berkeley: University of California Press, 2002.

White, Hayden. "The Fictions of Factual Representations." In *The Literature of Fact: Selected Papers from the English Institute,* ed. Angus Fletcher, 21–44. New York: Columbia University Press, 1976.

Wiedemann, Conrad. "Zwei jüdische Autobiographien im Deutschland des 18. Jahrhunderts: Glückel von Hameln und Salomon Maimon." *Juden in der deutschen Literatur: Ein deutsch-israelitisches Symposium,* 89–113. Frankfurt am Main: Suhrkamp, 1986.

Williams, Raymond. *The Country and the City.* New York: Oxford, 1973.

Wirth-Nesher, Hana, ed. *What Is Jewish Literature?* Philadelphia: Jewish Publication Society, 1994.

Witte, J. H. *Die merkwürdige Schicksale und die wissenschaftliche Bedeutung eines jüdischen Denkers aus der Kantischen Shule.* Berlin: H. R. Mecklenburg, 1876.

Wuthenow, Ralph-Rainer. *Das erinnerte Ich: Europäische Autobiographie und Selbstdarstellung im 18. Jahrhundert.* Munich: C. H. Beck, 1974.

Yaron, Reuven. "The Missing Husband in Jewish Law." In *Mélange à la Mémoire de Marcel-Henri Prévost,* 133–40. Paris: Presses Universitaires de France, 1982.

Ysaye, L. "Einiges aus den Memoiren der Glückel von Hameln." *Mitteilungen der Gesellschaft für jüdische Volkskunde* (Hamburg), 7, no. 1 (1901): 1–19.

Ziff, Larzer. *Writing in the New Nation: Prose, Print, and Politics in the Early United States.* New Haven: Yale University Press, 1991.

Zunser, Charles. "The Domestic Relations Court." In "Legal Aid Work." Special issue, *Annals of the American Academy of Political and Social Sciences* (Philadelphia), 1953 (March 1926).

———. "Family Desertion (Report on a Study of 423 Cases)." *Annals of the American Academy of Political and Social Sciences* (Philadelphia), 2318 (September 1929).

Index

Aaron ben Moshe, 20–21, 25

abandonment. See *agune* ("chained woman," including abandoned wife); children, deserted; deserting husbands/fathers; desertion, spousal

Abramovitsh, S.Y., xx, 49, 93, 174n5. See also *Travels of Benjamin the Third, The*

adventurer/adventurism: autonomy and, 50–51; demographic influences on, xx–xxi, 155–56; dual modeling of, 50; economic, 68–77; literary portrayals of, xx–xxiii, 50; petit-bourgeois, 66, 68–69; self-liberation of, 173n3. See also luftmentsh; *Menahkem-Mendl; Travels of Benjamin the Third, The*

aginut, xvii, 2, 5, 6, 155, 163n1. See also *agune* ("chained woman," including abandoned wife)

Aguna (Baron), 55

agune ("chained woman," including abandoned wife): children's welfare and, 117–19; class and, 158; Conservative solutions to problem of, 164n5, 164n8 (Ch.1); cultural environment of, xv–xvi; defined, 1, 163n1; divorces granted to, 160; as double exile, in Germany, 26–27; embedded narratives on, xvii; familial support of, 184n1; fear of rejection, 136; gender (in)equality and, 8–9; gender theory and, xv; incarcerated deserters and, 124–29; Jewish charities and, 125–26; in Jewish law, 2–9, 10, 36–37, 155; literary critics and, 63; as living widow, 168n13; luftmentsh and, 55–56, 63–64; male equivalent of, 8; powerlessness of, 82–85; in public forums, 112–19, 128, 129; as responsible for desertion, 93; self-censorship by, 113–14, 116–17, 128–29; shame/guilt felt by, 80–82, 96, 131, 153; *shekhine* as, 54–55; suicides of, 104–5; textual representation of, xiv–xvi, 1–2. See also *agune*, marginalization of; *specific texts*

Agune, Die (Grade), 1–2

agune, marginalization of, xv, xxii–xxiii, 1–3; in *Benjamin the Third*, 56–57, 59, 159–60; in "Gallery of Vanished Husbands," xxiii, 92–93, 99–100, 113–14, 160; in Jewish patriarchy, 153, 159–60; in Maimon *Autobiography*, xix, 11–12, 29–30, 35–36, 44–48; in *Menakhem-Mendl*, 59–60, 77, 159–60; by National Desertion Bureau, 103, 113–14

agune rights groups, 160, 165n24

Alter, Robert, 22

Altona (annexed by Denmark), 13–17, 19, 24, 169n28, 171n60

Amar, Shlomo, 160–61